1968 in Retrospect

Also by Gurminder K. Bhambra

RETHINKING MODERNITY: Postcolonialism and the Sociological Imagination

SILENCING HUMAN RIGHTS: Critical Engagements with a Contested Project (*co-edited with Robbie Shilliam*)

1968 in Retrospect
History, Theory, Alterity

Edited by

Gurminder K. Bhambra
University of Warwick, UK

and

Ipek Demir
University of Leicester, UK

Selection and editorial matter © Gurminder K. Bhambra and Ipek Demir 2009
Individual chapters © their respective authors

All rights reserved. No reproduction, copy or transmission of this publication may be made without written permission.

No portion of this publication may be reproduced, copied or transmitted save with written permission or in accordance with the provisions of the Copyright, Designs and Patents Act 1988, or under the terms of any licence permitting limited copying issued by the Copyright Licensing Agency, Saffron House, 6-10 Kirby Street, London EC1N 8TS.

Any person who does any unauthorized act in relation to this publication may be liable to criminal prosecution and civil claims for damages.

The authors have asserted their rights to be identified as the authors of this work in accordance with the Copyright, Designs and Patents Act 1988.

First published 2009 by
PALGRAVE MACMILLAN

Palgrave Macmillan in the UK is an imprint of Macmillan Publishers Limited, registered in England, company number 785998, of Houndmills, Basingstoke, Hampshire RG21 6XS.

Palgrave Macmillan in the US is a division of St Martin's Press LLC, 175 Fifth Avenue, New York, NY 10010.

Palgrave Macmillan is the global academic imprint of the above companies and has companies and representatives throughout the world.

Palgrave® and Macmillan® are registered trademarks in the United States, the United Kingdom, Europe and other countries.

ISBN-13: 978–0–230–22932–7 hardback

This book is printed on paper suitable for recycling and made from fully managed and sustained forest sources. Logging, pulping and manufacturing processes are expected to conform to the environmental regulations of the country of origin.

A catalogue record for this book is available from the British Library.

Library of Congress Cataloging-in-Publication Data
1968 in retrospect : history, theory, alterity / edited by
  Gurminder K Bhambra, Ipek Demir.
    p. cm.
  Includes bibliographical references and index.
  ISBN 978–0–230–22932–7 (alk. paper)
  1. Nineteen sixty-eight, A.D. 2. Social movements.
  3. Marginality, Social. 4. Culture conflict. I. Bhambra,
  Gurminder K., 1974– II. Demir, Ipek, 1972– III. Title:
  Nineteen sixty-eight in retrospect.
  HM881.A15 2009
  303.48′409046—dc22   2009013666

10 9 8 7 6 5 4 3 2 1
18 17 16 15 14 13 12 11 10 09

Printed and bound in Great Britain by
CPI Antony Rowe, Chippenham and Eastbourne

Contents

Notes on Contributors   vii

Introduction: 1968 in Retrospect   xi
Gurminder K. Bhambra and Ipek Demir

Part I   Rethinking Historical Narratives

1   Freedom Now! 1968 as a Turning Point for Black American Student Activism   3
Patricia Hill Collins

2   She's Leaving Home: Women's Sixties Renaissance   29
Lynne Segal

3   Subterranean Traditions Rising: The Year That Enid Blyton Died   43
Ken Plummer

Part II   Theoretical Engagements

4   From 1968 to 1951: How Habermas Transformed Marx into Parsons   59
John Holmwood

5   Critical Theory and Crisis Diagnosis: Key Exchanges Between Reason and Revolution after 1968   73
Tracey Skillington

6   On Totalitarianism: The Continuing Relevance of Herbert Marcuse   87
Sarah Hornstein

7   Everyone Longs for a Master: Lacan and 1968   100
Stephen Frosh

Part III   Other Voices

8   May 1968 and Algerian Immigrants in France: Trajectories of Mobilization and Encounter   115
Maud Anne Bracke

9	Turning to Africa: Politics and Student Resistance in Africa since 1968 *Leo Zeilig*	131
10	Riding the Waves: Feminism, Lesbian and Gay Politics, and the Transgender Debates *Sally Hines*	147
11	Subjectivization, State and Other: On the Limits of Our Political Imagination *Mihnea Panu*	160

Conclusion: When Did 1968 End? 175
William Outhwaite

Bibliography 184

Index 198

Notes on Contributors

Gurminder K. Bhambra is Assistant Professor of Sociology at the University of Warwick, UK, and convenor of the British Sociological Association's Theory Study Group. Her monograph, *Rethinking Modernity: Postcolonialism and the Sociological Imagination* (2007), won the 2008 BSA Philip Abrams Memorial Prize for best first book in Sociology and was shortlisted for the European Amalfi Prize for Sociology and Social Sciences. She is co-editor (with Dr Robbie Shilliam) of the interdisciplinary volume, *Silencing Human Rights: Critical Engagements with a Contested Project*.

Maud Anne Bracke is Lecturer of Modern European History at the University of Glasgow. She is the author of *Which Socialism, Whose Détente? West European Communism and the Czechoslovak Crisis of 1968* (2007), forthcoming in Italian translation, and has published articles on '1968', the Prague Spring and West European communism. She is currently working on immigrants and 1968, and on the role played by female workers during the Italian Hot Autumn of 1968.

Patricia Hill Collins is Distinguished University Professor at the University of Maryland, USA. She is also currently President of the American Sociological Association. Her research and scholarship have examined issues of race, gender, social class, sexuality and nation. Her first book, *Black Feminist Thought: Knowledge, Consciousness, and the Politics of Empowerment* (1990), won the Jessie Bernard Award of the American Sociological Association for significant scholarship in gender, and the C. Wright Mills Award for the Study of Social Problems. Her second book, *Race, Class, and Gender: An Anthology* (6th edn, 2007, edited with Margaret Andersen), is widely used. Her book *Black Sexual Politics: African Americans, Gender, and the New Racism* (2004) received the ASA's 2007 Distinguished Publication Award.

Ipek Demir is Lecturer of Sociology at the University of Leicester. Her work draws on political philosophy, social theory and epistemology. Her current research interests include a theoretical and empirical study of order and trust within science. Her publications include

'Incommensurabilities in the Work of Thomas Kuhn', *Studies in History and Philosophy of Science*, No. 39 (2008) and 'Thomas Kuhn's Construction of Scientific Communities' in S. Herbrechter and M. T. Higgins (eds) *Returning (to) Communities: Theory, Culture and Political Practice of the Communal* (2006).

Stephen Frosh is Pro-Vice-Master, Head of the School of Psychosocial Studies and Professor of Psychology at Birkbeck College, University of London. He is the author of many books and papers on psychosocial studies and on psychoanalysis, including *Hate and the 'Jewish Science': Anti-Semitism, Nazism and Psychoanalysis* (2005), *For and Against Psychoanalysis* (2006), *After Words* (2002) and *The Politics of Psychoanalysis* (1999).

Sally Hines is Lecturer in Sociology and Social Policy and the 'Centre for Interdisciplinary Gender Studies' (CIGS) at the University of Leeds, UK. She is currently working on a project funded by the Economic and Social Research Council, which is examining recent legislative shifts around sexuality and gender. She has published articles in *The Journal of Gender Studies, Sociology, Critical Social Policy* and *Sociological Research Online*, as well as a number of chapters in edited volumes. She is the author of *TransForming Gender: Transgender Practices of Identity, Intimacy and Care* (2007).

John Holmwood is Professor of Sociology at the University of Birmingham. His main research interests are in public sociology, the relation between social theory and explanation, and social stratification and inequality. He is the author of *Social Theory and Explanation* (with A. Stewart, 1991) and *Founding Sociology? Talcott Parsons and the Idea of General Theory* (1996) as well as other edited books and articles. He is currently working on a Leverhulme-funded project on 'The Moral Economy of Inequality'.

Sarah Hornstein is a PhD student in the Department of Sociology at York University in Toronto, Canada. She completed her Master's degree in Sociology at Simon Fraser University. Her primary interest is German social theory, particularly that of the Frankfurt School. She is currently planning a dissertation focusing on the Frankfurt School's theorization of totalitarianism and its relevance for understanding the dynamics of contemporary liberal democracy.

Notes on Contributors ix

William Outhwaite studied at the Universities of Oxford and Sussex. He taught at the University of Sussex from 1973 until 2007, at which point he took up the position of Professor of Sociology at Newcastle University. His research has engaged with debates in critical theory, the philosophy of social science, the history of social thought and contemporary Europe. His recent publications include *The Future of Society* (2006), and (with Larry Ray) *Social Theory and Postcommunism* (2005). He is the author of the book *European Society* (2008) and is planning further work on social change in Europe since 1989.

Mihnea Panu teaches sociology at Wilfrid Laurier University, Canada. He is interested in the mutually constitutive relations between truth, liberal governing and the formation of identity and in the possibilities for opening political spaces within this densely populated field. His present research analyses the relations between subjectivization and the governing of reproduction in the US.

Ken Plummer arrived at Essex in January 1975 to teach Social Psychology and the Sociology of Deviance. The following year he started a longstanding link with the Sociology Department at the University of California, Santa Barbara, where he also taught for many years. He has held many roles at Essex including Graduate Director and Head of Department, and has researched and written widely on sexuality. He has written or edited around fifteen books and over a hundred articles, including *Sexual Stigma* (1975); *The Making of the Modern Homosexual* (1981); *Symbolic Interactionism* Vols 1 and 2 (1991); *Modern Homosexualities Fragments of Lesbian and Gay Experience* (1992); *Chicago Sociology: Critical Assessments* (1997; 4 vols); *Telling Sexual Stories* (1995); *Sexualities* (2002; 4 vols); *Documents of Life-2: An Invitation to a Critical Humanism* (2001); *Intimate Citizenship* (2003); and (with John Macionis) *Sociology: A Global Introduction* (4th edn, 2008). In 1996, he set up the journal *Sexualities* and remains its editor.

Lynne Segal is Anniversary Professor of Psychology and Gender Studies at Birkbeck. Her research is in the interdisciplinary domain of gender studies and addresses the diversity of feminist scholarship, psychoanalytic dialogue and critical theory. She tackles issues of sexual difference, masculinity and its discontents, sexualities and culture, political identifications and cultural belongings. Her books include *Is the Future Female? Troubled Thoughts on Contemporary Feminism*; *Slow Motion: Changing Masculinities, Changing Men*; *Straight Sex: The Politics of Pleasure*; *Why*

Feminism? Gender, Psychology, Politics. Her book, *Making Trouble: Life & Politics* (2007), is a form of collective memoir covering her political generation of postwar rebels and dreamers who earlier helped to pioneer many of the contemporary ways of thinking about culture, politics and people, and today face dilemmas that highlight the paradoxical nature of all radical traditions and generational legacies.

Tracey Skillington has been in the Department of Sociology, University College Cork since September 2006. She is a former member of the Centre for European Social Research where she worked on a number of EU-funded international projects. Her interests include critical theory, cosmopolitanism, social movements, solidarity and collective learning. She is currently one of the editors of the *Irish Journal of Sociology*. She is the author of 'A critical comparison of the investigative gaze in three approaches to text analysis' in A. Bora and H. Hausendorf (eds) *Analyzing Citizenship Talk* (2006). Her forthcoming publications include 'Linking knowledge, communication and social learning: Critical theory's immanent critique of the administrative state' in S. O'Tuama (ed.) *Critical Turns in Critical Theory: New Directions in Social and Political Thought* (2009).

Leo Zeilig works in the Department of Sociology at the University of the Witwatersrand. He is also a research fellow at the Centre for Sociological Research in Johannesburg. He has published *Revolt and Protest: Student Politics and Activism in Sub-Saharan Africa* (2008) based on research conducted in Senegal and Zimbabwe.

Introduction: 1968 in Retrospect[1]

Gurminder K. Bhambra and Ipek Demir

What is the meaning of 1968? A tricky question. The editors weren't born, and those we've asked for advice claim to have been there and, therefore, their memories must be suspect![2] Yet, 1968 figures large in the social imaginary, perhaps especially that of sociology. The 1960s was the period when sociology had its first major expansion in the United Kingdom and, if that had taken place earlier in other Western European countries and the United States, it was also a period of expansion (Turner and Turner 1990). The wave of sociologists appointed in this period have related to 1968 in different ways; all carrying its memory, some its dreams and ambitions, and some defining themselves against its very premises. The sixties and '1968', in particular, have come to be seen as framing the 'culture wars' of the ensuing decades. As 1968 recedes into the past, however, it also becomes an object of historical enquiries that frequently challenge the (necessarily selective) memory of those who were part of it and, in the process, redefine the cultural contestations of that period and their connections to our present times. This volume addresses that mix of reflection upon past expectations alongside the identification of surprising new connections unnoticed at the time.

In one common representation of the past, the 1960s followed on from a period of social conformity and constraint in Western societies that had experienced the disruptions of war and the privations of the immediate post-war period. A generation born into subsequent affluence, the 'baby-boomers', came of age in their entry to institutions like the university which had hardly seemed to have caught up with the changing realities. The new universities in Britain created in the 1960s often mimicked the college forms of Oxford and Cambridge, but were soon to become centres of unrest, critical of what their universities sought to represent (see Thompson 1970). These new realities were also being shaped by the emerging women's and lesbian and gay movements' attempt to enlarge the scope of personal freedoms, while the availability of the contraceptive pill, among other things, furthered the transformation of both intimate relationships as well as cross-generational ones.

The relative affluence of their condition (with no fees to worry about and full grants, including, in the United Kingdom at least, housing allowances over the summer vacation!), and the belief in the secure future that awaited them, made it easier for students to vent their frustrations with a system that seemed to be at odds with their ideas and ideals (see Miles 1973; Outhwaite 2005).[3] The causes of dissatisfaction were different in different places, but the emerging protests seemed to spark off each other and exacerbate what was seen to be a general condition of the older generation just 'not getting' what the 'new' world was about. In Paris, for example, students protested at being treated like children with courses that had not been updated for decades and which did not appear relevant to understanding the profound social changes that were manifestly underway. 'Professors you are old and so is your culture' was one particularly pertinent comment on the perceived problems of the day! The generational struggle was also captured in Dylan's 'Times they are a changing' – 'don't criticize what you can't understand' – and The Who's 'My generation' – 'hope I die before I get old' – which provided the soundtrack of the period.[4]

The perception of society being at the brink of dramatic social change, however, did not come to pass in quite the way that had been expected. The leftist aspirations of the student protestors were dashed with the rise of the new right in the 1970s and 1980s. Thatcher and Reagan, for example, were seen as embodying this shift and provoked an almost visceral reaction in those who opposed them. Mrs Thatcher's famous comment, made in an interview in a British women's magazine, that there was 'no such thing as society, only individuals and their families' captured both the nature of a conservative reaction around family values and the possible displacement of sociology along with its object of study. 'What went wrong?' has often been the question associated with attempts to understand 1968 and its neoliberal aftermath. What went wrong such that it was the 'new right' that inherited the mantle in the period after what were seen as the most significant social protests of the time? (see Holmwood 1999)? The narrative trajectory that culminates in this question, however, is too simple and its simplicity obscures the other narratives that may help us to reframe the question asked and thus come to a different understanding both of that time and of its implications for ours.

The post-war period was also a period of movements of liberation from colonial rule and the creation of new states: new states which promised, even if they did not ultimately deliver, a new dawn for their peoples and for humanity and the bringing about of new opportunities and new experiences. As Jawaharlal Nehru, the first Prime Minister of India, said on the eve of independence at midnight on 14 August 1947,

> Long years ago we made a tryst with destiny, and now the time comes when we shall redeem our pledge, not wholly or in full measure, but very substantially. At the stroke of the midnight hour, when the world sleeps, India will awake to life and freedom. A moment comes, which comes but rarely in history, when we step out from the old to the new, when an age ends, and when the soul of a nation, long suppressed, finds utterance. It is fitting that at this solemn moment we take the pledge of dedication to the service of India and her people and to the still larger cause of humanity.

Newly independent countries and peoples, as well as those continuing to struggle for liberation from external oppressors and internal oppressions, were not afflicted with the same degree of solipsism as could be attributed to the students of the 1968 movements. Further, while the student movements might appear to be linked to new 'colonial' adventures such as the Vietnam War, their immediate context was also the ongoing 'old' colonial adventures. There was a war of independence *in* Europe, of Algeria from France and by implication from the European Community; movements against the Unilateral Declaration of Independence of Rhodesia and the establishment of a white supremacist regime in place of a colonial regime; as well as struggles for equality and liberty embodied in the US Black Civil Rights Movement. In this context, colonial struggles of liberation, broadly understood, become the central phenomenon of the post-war period, albeit one not typically addressed as constituting the context for the events of 1968.

This volume emerged out of a conference celebrating the 40th anniversary of 'the events' and re-examining 1968 in *global* perspective. In addressing the events of 1968, this volume seeks both to displace the dominant narratives of that period as well as to call into question the linear trajectories of history based on the attribution of significance to particular events in particular places. The displacement of 'centres', and a shift of attention to the 'peripheries', is a first step in the subsequent endeavour. Where the histories of 1968 have generally focused on the activism of white, male, heterosexual students, focusing on the activities of African American students in the United States, African students in Senegal and the Congo, on women's movements, on the emerging movements around sexuality and transgender issues, as well as on the activities of migrant labour in the metropolises, is a necessary corrective.

A global history organized by the markers of European and Western events is not, however, a *global* history and the extent to which the organizing framework, within which these new narratives are located, remains that of the 1968 of the West could be considered problematic. Yet, at the same time, we cannot simply do away with the markers of the old world. These markers have been, and are, significant for a reason – and those reasons need to be addressed in any subsequent reordering of them. Further, as the recent turn to global history demonstrates, particular events are always abstracted out of more complex and interconnected processes. Acknowledging the significance of '1968', then, is also to acknowledge the significance of a world structured around the dominance of the West and Western narratives. Seeing 1968 as a key moment in the history and narratives of freedom and protest is at once to privilege the actions of particular actors while also further silencing those actors and activities that are not (yet) recognized as 'world historical' (see Chapter 11, this volume).

The contributions to this volume are organized in terms of three different, but related, perspectives on 1968: history, politics and alterity. These perspectives tell the untold stories, forgotten aspects and unexplored accounts of 1968, and provide a different flavour of the time than that which is usually found within the standard narratives. More importantly, however, these narratives are as much about 'today' as they are about 'then' and link the relatively neglected histories of 1968 to our understandings and experiences of today. The first part addresses alternative historical narratives of 1968 which combine analyses of the politics and identity of race, gender and sexuality with personal reflections of the participants' own involvement in the events. The second part takes issue with selected theoretical debates which have been central to interpretations of the events and provides innovative re-readings and reinterpretations of them. The final part addresses 1968 from the perspective of peoples and places that have been neglected in the standard interpretations, as well as offering a chapter questioning the very positioning of 'other' narratives.

Patricia Hill Collins's chapter takes the activism of 1960s African-American youth and links it to the political activism of contemporary youth in the United States. She starts off by providing an analysis of, and identifying themes related to, the US Black student activism in the 1960s. Her chapter then uses this analysis both to inform her reading of contemporary youth activism associated with Barack Obama's presidential campaign and to illustrate continuing trends as well as differences between 1968 and 2008. She discusses how youth political activism takes place in many settings, depending on social constraints; how gender, race, class and age intersect and how these intersections need to be analysed in order to recognize the way in which multiple standpoints can contribute to an overall analysis and, at times, common politics. Further, she emphasizes the point about how the activism of youth needs to be understood in relation to political praxis. According to Collins, the reduced risks associated with being a political activist today, as well as the creative ways in which communications technologies enable contemporary youth to become citizen-journalists, are among the many differences which distinguish the political activism of 2008 from that of 1968.

Lynne Segal's chapter also sees continuities as well as ruptures in women's activism over the decades. Despite their historical invisibility in many accounts of the 1960s, women as a group were active in that period and women's liberation was clearly emerging in 1968. Her focus is on the struggles for women's liberation and its 'lagged' effect in the context of other political activities of the time. She argues, somewhat paradoxically, that women would become 'the decade's most decisive victors', even if some aspects of that victory could be seen more ambivalently today. In her chapter, Segal also pays attention to the way in which women and their activism have been erased from the subsequent accounts of that period. According to Segal, the 1960s was the seedbed for women's liberation and is implicated in the rising significance attached to gender, even if its political fruits were enjoyed much later and not necessarily in the terms initially fought for. In a similar vein, Ken Plummer explicitly links his personal experiences of the period with wider cultural changes that have occurred since the 1960s. His chapter starts off with a poem 'The Year That Enid Blyton Died' which delightfully describes and charts the texture and atmosphere of 1968 as well as providing an impression of what ensued, including an account of sociology's past and its 'heroes'. Plummer then moves on to discuss how the history of 1968 can be told in a multiplicity of ways. His story locates his own life in subterranean traditions, suggesting how the 'deviant imagination' of 1968 made possible certain conditions for the contemporary gains in gay rights and queer issues.

The second part addresses important, and perhaps neglected, aspects of theoretical developments associated with 1968. John Holmwood's chapter focuses on concepts which have dominated not only sociology, but also the consciousness and frame of mind of the 1968 generation, namely structure, conflict, action and change. Holmwood, however, tells an unexpected story examining how the theoretical shifts made by Habermas end up reproducing Parsonsian categories, even though Habermas had initially set out to oppose the structural-functionalist approach of Parsons. He puts forward the argument that Habermas's attempts to oppose the conservative and conformist undertones of Parsons by embracing agency, conflict and change failed as the initial Marxian voice in Habermas's writings was transformed into a Parsonsian one. The Habermasian effort to enhance 'communicative action' and to make ideas of agency, conflict and change, the hallmarks of the 1968 spirit, central to the sociological endeavour, has instead left a Parsonsian conservative stamp on sociology.

Tracey Skillington's and Sarah Hornstein's chapters, on the other hand, embrace the explicit theories of 1968, especially critical theory and its Frankfurt School origins. Skillington, for example, praises critical theory for its critique of instrumental reason and its reintroduction of normativity, drawing on the similarities between the May Movement and today's anti-globalization movements, such as Global Exchange. She is positive about critical theory's attempts to reconcile the universalistic elements of 'reason' with its situated, particular manifestations, and her chapter highlights how the struggles of 1968 embody this reconciliation and continue to live on in the anti-capitalist struggles of today. Hornstein's chapter, meanwhile, focuses on Herbert Marcuse who, for some, was *the* social theorist of 1968. Hornstein highlights the continuing relevance of Marcuse by engaging with the totalitarian quality of technological rationality. By way of differentiating between terroristic technocracies and non-terroristic technocracies, and by way of using Marcusean concepts of 'matter-of-factness', 'psychological neutrality' and 'repressive desublimation', Hornstein aims to highlight the continuing presence of domination and repression in 'democratic' advanced capitalist societies and, in so doing, brings to our attention the contemporary relevance of Marcuse and the possibility and the impossibility of freedom and revolution in 2008.

Stephen Frosh's chapter addresses the limitations and dilemmas of revolutionary activity by focusing on Lacan and 1968. Describing Lacan's frustration with 'rebellious' students, whom he saw as part of the system, Frosh tells us how Lacan considered psychoanalysis as the only revolutionary practice, one which was best placed to oppose totalization through allowing for a divided subject and through subverting the master's knowledge. But, when it came down to it, Lacan's apparent attempt to institute a radically democratic approach to psychoanalytic education foundered on the imaginary identifications others had with him, and perhaps on his own enjoyment of this identification. Like

Introduction: 1968 in Retrospect xvii

many revolutionary leaders, perhaps, he embodied the very mastery his movement was supposedly opposing.

The chapters in the third part on alterity take our engagement with untold stories and unheard accounts of 1968 a step further. In her chapter, Maud Anne Bracke examines the encounters between North African immigrants and the predominantly white student and union movements in France. Her chapter considers what the 1960s meant to immigrants themselves and argues that the events gave rise to an immigrant identity. Writing the story from their perspective, Bracke's chapter examines immigrant activism both during and after 1968, highlighting how the immigrant workers tried new forms of action to deal with their particular concerns and how the need for autonomous immigrant organizations emerged subsequently. Demands for non-discrimination at the workplace surfaced and came to be linked to broader, non-work-related issues such as racism and housing. By shifting the focus to immigrants themselves, Bracke also brings to our attention the contradictions between Orientalized (and romanticized) views of difference at the time and the universalized views of the left that held sway among the students and the trade unions in the 1960s.

Leo Zeilig's chapter focuses on student activists and social movements in Africa in the 1960s. He examines the role of the student-intelligentsia in the post-independence period in different African countries and also addresses the nature of their association with movements in Europe. Zeilig looks at how, a relatively privileged, student activism linked to wider social forces and, in the process, opened up the space for a new politics. The limitations of that convergence, however, were only fully made apparent in the subsequent decades in the struggles against neoliberalism and structural adjustment programmes. The 1968 generation, then, was not only motivated by different concerns in different places, but also had very different political trajectories and developments.

In her chapter, Sally Hines highlights the role of transgender people in the activism of the 1960s in the United States by discussing two events, the 'Compton's Cafeteria Riots' of 1966 in San Francisco and the 'Stonewall Riots' of 1969 in New York. She explores the active involvement of transgender people in the struggles of feminist, lesbian and gay activism and discusses the establishment of alliances between marginalized gender-identity groups. Her contribution also highlights the exclusions faced by transgender people from many lesbian and gay organizations in the 1960s, and the way in which the fragile alliances between these groups were disrupted, as well as emphasizing the creation of transgender-specific support services. In addition,

Hines considers the questions transgender theorizing and politics raise for today, including examining the gender and sexual binary model, the ontology of sex and gender, and the marginalization of those who are happy to occupy the gender boundary rather than deconstruct it.

The final chapter in this part questions the very notion of alterity privileged in the 1960s and the way in which this particular reading of it has structured what it is possible to say about 'others' and their place in the world and its histories. Mihnea Panu provocatively argues that the social imaginary of 1968, and its continuing legacy within social theoretical debates, works to maintain the very relations of power and domination that are ostensibly criticized within such debates. By focusing on Europe as the producer of the events of world-historical importance and structuring all other histories in relation to what occurs in Europe, we perpetuate the relations of domination established through Europe's colonial past. Panu links this theoretical perspective to a discussion of the politics of identity formation and the (limited) possibilities of ever moving beyond the structuring discourses of our times.

William Outhwaite, in conclusion, reflects on the different 'endings' of 1968 that have been articulated in dominant discourses as well as the endings that are implicit in the contributors' own narratives. He reflects on the nature of 1968 as a 'memory', beginning with the wry observation (that must be true for many) of what it was like to be there, sharing many of the motivations of other participants, but not be there, in the sense of missing where it was happening (or had happened) and just learning about it as reportage and 'newly minted' myth. However, 1968 differed from other key dates like 1989 with its vivid and defining event of the destruction of the Berlin Wall, or the 1917 Bolshevik Revolution. For Outhwaite, 1968 is more like 1848, another date that seemed only to inaugurate disappointment and yet lived on as a memory of the 'peoples' spring', more resonant, perhaps, because there were no specific consequences that could yield up a sense of betrayal of the values that had brought them into being. For Outhwaite, 1968's lasting significance, then, is its hope.

Fittingly, Barack Obama's political testament is called *The Audacity of Hope*. His election as President of the United States took place between the date of the conference and the publication of this volume of chapters. The election of the first Black president to a country scarred in its recent past by the legacies of slavery and social, economic and political apartheid is historic. Obama was seven years old in 1968 and is the first president since 1968 not himself to have been directly formed by the politics of the 1960s. The successful mobilization of young voters suggests that a generational change is underway and that politics has moved beyond the 'culture wars' of the earlier period. There appears to be a sense both that the baton has passed across generations and that the politics of the future will be significantly affected by the idealism of a new younger generation. Since it was 1968 that made the significance of generational politics so resonant, perhaps the election of Obama truly marks the end of 1968 as we have known it and allows for the possibilities of different histories and futures to be written.

Notes

1. The conference marked the relaunch of the British Sociological Association's Theory Study Group. Over 90 papers were presented, with 6 keynote speakers and close on 200 participants. The chapters collected here are indicative of the spread and quality of the debate over those two days in London and present, in different ways, one of the key themes under discussion: that of 'other' stories of 1968. We would like to thank our co-organizers, Helen Gregory, Stephen Kemp, Maki Kimura and Sasha Roseneil, as well as the administrative staff at the British Sociological Association, for their contribution in making this a successful event.
2. In writing this Introduction, we were assisted by the reflections of two people who *were* there and claim to remember – John Holmwood and William Outhwaite. We would like to acknowledge their contributions to this Introduction and absolve them of any responsibility for remaining errors: they have admitted to being there and so our reliance on their memory is solely our responsibility!
3. Although it must be recognized that this was the condition of the largely white, middle-class student movement; other student protests had different motivations (see Chapter 1, this volume).
4. A soundtrack of the conference was provided by Ste Nunn's mix of covers of tracks of the period as a tribute to the 'children of the revolution'.

Part I
Rethinking Historical Narratives

1
Freedom Now! 1968 as a Turning Point for Black American Student Activism[1]

Patricia Hill Collins

Two weeks before Barack Obama was elected the 44th President of the United States, ex-Secretary of State Colin Powell gave an unprecedented endorsement of Obama's campaign: 'I think we need a *generational change*, and I think Senator Obama has *captured the feelings of the young people of America*, and is reaching out in a more diverse, inclusive way across our society' (Halperin 2008). Obama's decisive victory suggests that Colin Powell may be onto something. In particular, the 2008 Presidential campaign galvanized American youth as an increasingly visible political force in US politics and, in the case of the Obama campaign, pushed a multi-ethnic youth population as potential voters and workers to the forefront of the campaign itself.[2] When seen against the backdrop of the seeming political quiescence of American youth in pre-2004 Presidential campaigns, the resurgence of visible political activism among youth was startling.[3] The November 2008 election not only was a watershed event for American electoral politics, it also may mark a substantial turning point in the political activism of American youth and the so-called Millennial Generation in particular.[4]

The year 1968 constituted a similar and significant turning point for youth activism. The year was a touchstone for the broader time period of the 1960s, one of massive social change that profoundly changed the dynamics of race, class, gender and sexuality in the United States.[5] Most people who were young adults in 1968 can point to at least one event that occurred during that year that, for them, held great personal significance. Each month brought yet another major political event, with 1968 itself symbolizing a constellation of social and political changes that began in the 1950s and continued into the 1970s.[6]

Moreover, the events of the 1950s through the 1970s typically had young people at their core. For example, young people were the ones who faced police dogs and fire hoses during demonstrations of the 1963–1964 campaigns in Birmingham, Alabama. Their images on television shocked many viewers out of their complacency. While Martin Luther King, Jr, composed his famous 'Letter from a Birmingham Jail,' more than one thousand students skipped school on 2 May to join the demonstrations, in what would come to be called the Children's Crusade. More than six hundred ended up in jail. The membership of the Black Panther Party for Self-Defense, widely recognized as a radical Black Nationalist organization, was founded and maintained by youth. Huey P. Newton and Bobby Seale were 24 and 30 years old, respectively, when they founded the party in 1966 calling for the protection of African American neighbourhoods from police brutality. The Young Lords, a similar group, was founded by Latino youth.[7] When Tom Hayden, a graduate student at the University of Michigan, launched Students for a Democratic Society (SDS) in 1960, he helped catalyse an anti-war movement against the War in Vietnam that spread far beyond his home campus.[8] Similarly, a heterogeneous constellation of young women, many of whom were politicized by their participation in the civil rights, anti-war, Black Power and Chicano social movements, launched a feminist movement that has catalysed widespread legal and social changes for women of all backgrounds. Campus organizing preceded the movement for gay and lesbian liberation, but the Stonewall Rebellion of June 1969 where gays and lesbians openly protested police actions gave a visible face to this hidden oppression.[9] Collectively, youth from diverse backgrounds and through heterogeneous means took the risks. We enjoy the benefits.

The centrality of American youth in the events of 1968 is clear. Yet the varying interpretations given to youth political activism from this period are now emerging. Enough time has passed that we can begin to take stock of that era. Depending on your social location and/or your point of view, 1968 was the year that youth either lost their minds or came to their senses or accomplished both simultaneously.

In the US context, I sense an emerging stock story, one that recasts this broad, politicized and unruly array of youth-oriented social movement activities through a narrow lens of apolitical, simple adolescent rebellion. As caricatured in the media, the sixties' youth apparently became mesmerized with drugs, free love and questionable politics; they were ungrateful hippies who disappointed their parents. From the perspective of White elites, this caricature held some validity. What does it mean when your own children turn on you and question the very institutions that you worked so hard to preserve for them?

For White middle-class youth, getting into good schools and getting good jobs was not something that they might hope to earn some day – education and good jobs were class property, part of White middle-class entitlement to be handed down from one generation to the next.[10] The task for elites lay in coming to terms with the seeming failure of the intergenerational transfer of wealth and power. For example, young middle-class White women became increasingly dissatisfied with attending college to find a mate with the hopes of settling peacefully in the suburbs. Their dissatisfaction with the 1950s catalysed their rebellion in the 1960s (Friedan 1963). Sociologist C. Wright Mills (1951) writes of the seemingly meaningless white-collar work that awaited young middle-class White men. In essence, some children of privilege used their education to seek greater freedoms within their race/class privilege (e.g., some strands of feminism and the identity politics of the gay/lesbian movement). In contrast, others turned their back on their race/class privilege by throwing in their lot with the most unfortunate (e.g., the White middle-class youth who participated in the voter registration drives in the Deep South), or directly challenging the authority of social institutions (e.g., student demonstrations at the 1968 Democratic National Convention).

Whether 2008 or 1968, I suggest that we remain cautious about identifying adolescent, intergenerational rebellion as the normative framework for explaining the political activism of American youth. An overemphasis on the political activities of college-educated, White middle-class youth flattens the heterogeneity of youth activism that occurred in multiple social locations and that was refracted through a lens of race, class, gender, sexuality and, in this instance, age. Viewing the growth of political consciousness among youth through the lens of one segment that stands for the larger group (in this case, the experiences of White, male, middle-class college students who were allegedly radicalized either by their leftist professors and/or a palpable fear of being drafted to fight in Vietnam) is short-sighted. Instead, this period offers an intriguing opportunity to rethink the significance of age as a structure of power via focusing on the coming to political consciousness of a heterogeneous constellation of American youth.

Here I want to focus on one phenomenon in this expanded frame of youth activism, namely, how 1968 constituted a turning point in Black American student activism that in turn signalled a shift in African American social movement politics. I do so because, when it comes to racial change in the United States, the political action of African American individuals and/or organized groups has been far more central in catalysing change than mainstream political thought typically recognizes.[11] I suggest that a closer look at African American youth activism does reinforce the theme of generational rebellion, but in the case of African American youth, their rebellion was against neither their parents nor their class privilege. Rather, I see the student activism of US Blacks as one component in intergenerational efforts by African Americans to disrupt racial business as usual in the United States and to change the terms of the intergenerational transfer of power.[12]

My argument is divided into three parts. First, by examining the significance of the construct of freedom as a visionary construct within African American politics and the struggle for education as its strategic, pragmatic counterpart, I sketch out an interpretive context for African American student activism.[13] Freedom constitutes a deep taproot of African American social and political thought and education has long operated as a crucial site for Black freedom struggle. Education remains a critical strategic tool for social mobility within American society, and the longstanding struggle to gain a quality education for African American students from day care through post-graduate education means that the political struggles of Black American youth have been simultaneously intellectual and political. Thus, US Black students have long been politically active in struggles to create the conditions for their own educational opportunities, a social location that demonstrates clear relationships between ideas, social structures and politics.[14] Moreover, this interpretive context of visionary pragmatism that links freedom and education draws on intersectional analyses of race, class and age. In essence, the race and class position of African American youth in the 1960s differentially positioned them in their understanding of politics, their own education, and their historical relationship with historically White institutions, specifically, colleges and universities.[15]

Second, I discuss core ideological tensions within US Black social and political thought around the contours of the freedom struggle that bubbled to the surface during the five-year period marked by Martin Luther King's 'I Have a Dream' speech at the 1963 March on Washington for Jobs and Freedom, to the assassinations of Malcolm X in 1965 and King in 1968. I suggest that, for African American youth, 1968 constituted a distinctive turning point in the intellectual and political history of US Blacks that pivoted not solely on the events in Vietnam or the assassination of Bobby Kennedy, but also on the meaning of the King assassination. Rather, patterns of Black American youth activism reflected longstanding ideological tensions within African American communities, in particular the ideological tensions within the emerging Black Power movement.

Third, I examine why King's assassination might have constituted a turning point for Black American student activism. In brief, King's assassination shifted ongoing debates among African American youth about the direction for Black freedom struggle by questioning the utility of integration as the expression of the vision of freedom and non-violence as the pragmatic strategy to achieve it. Black students on historically White campuses found themselves faced with a set of contradictions about the merits of integration and nationalism that were not simply ideological issues but that had pragmatic effects on their everyday lives. For US Black students who integrated historically White colleges and universities in the early 1960s, the college curriculum and its practices were not simply abstract issues of theory or ethics. Rather, struggles to desegregate historically White colleges and university campuses constituted expressions of Black freedom struggle. Claims for Black Studies programs and units reflect this phase of political struggle. Black students had to risk much to engage in campus politics. This placed them in a very different relationship to social movements than their middle-class White counterparts. It also led to very different decisions among African American students concerning how they would negotiate and change the contested racial terrain symbolized by 1968. Finally, I return to the theme of what lessons 1968 might hold for the unfolding political events of 2008.

I. Freedom, education and African American youth

Western intellectuals routinely analyse integration and nationalism as antithetical philosophies, weighing the relative merits of idea systems and then evaluating expressions of ideas in political behaviour. Instead, examining how African Americans actually use systems of ideas such as these within their everyday lived experience (often without using the terminology of nationalism or integration) constitutes a profitable approach to Black American politics.[16] When it came to the 1960s, conversations about the merits of integration and nationalism occurred neither exclusively among US Black leaders nor among Black American intellectuals. Rather, African Americans from all walks of life engaged in these debates, creating a vibrant, cross-generational and political public sphere in which African American leaders and intellectuals both were situated. This was not a top-down use of ideology, with intellectual fathers parsing out the merits of integration and nationalism and sharing this knowledge with the masses of US Blacks.[17] Moreover, this was not a new debate, but rather was one that had long permeated analyses of the US Black freedom struggle.

One fundamental contradiction of American democracy pivots on the promise of freedom juxtaposed to the differential treatment of indigenous peoples, of people of African descent, of Latinos and of immigrant populations.[18] For African Americans, this binary of freedom and slavery, of emancipation and captivity, operates as a core frame for African American social and political thought. African American history begins as a captivity narrative, the enslavement of people of African descent, their crystallization into an American ethnic group honed from both cultural similarities and a shared reality of racial oppression, and their struggle for literal and metaphoric freedom. On a basic level, anyone who has experienced captivity, being held against one's will and forced to engage in activities that one would be unlikely to choose, sees the significance of freedom. The construct of freedom was not simply a metaphor for Black American political theory, but also a construct that had literal resonance in lived African American experience. Within this context, 1968 was not an unusual, unprecedented event, but rather a visible rupture that exposed the contradictions of this foundational dilemma.[19]

The concept of *freedom* has multi-valent meanings within African American social and political thought.[20] Politically, the overarching goal of the protracted freedom struggle has been to gain first-class citizenship rights within democratic American institutions. The literal struggle for freedom is easily traced, with the construct of citizenship rights serving as a useful device for mapping this dimension of freedom struggle. The US Black freedom struggle can be traced as waves of ascendancy and repression, a forward and backward motion in time that constitutes a multi-textured achievement of an elusive freedom. During the period of slavery and of Jim Crow segregation, the goals of freedom struggles as well as the forms that they might take seemed clearer. Specifically, because the initial oppression of people of African descent consisted of enslaving their bodies, the US Black freedom struggle stressed emancipating Black American people's bodies from chattel slavery and gaining citizenship rights for newly recognized African American humanity. Upon emancipation, this new ethnic group of African Americans gained constitutionally protected, formal citizenship rights. However, the White Southern backlash against these newfound freedoms dashed African American hopes of experiencing first-class citizenship in the same way that Whites did. Instead, Jim Crow policies of legal racial segregation relegated African Americans to second-class citizenship. The 60-year civil rights struggles that gained momentum in response to the *Plessy v. Ferguson* Supreme Court decision in 1896 and that came to fruition in *Brown v. Board of Education* decision in 1954 framed sustained US Black activism to overturn racial segregation.

Education for African Americans has been an important focal point of this broader notion of freedom struggle. Each generation of African Americans faced a similar set of issues concerning the significance of education for empowerment. For slave youth, learning to read constituted a site of rebellion, a case aptly documented in the narratives of Frederick Douglass and others (Douglass 1962). For the emancipated children of former slaves, attending formal schools constituted the site of struggle. Because Southern governments refused to fund Negro education, ex-slaves supported their own institutions. Often the migration to urban areas of the South and to Northern cities was designed to provide better opportunities for youth, in particular the search for better schools.

The Civil Rights Movement of the 1950s constitutes a visible and important case of this broader history linking education with the empowerment needed for the freedom struggle. Not only did the Civil Rights Movement attract African American youth, the catalyst for the movement itself was a Supreme Court decision concerning separate but equal education. As the movement continued and the depth of resistance to racial integration became evident, African American youth could see how education constituted a crucial terrain of struggle. In this sense, Black American youth were not simply beneficiaries of the civil rights struggle, but instead could envision and often needed to become politically active as part of their coming of age narrative. In some cases, the involvement of youth in the political issues of the 1950s and 1960s took tragically palpable forms. For example, when *Jet* magazine published photographs such as the open casket of Emmet Till, a 14-year-old Black American boy who was murdered for allegedly looking at a White woman, or the debris left after the 1963 bombing of a Birmingham church that killed four African American girls in Sunday school, youth took notice. These images of murdered Black American children refuted the dominant ideology that American society was, in fact, 'separate and equal,' and that children were beyond politics itself. Instead, it was apparent that just as attacks on a few children symbolized the vulnerability of all Black American children to racist violence, that solutions to such structural patterns would not rest on helping children one at a time but mandated serious attention to group-based strategies.

Court-mandated racial integration encompassed a wide array of areas (housing, public accommodations, etc.), yet none was as controversial as desegregating public schools. By the mid-1960s, some public school districts had made tentative efforts to desegregate whereas others dug in their heels and refused. Southern Whites routinely defied court orders to desegregate schools, in some cases catalysing the need to send troops into Southern schools. A lone African American first-grade girl who needed federal troops to escort her to school, for example, desegregated the New Orleans public schools.

By the 1960s, historically White colleges and universities could no longer invoke a 'separate but equal' ideology to defend exclusionary policies. As the enrolment of African American students on historically White campuses increased, these early arrivers did not experience their college life as a respite from the real world. Instead, getting an education in these formerly segregated settings constituted an extension of the ongoing political struggles of the Civil Rights Movement. Their arrival in some sense represented a tangible victory. Individual African American college students may not have engaged in political struggle to gain access, like the case of the New Orleans first grader who desegregated her local public school; yet African American students who desegregated their campuses changed them, if only by being visible.[21]

Black American students may have been familiar with the general framework of freedom and the significance of education, but this generation that desegregated US colleges and universities in the 1960s also grappled with a particular manifestation of a longstanding ideological tension within African American social and political thought, namely the relative benefits of integration or Black Nationalism.

II. Integration and nationalism: Key ideological tensions of Black solidarity

African American students carried with them into newly desegregating institutions of higher education heterogeneous points of view on a variety of unresolved topics, including: (1) their duties and obligations as key figures in the 'race's' advancement, specifically, leadership; (2) the necessity for Black solidarity and Black unity among Black American youth in unwelcoming racial contexts; and (3) the special contributions, if any, required of Black youth as individuals for collective African American advancement. Many also came with social movement experience that involved substantial risk taking. In brief, many students also carried the tension between integration and nationalism into higher education settings where getting an education itself was inherently politicized.

Black freedom struggle not only focused on education, it also required variations of social and political solidarity. This core principle of US Black freedom struggle found its origins in this early struggle for African American emancipation. Central to the notion of solidarity is the assumption that African Americans comprise a historically constituted group who, because they share a common history of racial oppression as well as shared (albeit far from uniform) experience with institutionalized racism, have common interests. For example, African American women and men both experience racism, but often in gender-specific fashion. Similarly, social class differences among African Americans have long existed, yet these differences often disappeared in the face of uniform treatment by Whites. Slavery certainly stressed the need for solidarity – it made little sense to try and 'free' enslaved Black Americans one by one. Group-based political oppression mandates group-based political remedies.

The contemporary tendency, to juxtapose integration and nationalism as contradictory ideologies for African American political activism, is often interpreted as a deep-seated, ideological tension within African American social and political thought. In contrast, when contextualized within a broader framework of a US Black freedom struggle, these ideologies become redefined as tactical and strategic disagreements within a sustained commitment to the broader construct of freedom. Historically, notions of Black solidarity have accommodated bitterly opposed expressions of these seemingly antithetical perspectives. Yet integration and nationalism both share the ethical commitment to freedom for Black Americans as a collectivity (the freedom struggle is not an individualistic construct) and the necessity of some form of Black solidarity to get there.[22]

African American social and political thought holds many examples of African American leaders who counselled commitment to Black solidarity, but who expressed it by looking either inwards (diverse Black Nationalist agendas of community development); or outwards (issues oriented, social justice agendas, for example, integration); or in some cases, the necessity of coalitions among groups with seemingly different political ideologies and agendas. Stated differently, African American politics has long required a creative tension between nationalist projects that represent political mobilization by US Blacks in defence of African American interests and broader, social justice projects where US Blacks engage in issue-oriented alliances and coalitions for concerns such as employment, schooling, health care. For example, these tensions shape the corpus of work by African American journalist Ida Wells-Barnett. Wells-Barnett is best known for her anti-lynching activism, an outward-looking strategy that identified how racial segregation catalysed significant abuse of power. Yet, she also engaged in community development activities that were designed to uplift African American migrants in Chicago (see Collins 2002). It makes little sense to achieve equal access to unemployment or lack of discrimination in health clinics that are closed or that do not exist.

Rather than examining the virtues of various political philosophies based on their merits of logic and links to empirical verifiability, the test of African American social and political thought lay in its flexibility and pragmatic responses to historically specific situations.[23] Within this framework, the value of intellectual and political leaders often lay in their familiarity with these ideological perspectives and their ability to craft them in response to political needs. The freedom struggles of the 1950s and 1960s illustrate these tensions. For example, whereas Martin Luther King, Jr, is typically depicted as a 'non-violent integrationist,' Michael Dyson contends that King's work more accurately reflected an 'enlightened nationalism.' In explaining this concept, Dyson contends that King 'never succumbed to tribal loyalties that subverted the principles of fundamental equality and democracy for the citizenry of America. But he did embrace the need for Black people to organize themselves for the purposes of Black upward political economic mobility, and not in a selfish way, but in a fashion that would enhance the collective standing of the race' (Dyson 2003: 332). Dyson encourages us to resist the current tendency to categorize important leaders such as King within the narrow framework of 'race-only' politics. One need not throw out Black solidarity in order to pursue broader agendas of equality and democracy.

King was not alone. Within this same logic, Malcolm X, who is typically viewed as a nationalist, at the time of his assassination was developing a more complex and comprehensive view of Black American political struggle that did take note of broader social justice projects. In 'The Ballot or the Bullet,' Malcolm X (2000: 431) not only outlines the principles of Black Nationalism, but also asks his audience to question the culpability of the federal government in reinforcing racial oppression, and to search for new allies to fight the Black freedom struggle:

The same government that you go abroad to fight and die for is the government that is in a conspiracy to deprive you of your voting rights, deprive you of your economic opportunities, deprive you of decent housing, deprive you of decent education.... This government has failed the Negro. This so-called democracy has failed the Negro. And all these white liberals have definitely failed the Negro. So, where do we go from here? First, we need some friends. We need some new allies.

Malcolm X may have appeared to be especially hard on White liberals, but the subsequent capitulation of the Democratic Party to the conservative Republicans in the 1980s and 1990s suggests that he may not have been faroff. During that period, alliances with the White liberals who preached gradualism and assimilation apparently did not serve African Americans well. Identifying how the liberal agenda of continuing to petition the government was fundamentally flawed, Malcolm X counselled African Americans to seek new 'friends,' namely coalitions with groups who had a similar interest in social justice and could support a Black American freedom struggle.[24]

With hindsight, the perceived contradictions between these two ideological positions may be resolved somewhat by using a different language to describe the integration focal point. Strategies for racial integration are just that – strategies to achieve social justice for African Americans within a context of racism. The variations of nationalism deployed by African Americans also constitute strategies that seek similar ends. The way forward here may be to flesh out the links between the more robust construct of struggles for social justice that can take myriad forms (such as the US Black freedom struggle with its ideological poles of integration and nationalism). Linking both social justice and nationalist initiatives in this fashion within the broader context of a US Black freedom struggle that embraced a heterogeneous conception of Black solidarity enables us to map different configurations of thought and politics at distinctive historical junctures. The 1960s constituted an era where a variety of cross-cutting and consensus themes within African American social and political thought were questioned, reformed and transformed.

The early 1960s revealed the increasing tension between these two prominent ideological strands that emerged to shape the contours of Black American political struggle. Integration and nationalism, as expressed through social movement politics, were two sides of the same coin, a Janus-headed figure that was having increasing difficulty reining in the growing anger and upheaval in African American communities. The assassination of Malcolm X in 1963 did little to shut down growing sentiments towards nationalism, in part due to King's presence as a moderating influence on African Americans, as well as continuing anti-colonial struggles in Africa and the Third World that demonstrated the effectiveness of nationalism for political emancipation.[25]

II. 1968: The assassination of Martin Luther King, Jr, as a turning point in US Black student activism

By 1968, it was apparent that King himself was developing a more robust political analysis that increasingly recognized the significance of social class factors and American militarism in fostering the deeply entrenched problems that African Americans faced. King saw issues of American militarism (the War in Vietnam) and social class inequality as refracted through the specific contours of racial hierarchy in the United States, as foundational to African American disadvantage. More importantly, King increasingly organized around a more robust analysis of class and power, as evidenced by his planned participation in the Poor People's March on Washington, DC, that was cut short by his assassination. King's politics were not catalysed by a specific event that affected him personally (the threat of being drafted spurring middle-class White students to action, or the threat that perhaps one would not get the job that one expected all one's life, would be there when one got a degree). Rather, King's politics, although excised of its growing radicalism via media repackaging in short-cut phrases such as integration, man of peace and non-violence, constituted a significant shift in the social justice issues of multi-race, multi-class alliances among Americans.[26]

In this context, King's assassination in 1968 constituted a thunderbolt for many groups, but especially for African American college students. Virtually overnight, his death encouraged Black students not only to challenge strategies of racial integration as a core strategy for Black freedom struggle, but also to question their own placement in colleges and universities in the context of democratic politics. Like the elementary and high school students who integrated New Orleans, Little Rock and other Southern school districts, the arrival of Black students on historically White campuses was the tangible measure of civil rights itself. Yet the assassination of King placed the justification for civil rights at risk. The struggle might be long indeed if King, who was then seen by Black students as the voice of moderation, was killed. How long would the Black freedom struggle take with the one-at-a-time glacial pace of measured social change? Was the struggle going fast enough? Why not demand freedom now?

Patterns of African American student response to the assassination were varied. Yet it was clear that Black Nationalism rose in stature and became increasingly significant for African American students. Many of these actions have been recast through the lens of a redefined identity politics as a separatist, inward looking, narcissistic endeavour where African American students turned their back on the social justice traditions exemplified by Martin Luther King, Jr. I think that this is a re-reading of the past through the conservative frameworks of the present that have a vested interest in undermining histories of progressive political struggles, especially Black freedom struggles. Let me recount three examples from this period that illustrate the complexities of the times.[27]

The first demand that came from this period was the struggle for Black Studies itself. Recently, there have been efforts to rewrite this struggle as a multi-cultural endeavour and/or as a result of White philanthropic support for Black activism (Rooks 2006). Perhaps such support was more common in unusual settings, namely the multi-cultural setting of San Francisco or the moneyed halls of Princeton. Such efforts misread the significance of the racial segregation of American higher education of that period, one where the struggle for Black Studies was one of struggling for the inclusion of actual Black people as well as an effort to desegregate knowledge itself. In the 1960s, Black Studies initiatives focused on the institutional transformation of the very institutions of higher education. In this way, King's death radicalized Black students to demand not simply spots within the institution, leaving its structure basically unchanged, but rather transformation of those institutions so that they could not continue business as usual. Because the currency of universities is knowledge, attacking inequalities in the curriculum and how they in turn framed inequalities among students (admissions, testing, etc.) constituted core issues of early Black students' initiatives.

The second example comes from my own experiences with African American student protest at Harvard University. Students negotiated with the administration and subsequently occupied a building to protest the university's racially differential labour practices concerning its painters and painters' helpers. The painters were unionized and White while the painters' helpers were uniformly non-unionized African American workers. Although painters' helpers did virtually the same work, the unionized White painters were paid considerably more than the non-unionized African American painters' helpers. This example illustrates the broadening of the Black student political agenda from race to issues of class within Black American student politics. The focus of the struggle was to help the painters and the painters' helpers, not to gain more financial aid for students or hire some African American faculty role models. The focus here was not on forming alliances with the workers to figure out the best plan of attack on the state. Rather, the strategy was similar to that deployed by the (White) student movement, namely to use one's insider position to pressure the university to erase racial bias in its employment policies.

The third concerns the resurgence of modern Black Feminism, both across the diverse locations of integrationist and nationalist initiatives as well as an entity in its own right. It is important to keep in mind that politically active African American women moved among a variety of organizations. Chela Sandoval's (2000) analysis of differential movement as a way of doing theory and politics investigates this idea. There were iterations within social justice initiatives – African American women were in coalition with White women and other women of colour in the heterogeneity of feminist movement. Despite this movement, there also existed the need to organize on one's behalf, a tendency that pulls from the solidarity tradition. In their movement among various organizations, Black American women saw the limitations of those different organizations. There was a need to birth Black Feminism in dialogue with and in opposition to *both* the second wave feminist movement *and* the Black Nationalist movements.[28]

In this political context of cross-cutting and collaborative relationships among political movements, many African American women organized separate organizations that focused on their specific needs, but also kept those organizations in dialogue with multiple political groups. For example, The Combahee River Collective (1995), one signature analysis of intersectionality that emerged during this period of youth activism, issued a statement that argued for a politics that took race, gender, class and sexuality into account. This statement had great influence on US Black Feminism.

III. 1968 and 2008: A new turning point?

This brief survey of US Black student activism in 1968 might help identify productive themes for analysing contemporary political activism. What are the lessons from the 1960s generally and this brief foray into African American youth activism in particular that might inform our understanding of contemporary youth activism?

First, the political activism of youth takes heterogeneous forms depending on the opportunities and constraints inherent in their social locations. The period of the 1960s shows how tidy analyses that focus on the behaviour of one segment of the American youth population miss the theoretical and political significance of the heterogeneity of race, class, gender and sexuality that occurred *within* one age population. Many young people worked in mono-identity organizational settings (e.g., gender-only women's groups such as the National Organization for Women, or race-only Black Nationalist organizations such as the Black Panther Party); some worked in multi-cultural settings (e.g., grassroots social justice organizations); some moved among various organizations, and some simply took to the streets (e.g., riots). A much broader approach would examine the range of organizations where youth were active in non-school settings, for example, the young mothers who participated in the National Welfare Rights Organization, or in Association of Community Organizations for Reform Now (ACORN), or similar grassroots organizations.[29]

Not only is this true for 1968, it remains true today. Because US college campuses house many organizations ranging from the Young Republicans to students who want to end the genocide in Darfur, they provide numerous opportunities for youth activism. But other venues for youth activism exist around a range of specific issues ranging from HIV/AIDS awareness, to citizenship initiatives by immigrant youth and their allies, to environmental issues.[30] Since its emergence in the late 1970s, hip hop has been a site of contemporary Black youth activism by allowing inner city youth to give voice to their concerns and talk about life as they experienced it. In this sense, hip-hop culture can be seen as a site of cultural resistance (see, for example, Kitwana 2002; Clay 2006).

Second, any synthetic narrative about the political activism of youth requires examining multiple histories and the standpoints they might produce on a common political project. In this case, the shared ethos was the perceived need by youth in the 1950s and 1960s to engage in political activism in defence of social justice. Yet the social location of groups of youth, in fact, their very ability to recognize themselves as a group, suggests that individual and group placement within a matrix of domination of race, class, gender and age shaped the vision and patterns of political participation. It is important to keep in mind that had I written this narrative from the social location of gender and the feminist politics of the time, my 1968 story would have been quite different (see, for example, Valk 2008). Or had I examined the class politics of political activism among youth, one that sent poor and working class men not to college but to Vietnam, the version of youth activism would have been different yet again. Recognizing how the differential placement of youth within a matrix of domination framed the experiences of middle-class Latinas, poor gay White men, working-class African American women and similar groups suggests that any ideology that is seemingly shared by these groups (in this case, the meaning of political activism and the forms that it might take) is best developed by attending to this heterogeneity. Moreover, this same heterogeneity that shaped the differential placement of youth writ large, also framed dynamics *within* African American youth populations. In this sense, the narrative presented here is not meant to stand for African American youth as a population, but is one that shows a sliver of action by a youth population that is most visible within the broader story of youth activism. In essence, this one story refracted through intersecting power relations of race, class, gender and age requires similar stories that use the same framework of analysis.

A third and related theme for analysing contemporary political activism concerns the varying forms that political activism took in the 1960s as compared to today. This version of praxis, the recursive relationship between theory and practice, differed in the two periods. Social movements of the 1950s and 1960s were actively engaged in theorizing creative responses to social conditions; and theories in turn shaped political decision-making. For African American students, the relative merits of integration and nationalism were tested not solely through logic, but also through the crucible of experience in the Black freedom struggle. This framework of praxis grounded in a recursive relationship between theory and action both catalysed additional theoretical perspectives (the case of Black Feminism) and shifted the terms of political participation (African American women who participated in multiple organizations).[31]

For politically active 1960s youth, face-to-face organizing was crucial. Politically active youth in the South faced dangerous, often life-threatening situations. It is important to remember that the Civil Rights Movement revealed how recalcitrant various levels of the US government could be in protecting its African American citizens. In some cases, the government condoned the murder of US Blacks by not investigating cases. African American students were at special risk, and thus could not count on fair treatment in schools and jobs as well as protection by the police. With the government infiltrating youth groups, personal contact was an element of building trust. Politically active 1960s youth also effectively used the mass media that was available to them for political ends. African American youth were a large part of the Civil Rights Movement, and the Civil Rights Movement was one of the first social movements to be televised (the television coverage of Birmingham youth being attacked by dogs and sprayed with fire hoses comes to mind). Yet news of their local political activities was screened by a small number of mass media venues.

The lessons for contemporary political praxis are provocative. For contemporary youth, the recursive connections between ideas and society, social problems and intellectual production, persist, but the reduced dangers of political activity coupled with new communications technologies have enabled new ways of organizing. New possibilities exist for an innovative synergy between face-to-face organizing and the use of media. A more decentralized communications technology enables contemporary youth to organize *both* locally (on college campuses, in their neighbourhoods, etc.) *and* in imagined political space. In essence, many have gained valuable experience in this kind of praxis, in a different political context and by using dramatically different organizational tools.

The Obama campaign illustrates this emerging form of praxis. On the one hand, the Obama campaign utilized tried-and-true techniques of having people organize their neighbours and friends. This form of organizing creates a trustworthy cadre of people who participate in political communities. Because Obama ran a grassroots campaign, youth volunteers and paid staff practised problem solving about the nuts and bolts of political participation. They canvassed, made phone calls and learned the ropes of face-to-face community organizing. Their efforts to identify and work directly with voters in turn had important implications for the success of the campaign.

On the other hand, because a sizeable portion of the Millennial Generation and their immediate generational predecessors grew up with computers, the Internet and cell phones, the Obama campaign was able to draw upon the technical sophistication of youth volunteers and campaign workers.[32] An arsenal of communications tools that were unavailable 20 years ago dramatically changed the contours of community organizing. For example, the Internet created unprecedented social networks (MySpace, Facebook, etc.) as well as numerous written and visual opportunities for youth to become citizen-journalists (blogs, YouTube, etc.). The actual campaign relied on email and text messaging, two relatively inexpensive mechanisms for communicating with large numbers of people instantaneously. For example, Obama supporters could sign up to receive an early text message announcing Obama's Vice Presidential running mate; or those attending the convention were told to text friends and family to watch the speeches.[33] The Obama team seems to be carrying over the use of technology from the campaign into the Presidency. Like the campaign website, the transition team has set up a post-election website, http://change.gov/, that contains a newsroom blog with YouTube videos of events since the election. The website also has a section where visitors can share their visions for the country.

Increased youth activism in the 1960s and today suggests a fourth significant theme for analysing contemporary political activism, namely the intergenerational transfer of power. In essence, youth political activism of the 1960s was a response against efforts in the 1950s to reinstall seemingly conservative values in American families, neighbourhoods and political institutions. African Americans, Latinos and women in particular had enjoyed new freedoms during the Second World War and simply could not go back to former ways of being. Similarly, the deeply conservative turn within American politics symbolized by the 1980 election of President Ronald Reagan can be seen as a direct response to the radicalism of 1968. This cycling of political positions among liberal and conservative ideologies suggests that there is considerable reason for optimism that a more multi-cultural, multi-ethnic and tolerant US population that has been raised in a different political and media context may in fact wield the reins of power differently.

The unprecedented 2008 Presidential election suggests that such a shift is at hand. The 2008 election may mark the coming of age of a generation of youth whose adult memories have been shaped by a combination of post 9/11 rhetoric, of environmental degradation and a Janus-headed mass media that simultaneously homogenizes global culture and provides a dizzying array of digital tools with which to navigate it. We may be in yet another awakening of youth politics, this time refracted not primarily through issues oriented, social justice themes expressed via social movement activities, but rather through electoral politics itself.[34]

At the same time, we must be cautious not to vest unreasonably high expectations in either the youngest members of Obama's coalition or any one charismatic leader. Frantz Fanon, an intellectual whose ideas inspired African American youth movements of the 1960s, points to the dangers of seeing independence (or in this case, the 2008 election) as the inherently positive defining moment of a generational freedom struggle. In *The Wretched of the Earth*, Fanon (1963: 112) says,

> Before independence, the leader, as a rule, personified the aspirations of the people – independence, political freedom, and national dignity. But in the aftermath of independence, far from actually

embodying the needs of the people, far from establishing himself as the promoter of the actual dignity of the people, which is founded on bread, land, and putting the country back into their sacred hands, the leader will unmask his inner purpose: to be the CEO of the company of profiteers composed of a national bourgeoisie intent only on getting the most out of the situation... His honesty, which is purely a frame of mind, gradually crumbles. The leader is so out of touch with the masses that he manages to convince himself they resent his authority and question the services he has rendered to the country.

Certainly, Fanon identifies a crucial danger for a generational shift in power. Many newly independent nation-states found that the leadership and forms of political activism organization that effectively brought about the transfer of power were less effective in governing.[35] Yet because this story is still being written, it need not be the way Fanon predicts.

Finally, this foray into youth activism of 1968 raises questions about the significance of specific political events as defining moments in the political self-understandings and behaviour of a generation. Like others of my cohort, I remember 1968 as a year of student upheavals that signalled a shift in social movement politics among youth. Yet, as evidenced by emerging research on 1968, political activism by youth was not solely an American phenomenon but rather signalled something far broader. Similar youth movements in France, Bengal, Pakistan, Senegal, South Africa and other locations suggest that a global phenomenon of youth activism was at play in 1968.[36] Unlike contemporary youth, we lacked the communications technology to craft a global movement. As I write this chapter, it is simply too early to tell from within this historic moment. But when we look back on 2008, we might ask, in what ways did 2008 constitute a turning point, for those who came of age, but also who aspired to come to power?

Notes

1. I would like to thank Kendra Barber, University of Maryland College Park, Department of Sociology, for invaluable research and editorial assistance for this chapter.
2. An estimated 24 million Americans aged 18–29 voted in this election, reflecting an increase in youth turnout by at least 2.2 million over 2004. That puts youth turnout somewhere between 49.3 and 54.5 per cent, meaning 19 per cent more young people voted this year than in 2004. Exit polls show 66 per cent of voters aged 18–29 preferred Obama and 32 per cent preferred McCain (Dahl 2008). Thus, it is safe to say that the Obama campaign relied

on a large percentage of youth workers and voters. At the same time, it is premature to assess the specific demographics by cohort (Generation X, the Millennial Generation, the Hip-Hop Generation) of political participation, primarily because the significance of this youth vote has only recently been recognized.
3. This belief may have been fuelled by the visibility of hip-hop culture in the 1990s and its expressions of social protest. For discussions of this generational analysis, see Kitwana (2002), Bynoe (2004) and Clay (2006). For a provocative analysis of the potential political behaviour of African Americans in the Hip-Hop Generation, see Goff (2008).
4. In his book, *Youth to Power: How Today's Young Voters are Building Tomorrow's Progressive Majority*, political activist Michael Connery provides a generational analysis of youth activism in the United States. Connery makes a distinction between the era of Generation X where, throughout the 1980s and 1990s, volunteerism and civic engagement among young people went into a steep decline, and the Millennial Generation. After the 2000 election and in 2004, young voter turnout began to increase. Connery contends that this new Millennial Generation is redefining civic participation and the growth of progressive youth activism (Connery 2008: 9–10). Using Connery's argument, the Obama campaign did not lead the Millennial Generation, a trend that preceded Obama's decision to run for president, but rather recognized the trend and worked with it. For another analysis of the Millennial Generation, see Howe and Strauss (2000).
5. In this chapter, I use the '1960s' as a shorthand term for the three decades of youth activism beginning in the 1950s with the Civil Rights Movement and continuing into the 1970s with the feminist and gay and lesbian movements. The 1960s constitutes the peak of political activity for this period.
6. A brief synopsis of the events of 1968 includes the following: on 31 January, the Viet Cong opened the Tet Offensive by attacking major cities in south Vietnam, a move that triggered President Lyndon B. Johnson's call for peace negotiations. On 31 March, Johnson announced that he would not run for re-election. On 4 April, Martin Luther King, Jr, was assassinated in Memphis, Tennessee, a move that led to riots in Washington, DC, and other cities. In June, Robert F. Kennedy, former US attorney general and US senator from New York, was assassinated while campaigning for the Democratic presidential nomination. In August, the Democratic National Convention encountered clashes between Vietnam War protesters and the Chicago police force. Over hundred demonstrators were arrested and over hundred more were injured. At Mexico City's Summer Olympic Games in October, African American sprinters Tommie Smith and John Carlos won gold and bronze medals, respectively, and then raised their hands in the Black Power fist during the playing of the national anthem.
7. See, for example, Abramson *et al.* (1971). For an analysis of the Brown Berets, a group founded by Chicano youth who modelled themselves after the Black Panther Party, see Muñoz (1989).
8. Students for a Democratic Society (SDS), a student activist movement in the United States, was one of the main iconic representations of the country's New Left. The organization developed and expanded rapidly in

the mid-1960s before dissolving at its last convention in 1969. Though various organizations have been formed in subsequent years as proposed national networks for left-wing student organizing, none has approached the scale of SDS, and most have lasted a few years at best. For a discussion of these issues, see Calvert (1991).
9. Students at certain colleges began to see the importance of equal rights for LGBT (Lesbian, Gay, Bisexual and Transgender) people. The first student gay rights group, the Student Homophile League (SHL), was formed in 1967 at Columbia University, organized by a student, Stephen Donaldson. While the SHL attracted negative attention from the media, it inspired other gay activists to begin SHL chapters at different universities. For an overview, see Dynes (2002) or Beemyn (2003).
10. For a discussion of whiteness as property, see Harris (1993).
11. Prematurely embracing adolescent rebellion as the social theory explaining the 1960s youth activism identifies blind spots in Western social theory concerning not just age (youth), but also the politics of race and Black political activism. For example, paths to Black American student activism certainly resembled and intersected those followed by White middle-class students, yet one is not derivative of or a special case of the other. We must be careful not to develop analyses of youth activism that constitute yet another example of how Western social theory misreads racial politics. As Jalali and Lipset flatly assert, 'race and ethnicity provide the most striking example of a general failure among experts to anticipate social developments in varying types of societies' (1998: 317). Much evidence supports their thesis. For example, assuming that the importance of ethnicity would decrease in conjunction with modernization, the sociology of race and ethnicity seemed unprepared for the resurgence of racial/ethnic conflict in the 1990s. Conflicts in places as diverse as Yugoslavia, Rwanda, Canada, Sri Lanka and Malaysia challenged the theoretical consensus among Marxist and non-Marxist scholars alike that industrialization, urbanization and education would foster racial and ethnic group integration into emerging democracies (Jalali and Lipset 1998). American sociology in the 1950s provides an especially glaring example of this myopia. Its preoccupation with racial attitudes held by White Americans apparently blinded it to the rumblings of African American unrest that exploded into sit-ins, marches, protest rallies, and a sustained civil rights movement in its own backyard. As James McKee points out, 'the sociologists of race relations had not simply failed to predict a specific event; rather, they had grievously misread a significant historical development. The race relations that appeared in their writings were incongruent with the race relations to be found in the society around them' (1993: 2).
12. In this chapter, I capitalize the terms *African American*, *Black American* and *US Blacks* and use all three interchangeably to describe the group of 35 million people. According to the 2000 Census, there are 34,658,190 people who are Black/African American alone, but 36,419,434 who are Black/African American alone or in combination with other racial categories. http://www.census.gov/population/www/cen2000/briefs/phc-t8/tables/tab03.pdf. I use the criteria of a social group whose experience in the United States has been shaped by the African Slave Trade, American slavery, and/or history with legal and *de jure* racial segregation. These patterns

of capitalization parallel similar terms that are routinely used to describe US racial/ethnic groups, for example, Irish Americans, Puerto Ricans, Mexican Americans and Asian Americans. The controversies revolve on the capitalization of 'Black,' one that resembles debates a century ago about the need to capitalize 'negro.' I am aware of the debates about the social construction of race and the use of the term 'Black.' For a developed analysis of the nuances of these debates, see my comprehensive discussion of the construct of 'social Blackness' in Collins (forthcoming).

13. Here I invoke the idea of *visionary pragmatism* that I argue has been central to African American women's theory and practice. For discussions of this construct, see my discussions in *Fighting Words* (Collins 1998) and in the Afterword of *Another Kind of Public Education* (Collins forthcoming). For an edited volume that further develops this construct, see James *et al* (1993).

14. African American intellectuals confront similar issues, but not about access to education itself, but rather access to intellectual freedom. US Black activism has required struggles to create the conditions that foster one's intellectual production.

15. This activism also invokes a different conception of praxis, one that is grounded in African American social and political thought specifically, but that also has been influenced by broader traditions of American pragmatism. For two classic works in American pragmatism that invoke this notion of praxis, see Mills (2000) and Dewey (1954). The centrality of African Americans to American pragmatism has been overlooked. For analysis of pragmatism and race, see the essays in Lawson and Koch (2004).

16. For representative work in traditional approaches to integration and nationalism as philosophies, see Shelby (2005). For an example of how a population might use ideology to craft its everyday lived experience, see my analysis of how Afrocentrism, a specific variety of Black Cultural Nationalism, has been used by African Americans as a civil religion (Collins 2006: 75–94).

17. I refer to this approach as a 'family lineage' model of knowledge production. Under this approach, we study the ideas of prominent thinkers by examining which intellectuals influenced them, and then aim to identify which thinkers they 'trained' or influenced. This approach privileges the ideas of Western White men joined together in a socially constructed family lineage of intellectual fathers and sons. This routine intellectual history model works less perfectly for analysing the ideas and actions of politically active groups. Here I use a social history or social context model as more useful in examining African American student activism, namely, the recursive relationship between social location, ideas and political behaviour. In its focus on preparing citizenry for American democracy, American pragmatism argued for this approach to ideas and action. See, for example, Mills (2000) and Dewey (1954).

18. For African Americans, the vision of freedom takes a palpable form and frames pragmatic action. It is a form of visionary pragmatism and has been a collective vision that sustains the struggle for freedom from one generation to the next. There is a pragmatic element to this vision so that one tempers one's political activity around the historical times. For two analyses of the significance of the concept of freedom to African American political struggle, see Kelley (2002) and King (1996). Also, consult the speeches of

Martin Luther King, Jr, for examples of how King repeatedly refers to the term 'freedom' as part of civil rights (Carson and Shepard 2002). Also, see note 16.
19. Here I am following a social movements philosophy that sees social movements as having phases of visibility and abeyance that flow into one another. Within this framework, social movements for social justice, for example, will be ongoing as long as social justice has not been achieved. Outsiders can see phases of quiescence or 'peace' as evidence for the death of a movement yet such periods may signal a different phase. For a discussion of this concept applied to the US women's movement, see Taylor (1989).
20. Before I discuss education and its relationship to freedom and African American freedom struggle, I want to provide an interpretive framework. For one, African American thinkers often use the construct of freedom to describe the broad array of political activities within African American thought and politics. Specifically, for histories of African American politics that implicitly use this notion of freedom struggle, see Berry (1994) and Franklin (1992). For two distinctive analyses of the centrality of freedom for African American politics, see Kelley (2002) and King (1996). As a concept, freedom has objective and subjective resonance throughout African American culture, as in poet Nikki Giovanni's plaintive cry in her 'Woman Poem' during the Black Arts Movement, 'I wish I knew how it would feel to be free' (Giovanni 1968). Despite the centrality of the term *freedom* within African American history, I use the term freedom carefully. Because freedom is such a powerful word that can invoke subjective meanings, politicians and protest groups alike appropriate the term and use it to advance their own political agendas. For example, the Bush administration (2000–2008) invaded Iraq in search of weapons of mass destruction under the heading 'Operation Iraqi Freedom.' Freedom is a slippery concept – freedom from what, freedom to do what, for what purpose. In a context where representations and ideas play such an important part in a society that disproportionately ghettoizes and locks up African Americans, consciousness as a sphere of freedom takes on added importance. My discussion of 'The Power of a Free Mind' is designed to investigate this dimension of freedom struggle (Collins 2004: 303–7).
21. In 1964, there were an estimated 15,000 Black students enrolled in predominately White colleges in the South, representing a fourfold increase since 1957. Meanwhile, African American undergraduate enrolments in Northern colleges had increased from around 45,000 in 1954 to almost 95,000 in 1967–1968. The number of Black Americans attending White colleges in the South during the first half of the decade of the sixties rose from 3000 in 1960 to 24,000 in 1965, and to 98,000 by 1970. Between 1965 and 1970, African American enrolment in White institutions more than tripled. Simultaneously, African American enrolments in historically Black colleges and universities had dropped from 82 per cent of all college-attending Blacks to 60 per cent between 1965 and 1970; it declined to 40 per cent by 1978 (Lucas 1994: 241–2). For a review of research that discusses the backgrounds and political activism of Black students attending predominately White universities, see Willie and Cunnigen (1981).

22. For a substantive, philosophical analysis of African American solidarity that develops the ideas sketched out here, see Shelby (2005). I suspect that the need for group-based politics is more difficult to see in the contemporary context. In the contemporary period of post-structural analysis, the very construct of group presented in this survey has come under attack, and if one dismantles the recognition of a shared group status, one simultaneously dismantles its politics (Collins 1998: 201–8).
23. It also explains the seeming contradictions within the intellectual and political work of individual African American thinkers. One might begin as a Black Nationalist and advocate for Black solidarity but will quickly see that, under conditions of contemporary globalization, freedom can never be won through a simplistic separatist agenda. This seems to be the path that Malcolm X was following during the last year of his life after he broke with the Nation of Islam. See the end of *The Autobiography of Malcolm X* (1965). Conversely, one might begin analysis within a framework of integration and human rights, yet see that if African Americans fail to advocate on their own behalf, the state is likely to remain unresponsive. Some of the later speeches of Martin Luther King, Jr, suggest that he was increasingly responsive to nationalist perspectives. For example, in 'Where Do We Go From Here?' one of his later speeches, King speaks of Operation Breadbasket and economic boycotts of recalcitrant companies. He asks his largely African American audience to stand in solidarity and use economic power. See Carson and Shepard (2002: 185–6). Neither figure arrived at a destination, but both were assessing the possible links between integration and nationalism.
24. Given how Malcolm X is routinely treated as a Black Nationalist separatist, it is noteworthy that he titled this famous speech 'The Ballot or the Bullet.' The undue attention given to the bullet may have been catalysed by Fanon's discussion of revolutionary violence as a route to Black male subjecthood (Fanon 1963). Yet Malcolm X's focus on the ballot, while seemed to be slower and reformist, also constitutes a political choice.
25. The work of Frantz Fanon was especially significant for nationalist groups like the Black Panthers who often cast their political projects in the context of domestic decolonization. For representative work, see Fanon (1963).
26. For an especially suggestive speech that captures King's deepening radicalism, see his 'Beyond Vietnam' speech (Carson and Shepard 2002: 133–64). Also, for a revisionist analysis of King that identifies his radicalism, see Dyson (2000).
27. For a sample of work on African American student activism, see Anderson-Bricker (1999), Franklin (2003) and Rosenthal (1975).
28. For an analysis of these trends in Black Feminism, see Collins (2006). For an historical analysis of how African American women were positioned within these relations, see Valk (2008).
29. For example, ACORN was started in 1970 (http://acorn.org/index.php?id=12447&L=0%2Findex.php%3Fid%3D4201). For an analysis of women's activism among various groups, see Valk (2008).
30. For example, for AIDS awareness, see the Youth Force as one example of a global youth organization centred around HIV/AIDS activism, http://youthaids2008.org/en/about/background.html. For an example of

citizenship activism by immigrant youth, see 'Walkouts May Signal Rebirth of Youth Activism' by Lourdes Medrano, Arizona Daily Star, 3/31/06, http://www.nusd.k12.az.us/schools/nhs/gthomson.class/articles/first.amend/ Walkouts.signal.rebirth.youth.activism.pdf. For environmental issues, consult the Student Environmental Action Coalition or SEAC, a grassroots, youth organization based in the US and Canada, http://www.seac.org/. For work on queer activism, especially various Gay-Straight alliances in high schools and colleges, as well as LGBT organizations on college campuses, see Driver (2008). For an overview of youth activism, see Ginwright, Noguera and Cammarota (2006).
31. There was a more robust space for a public sociology and the praxis that it reflects and engenders.
32. For example, Kendra Barber reports that one of the Obama emails that she received during the campaign offered her the opportunity to be trained in grassroots organizing. Volunteers were offered a place to stay for several days during training, after which they were expected to return to their home communities and organize.
33. Just as politically active youth of the 1960s and 1970s rejected the family lineage model of legitimated knowledge, so might politically active youth of today have no need for the gate keeping, interpretive processes of editorial pages of local newspapers, or television pundits on the nightly news. There are many ways to make and obtain news, with the notion of the citizen-journalist emerging as an especially crucial area among youth. For example, access to cell phones with digital cameras created entirely new communications possibilities for political organizing.
34. For an interesting analysis of how Obama connects with the Millennial Generation, see *Millennial Makeover: MySpace, YouTube, and the Future of American Politics* (http://www.millennialmakeover.com/Articles/Newsweek%20McCain, %20Obama%20and%20the%20Millennial%20Generation.htm). See an article on this site by Andrew Romano called 'McCain, Obama, and the Millennial Makeover' that talks about Obama having millennial values. In a 2008 *Newsweek* article titled 'He's One of Us Now,' Romero argues that Obama is the first millennial to run for president. He said 'my point in the piece wasn't to alter the space-time continuum by suggesting that Obama is a millennial; obviously he's too old for that. Instead it was, as I wrote then, to show "how fully and seamlessly he embodies the attitudes, aspirations and shortcomings of the generation that's rallied around him"' (http://www.newsweek.com/id/109589/output/print).
35. Robert Mugabe's failed state in Zimbabwe provides an especially stark example. The trajectory of Mugabe's rule raises additional questions about how and why politically active student leaders often become conservative when they govern. Karl Mannheim sketches out a preliminary explanation for this phenomenon. Mannheim notes, 'It appears to be a generally valid law of the structure of intellectual development that when new groups gain entry into an already established situation they do not take over without further ado the ideologies which have already been elaborated for this situation, but rather they adapt the ideas which they bring with them through their traditions to the new situation... When these strata had come to occupy the social position previously held by

the conservatives, they quite spontaneously developed a feeling for life and modes of thought which were structurally related to conservatism' (Mannheim 1954: 249).
36. Several papers presented at the *1968: Impact and Implications* Conference that catalysed this volume examined this question of particular expressions of youth activism in different national settings.

2
She's Leaving Home: Women's Sixties Renaissance

Lynne Segal

It is rather amazing to be at a celebration of 1968 that begins, and also ends, with reflections by feminists on women's position in the Sixties. Certainly, it is usually not women who are highlighted in reflections upon what became the iconic year of that momentous decade. Yet, far from it being simply tokenism to ensure the inclusion of a few women's voices, retrospectively, it now seems quite essential to draw attention to women's place in Sixties memorabilia. Merely saying so, however, brings to light at least two things. First of all, it confirms how distant we are now from the structures of feeling 40 years ago; second, and most interestingly, it indicates how memory itself mutates, allowing us to look back and see the past differently, differently from how it was seen at the time, or even how we might once ourselves have looked back upon the era.

We live in nostalgic times, that much is certain, when that eager walk backwards, down memory lane, has never been more popular, nor memoir-writing as fashionable. Accordingly, the academy is blooming with life-writing courses, and few literature options remain unaffected by the autobiographical turn. Today, 'the past is selling better than the future', Andreas Huyssen (2003: 13) remarked a few years ago, pondering the perilous politics of memory. It is as if, the historian Mark Mazower echoes, the only *new* worlds still to be discovered lie behind us. Even the 'New' of New Labour is now already the past. It has become merely that blip that sadly failed to differentiate itself from corporate capital's triumphant post-Seventies' neo-liberal assault on any Keynesian alternatives, or from recent US-led neo-imperial military ventures, as today's enthusiastic demolition of Gordon Brown testifies. Thus, in these backward glances, there is also much mourning, but most especially, and

29

for obvious reasons, mourning coming from the Left, whatever its formation.

I. The New Left and its influence

With its attention to culture, to sexuality and everyday life, to self-help, participatory democracy and direct action (with CND, the Campaign Against Nuclear Disarmament – those colourful Aldermaston Marches – its first major movement in the UK) the New Left of the Sixties was, of course, implicated in the rising importance attached to personal life. Belatedly so obvious, the *material* underpinning of this political shift was the spectacular rise of mass markets and consumer spending in the Sixties. Launching *New Left Review*, in 1960, for instance, its founding editor, the then 28-year-old Stuart Hall, could register his high utopian hopes, seeing this New Left as motivated not so much by 'the need to escape immiseration', but rather by its dedication to creating an egalitarian society of 'conscious thinking human beings', people who would be able to create their own 'self-determining lives, which would prove more than something one passes through like tea through a strainer' (1989: 33). 'Creativity', 'self-determination', now there were two words for a young woman to brood over in the Sixties: situated as she still was then either as 'mother's little helper' or awaiting the arrival of her one-true-love, if not, all of a sudden, newly perplexed by the images of 'herself' freshly stylized as buxom pneumatic chick, then also increasingly adorning counter-cultural radical porn. With its very distinct focus on personal life, psychoanalytic thought would also penetrate more widely than ever before into the language of this New Left, and well beyond, as Eli Zaretsky (2008) has recorded in all of his writing. (Paradoxically, he adds, its popular influence spread during the very decade that also marked the beginning of the decline of psychoanalysis as a profession – despite its growth in more affluent pockets of Latin America). Finally, the Sixties was implicated in the rise of the domain of personal life, as we'll see, also because this was the decade which, above all (as Juliet Mitchell's reflections also highlight), provided the seed-bed for Western feminism: the movement that would do most to consummate that union between personal life and politics, politics and personal life, as that enduringly Sixties' rebel girl, Sheila Rowbotham (1973), captured so memorably in the title of one of her classic books, *Women's Consciousness, Man's World*. This book was an offprint of writing she had begun at the close of the Sixties, which had been published the previous year, *Women, Resistance and Revolution* (1972).

Of course, as we should know by now, not only memory, but history too has its blind spots, even for those rigorously attentive to its more neglected byways. What is lost almost always includes the precise texture of emancipatory struggles, those upsurges so swiftly disregarded or misrepresented once their initial fervour fades. Yet the Sixties *is* a little different. The legacies of that decade live on, whether seen, as it often is, and most usefully can be, as encompassing what some historians call the 'long Sixties', the 20 years of popular protest movements stretching from the rise of the New Left in 1956 to the beginning of the decline of such movements in 1976, or compressed into its flashpoint, in France, May 1968. They persist if only because they remain, after all these years, still so fiercely contested – the Sixties' spirit as precious to the libertarian Left as it is anathema to the Right. Today, suitably, Nikolas Sarkosy replaces Margaret Thatcher, as the decade's chief scold; indeed, the goal of his 'renewal' process was, he claimed, 'to do away with May '68, once and for all' (quoted in Badiou 2008: 34). Since its high points originated in confrontational, often anarchic, challenges aiming to disrupt the prevailing order of just about everything, of course, any systematic accounting of the decade violates exactly that chaotic and confused excitement seen as emblematic of Sixties' rebellion. Yet, while most historical texts readily encompass the diversity and distinctiveness of most of the engagements and revolts of its varied activists, there is one cluster that tends to fall beneath the usual radar of analysis, whatever direction it comes from. The historical accounting, the familiar memorabilia, of the Sixties, and even more so of May 1968, all place men *definitively*, men *exclusively*, at the centre of both the decade and its defining year.

II. Predators and prey

With the conference generating this collection one of the main exceptions, the commemorations and publications on 1968 in this new millennium have mostly mirrored the traditional accounting. We see again the imprimatur of the decade reduced to student graffiti adorning those Parisian walls, 40 years ago. Their once imaginative, now *rather* tired and untroubling slogans urge us forward once again into gardens of earthly delight, on the back of tigers of wrath: 'Be Realistic, Demand the Impossible', 'Live without Dead Time', 'Form Dream Committees', and all the rest of it. There is, however, the usual neglect of that group which appears, perhaps surprisingly, in almost equal numbers alongside, although clearly distinct from, the angry and rebellious young men whose names reappear in the scholarly and popular re-staging of those years. Yes, of course, of course, women were there. What were they doing, what were they thinking, that particular band of humanity, those with the bright eyes and smooth faces, long-legged in their miniskirts, often dancing so wildly to the drumbeat of Sixties' rock; later reappearing marching in step with male comrades, usually listening just as eagerly to the rising figures of the Left, those hurling their passionately defiant words from formal platforms, at barricades, astride the bonnets of overturned cars?

If you want to project your most lascivious fantasies onto them, you can imagine some ineluctable connection between these energetic young women and the iconography of female bodies – always stripped-down, prone, perpetually servicing, men – in the sexist litter saturating much of the 'underground' or alternative press of the time. Its nadir was, perhaps, one drawn-out, dreary strip from 'May '68', concluding:

> Some comrades from the council for maintaining the occupations are going to come and fuck me violently. Judging by their practice, their theories must be truly radical.
> (Stansill and Mairowitz 1971: 141)

Radical? Radicalizing, beyond a doubt, in that the graphic display of so much infantile braggadocio, with its projected predatory presumptions no longer securely hidden behind syrupy sentimentality, was already helping to generate its own comeuppance. Women's presence during those years, when madness was declared the new sanity, must have amounted to much more than their depiction as masturbatory aids and sources of male bonding for those busy drafting or eagerly absorbing outlaw manifestos. Much more. For even as so many male militants were already worrying that their revolution was over before the decade itself was out, scores of women were simultaneously suggesting that the spirit of the Sixties was crucial for them. 'Freedom Now! We love you!' young women in the Students for a Democratic Society (SDS), the radical students' movement in the USA, concluded a collective statement addressing their male comrades in the summer of 1967. Given that their main concern was the destructive impact of what they newly identified as 'male chauvinism', it was a love that for many years went unrequited, merely mocked and rejected by most of those to whom it was proffered. Whisper it softly, in today's cultures of blame and victimhood, but such defensive derision would eventually rebound, for it was women who in the end could perhaps be seen as that decade's most decisive victors. Something in the Sixties' air, as well as that small packet of pills in their handbag or by their bedsides, was giving women a new found energy. It was the spirit some took with them into the Seventies, as they marched by then so much more confidently along the very same pathways they had trod during the previous decade, although making several critical swerves, all the while mouthing many of the same words, although with certain crucial new catchphrases – 'Women Hold Up Half the Sky', for one.

Now, if there is any agreement about the Sixties, it is that this was a time of sexual challenge to the prudery, hypocrisy and stolid family conservatism dominating the post-war Fifties' world. But here, strangely, a point missed by many (though not by the American novelist Norman Mailer (1971), who early on articulated his fear that men might in the end lose out to the whirr of the vibrator) is that it was only women's determination to seek sexual pleasure outside marriage, and to flaunt it, which was actually really new. Double standards had long since made straight men's engagement in sex outside marriage, an activity that was tolerated, if not encouraged. That Sixties' women were far from the mere passive objects of men's desire (notwithstanding the surrounding priapic iconography) was affirmed by various feminist writers when asked to commemorate '1968', some 20 years ago. Angela Carter, for one, then rejoiced that this was a time when sexual pleasure was suddenly divorced not only from reproduction, but also from women needing to use it for 'status, security, all the foul traps men lay for women in order to trap them into permanent relationships' (1988: 214). Sheila Rowbotham, somewhat similarly, described how she and her friends struggled throughout the Sixties 'with all the contradictory versions of sex, morality and what being a woman was meant to be about' (1988: 26), determined to outwit the conspiracy of fathers, teachers, ministers and dons, trying to keep them chaste. Almost at once, other sexual dissidents, first of all those identifying as gay men and lesbians, were also not only asserting their own rights to sexual freedom, but making common cause with oppressed people more generally: 'Free Our Sisters, Free Ourselves', North American Gay Liberation Front marches yelled outside the Women's House of Detention in June 1970, at very first gay march on the anniversary of the Stonewall Bar riot in 1969 (Kunzel 2008). These joyful years of rising movement politics were, at least in the beginning, a time for making links with all those other outsiders in the world, not primarily for asserting differences.

'She's Leaving Home', the Beatles chorused in 1967, and indeed, she was; young women were just on the verge of that mass exit. Over the next few years, ever more single young women began fighting with parents and other authorities to establish that it was possible, if still certainly often perilous, to leave home, have sex, and much else besides (though not yet to obtain a mortgage or other forms of basic financial backing) free from dependence on some man who had authority over them. As the meticulous historian of the Sixties, Arthur Marwick, reports (using figures from West Germany, the place where he grew up), the ultimate success of these intrepid sexual pioneers appears in numerous surveys tracking their enduring cultural impact. In 1967, 65 per cent of single German women still disapproved of cohabitation, but a mere 6 years later only 2 per cent of women had any such objections. Always already on a somewhat different playing field, for single men the figure dropped somewhat less precipitously, though also significantly, from 43 per cent to 5 per cent (Marwick 1998: 805). At least as importantly, women working alongside or within the various civil rights, anti-racist, anti-imperialist and, eventually most importantly of all, the anti-Vietnam War movements of the Sixties, had also been learning how to organize, work politically, and how to bond with each other – if at first rather hesitantly. The direct action involved in such political work often combined with at least some attachment to the various avant-garde stirrings of the alternative cultural scene, while women in particular were already especially prominent in some of the grass-roots community projects of the Sixties: 'I find myself happier than I ever dreamed I could be', Alix Kates Shulman (1978) begins her semi-fictionalized memoir of women's political awakening in the Sixties, *Burning Questions*. She was not alone. It is this harnessing of energy amongst women, a time when for many women the space between suddenly desiring change and believing it could happen was shrinking, which slips out of Sixties' accounting, though it is obvious when women write their own accounts of the decade, as Sheila Rowbotham's (2000) superb memoir of the decade exemplifies.

III. Lost in the slipstream

Symptomatic of the slippage, with women again bleached out of the picture, is one of the most recent scholarly overviews of the Sixties, Gerd-Rainer Horn's *The Spirit of '68: Rebellion in Europe and North America, 1956–1976'*, which appeared in 2007. This book attempts a far-reaching analysis and appraisal of the political and cultural achievements, defeats and thwarted aspirations of struggles over these 20 years, while also considering whether some of its lost causes could ever be regenerated once more. Horn opens his account with the restless desires of those cultural rebels, beats, outcasts and dropouts, challenging the heightened conformism and bourgeois respectability of the Fifties post-war years. I am familiar with his object of study here, as I began my own political life amongst the vestiges of just such cultural and political rebels, down among the bohemians and 'wild men' of the Sydney Push in the early 1960s. In the years before she became famous, these were the dissidents who also first influenced Germaine Greer, with their own distinct brand of pessimistic anarchism, determined to reject authority wherever they found it, since they believed that whoever got any grip on political power would always come to abuse it in self-serving ways. The influence of this form of free-thinking, anti-authoritarianism, equally critical of marriage, religion and the State, on the women such as myself who encountered it, is something I write about in my book *Making Trouble* (Segal 2007). For me, as for Greer, such Sixties' encounters would serve as part of the pathway on the road to feminism, once women found their own collective voices from the close of the Sixties.

Horn's own survey moves on from the beat generation and other cultural rebels in the USA, to highlight the significance of the detached political disdain enlivening the ultra-libertarian, anti-capitalist Situationist texts of Guy Debord and Raoul Vaneigem, before ranging broadly across the Sixties' landscape of civil rights alliances, Black liberation and student struggles in North America, as well as the various workers struggles, anti-war movements and student insurgencies that sprung so vibrantly to life across Europe. Although the eyes of the world fixated on the dramatic, three weeks of students and workers' uprisings in France in 1968, Horn points out that other labour struggles actually lasted far longer, such as struggles of the Italian labour movement, which continued for eight years, making Italy's unionized workforce the best protected and most democratically organized in Europe. Horn correctly identifies the Sixties' spirit in its rejection of the authoritarianism, cultural conservatism and extreme moderation of the Old Left (whether nominally communist or social democratic) alongside its commitment to direct action, participatory democracy and, above all, the autonomy of the collective resistance of diverse movement struggles, all beginning from their own specific sites of resistance. Yet, here is his only striking omission, women's presence over this period receives little more than a single page in his penultimate chapter, which is all the more surprising when women's liberation as an organized movement had itself peaked *before* (rather than after) the endpoint of Horn's survey, in 1976.

All over again, it is still necessary to emphasize that the spirit of the Sixties was the cradle of feminism. Women's liberation did not emerge merely as a reaction against the supposed 'male' priorities of that decade. Women were already there, already fighting, organizing and beginning to think collectively, both with and without men. Although it was primarily movement politics in the USA that would in the early years serve as the main inspiration for women's movements around the world, there were already feminist stirrings everywhere. The diverse Marxist currents so often in the forefront of the radical workers and student uprisings in Europe, for sure, usually were, and often remained, much less open to prioritizing any distinctive women's perspectives, although within them women were also transformed simply by the struggles themselves. Describing the break-down of her usual feminine passivity in Paris in May 1968, the American-born, subsequent British literary agent, Anne McDermid, recalls her activities trying to beat back the phalanx of Dalek-like French police bearing down on protesters: 'I threw the *pavé* with all the force I could muster and the shriek of triumph in my ears was probably my own' (1988: 209).

It was certainly in her own voice, we know, that Juliet Mitchell wrote her influential feminist text, 'Women, the Longest Revolution' for *New Left Review* in the mid-Sixties, followed a few years later by the articles Sheila Rowbotham published in the radical magazine *Black Dwarf*, heralding *The Year of the Militant Woman*, which hit the street in 1969. Along with most other women caught up in Sixties' radicalism, the books that these avatars of women's liberation were reading during that decade almost always included Simone de Beauvoir's *The Second Sex* (1988).

Twenty years after she penned them, de Beauvoir's words in that text, which has stayed in print for over 50 years, provided almost the founding text for women's liberation. Around the world, she became legendary in her own lifetime for many Sixties' women, as the self-styled 'liberated' woman, choosing to remain sexually active and single, in pursuit of a free and independent life. Recalling their youthful Sixties selves, there is hardly a single well-known first-wave feminist who did not subsequently acknowledge her influence on their younger selves: 'It was a siren call', Kate Millett claimed (quoted in Forster and Sutton 1989), alighting upon *The Second Sex* in New York in the 1960s; 'I was seized by a desire to imitate her', Lisa Appignanesi (1988: 2) recalls her Canadian teenage years in the Sixties; '[We] were grateful, regaled, awestruck and disturbed... [Her] denunciations opened windows on to a great gale of air. We shouted *yes*', Sylvia Lawson (2002: 153–4) relives her delight on discovering *The Second Sex* as a young middle-class mother in my own home-town, Sydney, in 1960, immediately sharing her reading with friends. 'For us, the young women in the 1960s who became the Women's Liberationists of the 1970s, her life was truly exemplary, to be pondered and explored for clues [on] how to live differently', another Australian feminist, Ann Curthoys (2000: 11), later wrote. Sheila Rowbotham (1973) sums it all up in *Women's Consciousness, Man's World*: 'she demonstrated an art of living'. '[She] indicated a new and transformed possibility – the movement from passivity into freedom'. Doris Lessing's novels also served to enlighten many Sixties' women of the challenges lying ahead, especially for women caught up in radical politics, as she had been in the 1950s, in what was then the Southern Rhodesian Communist Party. Influential as her books remained for feminists, however, Lessing herself, quite unlike de Beauvoir, always had a far more ambivalent, even hostile, attitude towards the young women who followed in her wake (see Segal 2007: ch. 5).

IV. Women's Sixties' radicalism

Women's Liberation thus had its origins fully within many of the political and cultural currents of the 1960s, at least within all of those which overflowed into the 1970s. For even as the sardonic Situationist-inspired slogans that now provide the routine backdrop for periodizing of the Sixties were racing around the world, we can, if we choose to, easily unearth a few other, more sharply combative slogans, which were first uttered at much the same time, before they were anxiously, actively repressed, almost never to reappear in the memorializing of that time. 'Liberate socialist eminences from their bourgeois cocks', was the slogan unfurled at the Socialist German Student Organization, in 1968, as Helke Sander along with other women addressed their male comrades. The swift burial which followed their performance is hardly surprising, especially as the slogan itself was accompanied by a poster containing graphic representations of just how this liberation could be achieved (quoted in Harrigan 1982: 42). Hidden from history such slogans remain, yet they expressed one of the more lasting revolts from 1968, if one that would, mercifully, be somewhat tamed as the decades rolled on.

Back in the USA, women were crossing class and race barriers to stand up for each other. In 1965 Mary King and Casey Hayden had written a widely circulated document on the status of women in the Student Non-violence Co-ordinating Committee (SNCC) to register Black voters. One of their number, Barbara Epstein, would later recall the strength White women, such as herself, gained from supporting Black women when involved in voter-registration campaigns in the Southern states in the mid-Sixties:

> I lived with local families, often at some risk to them...I had a lot to observe. Black women seemed different from white women. They seemed stronger. More important... They occupied more social space than white women... In effect the Black women I saw and worked with provided a different model of what it meant to be a woman in our society. This opened up a whole realm of possibilities.
> (Epstein 1998: 175)

Later, White feminists participated in the rallies held in support of jailed Black Panther sisters, such as Joan Bird, and raised money to pay their bail, at the close of the decade. In the USA, as elsewhere, women fighters in Vietnam provided other models for women in the Sixties, as life-long feminist and anti-war activist, Leslie Cagan, recalls when describing the electrifying impact of meeting some of them in Bulgaria in the spring of 1968. Strength was certainly necessary if women were to withstand the heckling some received if and when they dared to rise to speak at student meetings, as the late New York feminist, Ellen Willis, reported of such attempt in early 1969: 'The men go crazy. "Take it off! Take it off the stage and fuck her!". They yell and guffaw at unwitting double entendres like "We must take to the streets"' (Willis, quoted in Popkin 1979: 198). Sheila Rowbotham had similarly found herself 'an object of derision' when speaking at a British student rally in 1968, recalling: 'It was like a living nightmare. Stubbornness kept me in front of the microphone...Somehow through the whistling and laughter I managed to speak about [the under-funding of] further education' (2000: 188).

The American feminist, Amy Popkin (1979), later commented on the 'second-level' chauvinism soon evident at student meetings, which meant that women would not be taken seriously when they reported on anything other than the problem of men's sexism. No matter, women were getting on with their activism anyway, with the rhizomic spread of feminism throwing its shoots first of all right across the USA, as another member of New York Radical Women's group, Ros Baxandall (1998), writes, describing her own work with other mothers in 1967, setting up Liberation Nursery, the first feminist day care centre on the Lower East Side of Manhattan. In the USA, 1968 was the year that Jo Freeman published the first national newsletter *Voices of the Women's Liberation Movement* in Chicago; *No More Fun & Games: A Journal of Female Liberation* appeared some months later in Boston, the movement staged its first widely reported protest (at the Miss America pageant in Atlantic City); Shulamith Firestone published her 'Women and the Radical Movement'; Adrienne Rich wrote her poem, 'Planetarium', which began, 'A woman in the shape of a monster/a monster in the shape of a woman/the skies are full of them' (Rich 2008). And so they were, all of a sudden, raining women. 'WOMEN OF THE WORLD UNITE – WE HAVE NOTHING TO LOSE BUT OUR MEN!' was yet another banner unfurled in the USA in 1968. Unite they surely did, continuing many of the old struggles, but losing some of the men they had fought with, who dropped faster by the wayside. As the radical Sixties balladeer, Joan Baez, addressed her old comrade and lover, Bob Dylan, in 1972: 'You left us marching on the road and said how heavy was the load/The years were young, the struggle barely had its start/...And we're still marching in the streets with little victories and big defeats/But there is joy and there is hope and there's a place for you' (Baez 2008). Bobby, however, like many other men from those years, had long since left it to the women to march on alone.

V. Feminism in context

The growth of Women's Liberation, I have been arguing, needs to be placed within that Sixties' context in which it first appeared. 'Form Dream Committees', 'Be Realistic, Demand the Impossible', could be interpreted anew once women's needs and interests came to the fore. Feminists drew up their plans to transform society and also their own lives, at one and the same time: 'Under the movement's spell we sometimes fancied raising our children together and growing old in joyful women's communities that would satisfy all our needs for companionship, sex, autonomy, power, family, free of oppressive – or merely dull – marriages' (Shulman 1998). This particular feminist spin on Sixties' utopian dreams comes from the recollections of Alix Kates Shulman who at the close of the Sixties was a full-time housewife with two young children, and also a member of the New York dream committee, the Redstockings collective. It was, for instance, with typical Sixties, yet also fundamentally, 'feminist irony, idealism, audacity and glee', as she later reports, that Shulman sat down in 1969 to write her instantly infamous

'Marriage Agreement' (signed by herself and her then husband). It would be reprinted in many women's magazines and journals over the next few years, generating over two thousand letters in one magazine alone, the national women's lifestyle journal *Redbook*. The long list of principles comprising the 'Agreement' all expanded upon men and women's equal sharing of the possibilities for paid work and of the pleasures and the burdens of childcare and housework: 'As parents we believe we must share all responsibility for taking care of our children and home – not only the work but also the responsibility' (Shulman 1998: 292). Radical men had for years declared that women's demands for shared housework were pointlessly utopian when, within the blink of an eyelid, it was just such demands that were being popularly discussed across the USA.

So while it is in many ways correct to see the agendas of women's liberation as significantly breaking away from aspects of Sixties' politics, it is equally right to see their continuities. It was the political currents and theories of the Sixties, in Britain filtering down, especially, from Raymond Williams, E. P. Thompson and Stuart Hall, that had emphasized the role of culture in politics, stressed the significance of cross-class alliances, the need to respond to calls for direct action and the building of networks of solidarity over forms of party building. These were precisely the political perspectives and strategies favoured by feminists as they began to differentiate themselves, to a degree, from the revolutionary posturing of some of the best-known male militants and their comrades. Moreover, behind the braggadocio, many Sixties' men themselves were early on rather receptive to the feminists soon in their midst. The Sixties' poet and radical activist, Kenneth Pitchford, for example, was fully supportive of his wife, Robin Morgan, when in the late 1960s she moved from the American anti-war Left, and her own contributions to its alternative counter-cultural journals, to become a founding member of New York's Radical Women. Indeed, it was Pitchford, together with Morgan, who fashioned what became, and remained, the women's liberation symbol, that raised, clenched fist inside the female symbol (see DuPlessis and Snitow 1998: 501). This iconography alone underscored the origins of second-wave feminism within, quite as much as against, that spontaneous, directly confrontational, Sixties' spirit.

Men were certainly being challenged, but it was some men, alongside women, at least for quite a while, who followed feminists in trying to work to unify anti-war, anti-racist and Left politics with women's liberation. In Britain, it was even clearer that it was the institutions and publications of the New Left, with their emphasis on building socialism from below, in the here and now, which created the indispensable catalyst for women's liberation. For example, it was that indefatigable New Left dynamo, Rafael Samuel who, with his founding of the *History Workshop Journal* and alternative people's history conferences, had helped provide a public platform for many new rebel voices, but especially for women's liberation. Indeed, it was at a History Workshop Conference in 1969 that Sheila Rowbotham successfully proposed what would become the first ever National Women's Liberation Conference to be held in Britain, which took place at Ruskin College, Oxford, where Samuel worked. Setting a pattern that would be followed at all the national women's conferences in subsequent years, it was Left men who ran the crèche at that first conference. It was certainly the chauvinist male bonding and blatant sexism of Sixties' radical men that had forced militancy upon women. It was also true that it would take most women many years to overcome their apprehension and timidity, if and when confronting mixed Left gatherings, and some of them never did attempt it. Nevertheless, it was precisely within those Sixties' publications that women announced that their time had now come to fight their battles on their own. Just as Juliet Mitchell had been the sole woman on the editorial board of *New Left Review* when she wrote 'The Longest Revolution', so it was when Sheila Rowbotham was serving as the sole woman on the editorial board of the radical Left magazine, *Black Dwarf*, headed up by Britain's then best-known student radical, Tariq Ali, that she was able to solicit and write articles for an issue of the *Dwarf* heralding *The Year of the Militant Woman*, which appeared in 1969. Preparing for that special issue, Rowbotham had read through Lessing and de Beauvoir, eagerly searching for ideas on how to bring women's personal issues to politics, while at the same time interviewing women sewing machinists on strike at Ford factories, and other militant working-class women who, alongside female guerrilla fighters in Vietnam, provided early role models for Women's Liberation (Rowbotham 2000: 209).

The rest is history. Many other women quickly joined the ranks of these earliest militant women. 1969 was the year the young Australian in Britain, Germaine Greer (then working with the quintessentially Sixties' radical porn magazine *SUCK*), was busy writing *The Female Eunuch* (1971), which became an instant bestseller in mainstream culture, popular with men and women. This was also the year that the first Women's Liberation groups appeared in the UK, a year after they became visible in the USA. Just for a change, as Rowbotham would later wryly note, the assertive predictions of a Left paper 'had been vindicated by history' (2000: 252). That year, 1969, *was* the turning point in the rebirth of the 'militant woman' in Britain, just as 1968 had proved its decisive moment in the USA. Like it or loathe it, memorialize or disavow it, despite and because of all its hitherto unexamined male chauvinism, the Sixties was the decade that nurtured women's liberation.

3
Subterranean Traditions Rising: The Year That Enid Blyton Died[1]

Ken Plummer

I. The year that Enid Blyton died

So these are the times and the tales of our lives.
Contested. Contingent. Creative and thriving.
Progressing. Regressing. And usually surviving.
Incorrigibly plural. Intransigently vast.
These are the tales of how we order our past,
the moments we might have as the futures unfold,
the hopes for the world if our visions are bold.
These movements, these changes that never will end,
and years that fly by, and the moments we spend.
The stories we tell and the memories we mend.
So here is a year overflowing with symbols,
effervescent and striking.
A world in the making, a world for our liking.
Yes. These are the times and the tales of our lives.

So this is the year that Enid Blyton had died.
Poor Noddy's demise – and the fabulous five.
Three and a half billion were struggling to live.
As spacemen and lunar trips have so much to give,
we saw transplant surgery and the strength of Apartheid.
In Africa, as usual, the millions had died.
Famine in Biafra and Asian Kenyans to flee.
This was also the time of the new liberty.
And the cold war hung in the heat of the night
as the tanks poured into Prague to scare all in their sight.
In Vietnam, many were killed in My Lai;
While the Cultural Revolution led millions to die.

The Pope told us all not to use contraception-
whilst nudity in *Hair* won a world wide reception.
Warhol was shot, Martin Luther King dead;
Enoch Powell raged in his rivers of red.
Then, as now and throughout all the times,
humanity keeps moving along with its crimes.
Yes, these are the horrors and joys that we make in our lives.

But these were also the times of the student protests
as marches and sit ins unleashed civil unrests.
The whole world was watching and media pervaded
as universities grew and then got invaded.
Across all the globe the students were rising
and the stances they took refused compromising.
In France, Marxist Situationism rose up from the floor,
US students rose up against the poor and the war
In Italy, Turin and Trento bloody battles engaged,
and Mexico City had students enraged.
While Warwick Limited signposted the future of money,
of big companies, big industry and something quite funny;
Yes this was the start of the university market
to turn learning and knowledge into a measurable target.
And just when I got my degree, to set us all free,
Discursive deconstruction came looking for me.

Yes this was the time of bourgeois ideology
and that consensual nonsense we called sociology.
Parsonsian drivel was mocked with the jeers
whilst Marxism rose up and was given three cheers.
Banned in China, the left was so right.
Denying again the darkness of night.
Banned in China, the West had it wrong-
wear Mao Tse Tung Uniforms and start to feel strong.
The culture and its Maoist revolution
showed communism was no easy solution.
We made Marx our hero and wore Maoist dress.
a coming crisis was everyone's guess.
And a paradigm shift to get out of the mess.
Mundane consensus became radical orthodoxy
a coming crisis in Western sociology–
consensus and conflicts, and action and structure
the clichés of a legitimation crisis.

So this was the march of the sixty eight dreamers.
Anarchistic believers and socialist schemers.
The calls that they made were stark and dead clear.
Post colonial anger began to appear.
End war. Kill Capitalism. And stop the technology.
And bring to an end bourgeois sociology.
The pedagogy of the oppressed was liberated here.
The politics of experience was set into gear.
The History Man and the NDC would appear.
Yes these were the days of the subaltern rising.
Of marginal women and men now arriving.
Subterranean tribes now leaving the zoo,
Bohemians and radicals, delinquents too,
Outsiders and strangers with different views-
spreading the news of the rights now to choose.
Empowering voices. And plausible choices.
Dominant hegemonies once taken for granted.
Subterranean traditions now queering the slanted.
Active and pushing and changing the spacing;
Ideas from the past must now need replacing.
When everyday life shatters each second of living,
the margins merging, the queers unforgiving.
Greenpeace and Greenham and Gay Liberation,
fighting back for a much better nation.
In a world that they had never ever made.
Migrants of time, generational divides
Holding on to their places, protecting their spaces,
defending their races. The ones before
they can hardly see. The ones to come will just disagree-
rejecting and fighting, resisting the new.
Delinquent, declining and gone to the dogs.
Each generation unique and then lost.
Each generation is lost at its cost -
as each generation must do it again,
and face all the pain – all over again.
As they bump and they jump and they thump
on the old – and the new.

So these are the times and the tales of our lives.
As the walls came down and capitalism spread
to lands where before it had been hopelessly dead.
Vietnam may have ended but the wars kept on going.

The deaths of the millions kept flowing and flowing.
Our lap tops and iPods and gadgetry gizmos,
our Starbucks and Googles and terrible quiz shows,
our markets and shopping where all lives could flourish
with sushi and dim-sum and nachos to nourish.
Inequalities widened with billionaire fools,
and the life of the mind must now follow rules
provided by managers – who run all our schools.
We live with RAE. And are all made professors.
We lead lives over run by quality assessors.
So these are the times and the tales of our lives.

Spectacular tales and multiple voices
Effervescent moments and plausible choices
Mosaics and patchworks and kaleidoscopes playing
Grand designs, total structures collapsed and decaying.
And linear lines fragment into fractures
Symbolic, shambolic, semiotic, systolic.
This is the march of the times

And these are the dreams for the rest of the time.
  Utopias imagined will never arrive.
    But the dream and the drama will help us survive.
      And everyday life will keep us alive.
        Cultivate capabilities and the rights of all people.
          Weaken the deepening of all social inequalities.
            Be cosmopolitan and live with our differences.
          And love one another or die.

Yes these are the times and the tales of our lives.
Contested. Contingent. Creative. And thriving.
Progressing. Regressing. And sometimes surviving.
Incorrigibly plural. Intransigently vast.
These are the tales of how we order our past.
And the moments we might have as futures unfold.
And the hopes of the world if our visions are bold.
The movements, the changes that never will end;
The years that fly by and the moments we spend,
The stories we tell and the memories we mend,
The chances and whispers and dreams we construct,
World changin' and movin': worlds won and worlds lost.
These are the times and the tales of our lives

II. Subterranean traditions rising

> We cannot make heaven on earth. What we can do instead is, I believe, to make life a little less terrible and a little less unjust in every generation. A good deal can be achieved in this way.
>
> Karl Popper

Lives, stories, standpoints and generational perspectives all interconnect, and as such there can be no one meaning of 1968 – nor even a dominant one. My story – as a child of 1968 – is like some others but different from most. There is both a uniqueness and a generality. In this chapter, I start with some aspects of my own perspective and experience, and then move out to a wider sense of generations and their rebellious pasts. All tales are told from a standpoint, one of many possibilities, and mine is that of a sixties' queer with a sociological eye.

1968: Fragment of a life story

Now, in 2008, I am a retired Professor of Sociology. For the past 40 years I have been teaching, thinking and writing about the stories we tell of society – and especially of our queer and sexual lives, and the identities we forge around them. I am, what I call, a critical humanist – which means I like to focus on real embodied human beings living their everyday lives through pain and joy in historically structured moments. I am interested in embodied humanly made social worlds, the interactive webs and negotiated orders we creatively weave them into, and their linkages with wider historical social patterns (structures). I believe that everything we do as humans (and indeed, reflexively, as sociologists) is saturated with creativity and action, language and materiality, ethics and power, ceaseless change and contingency, and multifarious plurality. I see societies as heaving webs of ever changing stories and human life as always being on the boil. There is nothing fixed, static, essential or tidily coherent about any of it. We are compelled to write ever changing tales from our various perspectives (or standpoints): sociology always fails badly when it over-generalizes. Epistemologically, sociologists can only ever have partial perspectives, stories, accounts of this world; but we need to make them as good as they can be. Human beings are always engaged in continuous permutations of action. I worry that sociology can sometimes be driven by too much form, too much method, too much theory, too much abstraction, too much generality. And not enough precarious human social life.

So now go back 40 years. To 1968. My life. Here is the start of an auto/ethnography. There is absolutely nothing straightforward about this, and it stands in a very odd relation to the 'events of 1968', most of which had no involvement with student lives, let alone 'the student conflicts'. I was 21 coming on 22. I was in the middle of my 'coming out as gay' stage of life, my identity being shaped as a young gay man. In the UK – and my story has to be primarily a UK story – 1968 was a year after the Sexual Offences Act which made homosexuality a little more legal than before; and 1968 was two years before the London Gay Liberation Front was formed at the London School of Economics (LSE) and where I was to be very involved. It may have been a harbinger of the Gay and Lesbian Movement, and one of the most critical moments of my life. But it did not exist in 1968. I had however, during Roy Jenkins's significant tenure as Home Secretary, been released from being a criminal.

After graduating in 1967, I started work first as a Careers Officer, and then as a Community Service Volunteer in Ilkeston, Derbyshire. In October, I began my PhD (on gay life after the law change) at the LSE, teaching at Enfield College (soon to become Middlesex Polytechnic), and living at home with my mum and dad (but soon to rent a small flat in Marble Arch – where I also worked part time as an usher at the Odeon Marble Arch – home at that time of big screen blockbusters like *Hello Dolly, West Side Story* and the reworked *Gone With the Wind!*). I had come out into the gay scene and gay life in and around Soho and the trendy Carnaby Street of 1966 when I was 20. My first gay sex came through buying a porn magazine in Soho, writing to the publisher, meeting him and his friends and being taken to a gay bar – The A & B, in Wardour Street (later I learned it was more popularly known as the Arsehole and Buggery!). I volunteered and worked at the Homosexual Law Reform Society Office – the Albany Trust – at 32 Shaftesbury Avenue, where I met Anthony Grey and the early law reformers.

My intellectual mentors at that time were limited. As an undergraduate I was taught by Stan Cohen, Roy Bailey, Jeanne Gregory, Adrienne Mead, Alf Holt, Tessa Blackstone, Rachel Parry and Jock Young – a lively group of renegades newly graduated from the LSE. I met Michael Schofield, a freelance researcher, who had published three key texts on gay life during the 1950s and 1960s as well as a popular book of the time (1966) called *The Sexual Behaviour of Young People*. In 1968, I started my PhD first with David Downes and then primarily with Paul Rock, both of whom have recently retired from the LSE. I was on the edge of the National Deviancy Conference – which in the UK was the most radical group of sociological thinkers and activists at that time.

Stan, Paul and Jock were my mentors and through them I was introduced to symbolic interactionism – especially in the work of Howard S. Becker, Erving Goffman, John Gagnon and William Simon, and Herbert Blumer. Theatrically, this was the year I danced on the stage of *Hair*, saw the trail blazing play *The Boys in the Band*, and fell in love with *Hello Dolly*. *The Sound of Music* topped the LP charts. It was the time of the Supremes, Motown, Simon and Garfunkel and Dusty Springfield. I never liked the Rolling Stones much but I did see the Beatles. I suppose I was fashion-conscious, a bit of a trendy little mover with platform shoes, wide flairs, bright colours and very long curly hair. I guess I was a political liberal; my mates in the academic world were all members of leftist groups, and I aspired to be one of them – but secretly I had my doubts. Marxism became my intellectual ghost in the cupboard – I have spent most of my life in fact wanting to be a Marxist, and not quite being able to make it: intellectually, politically or emotionally! Being gay made me a young engaged person and I was definitely on the side of all the liberal causes of that time with a very strong left leaning.

1968: A multiplicity of stories

So this is a bit of my story, my identity and my standpoint: what were the stories of others at this time? What did these human beings – my species, three and a half billion at that time (it is now nearly double that) – make of the year 1968? Many, many stories were told. As always. There is never the unified story that some sociologists so desperately seek. It is easy to collapse into a narrative of student rebellion and the clichéd stories that have been published. As always. But very different and multiple stories could be told. It was, in fact, the year that Enid Blyton died – that cosy middle-class author who had shaped the childhood worlds of millions of children with *Noddy* and the *Famous Five*, the sixth bestselling author of all time with thousands of global translations. In a way, her death signalled the end of postwar middle-class suburban safety. For those in Sicily, it was a different story. It was the year of a major earthquake and Mount Etna doing its usual damage: hundreds died, thousands were injured and all lived daily in the glory and fear of the eruptions of Mount Etna. In Africa, war-torn Biafra came into being in southern Nigeria for a scant three years: probably a million died of something we now call genocide from starvation, war and neglect. Biafra became the byword for human suffering. And thousands of exiled Asian Kenyans fled to England – to swim into Enoch Powell's 'Rivers of Blood'.

It was the time of the Cold War – of capitalist Amerika and communist Russia and China. In Prague, some 165,000 soldiers and 4,600 Russian tanks rolled over the Czechs to stop 'socialism with a human face'. In the USA, Martin Luther King was assassinated on the day of my birthday; Robert Kennedy, a month later: all the wailing and the weeping and the wondering. A few sociologists in England dressed up in Mao Tse Tung uniforms to celebrate Maoism whilst in China, Mao pushed forward his Great Leaping Cultural Revolution purging and slaughtering millions. For a few it meant that for the first time in world history a life could be saved by what has come to be known as transplant surgery. For a few others it meant flying to the Moon and photographing the Earth. For most, everywhere, it meant the daily dangers, drudgery and delights of life: work, love and play. Maybe it was indeed a special year with special stories? No: 'history' is like that; what of 1066? Or 1588? Or 1789? Or 1914? Or 1939? Or 1989? Or 2001? Or anytime? Time flies. Life moves. Stories are told. People come. People go. Nothing changes. Everything changes.

And what was 1968 not? I knew nothing of AIDS, Muslims, McDonalds, Channel Four or colour TV. I did not buy a computer or a video till 16 years later. I had not travelled outside of the UK – or been on a plane. My old school had been a second-rate grammar school – but it was about to become a comprehensive school; my old college was just about to become a new polytechnic (which in turn would become a university in the late eighties). I lived in a different world to those who followed and preceded: we are all immigrants in time. We all function with our own generational standpoints.

1968: Symbolic effervescence

But 1968 was surely a spectacularly symbolic year even if it is only one blip in the grand march of time. It was a year when the whole world was watching – as it does now all the time. For a few it has come to stand for an awful lot. But in many ways it has become an overloaded symbol, fraught with multiple meanings and tensions. '1968' is perhaps best seen as one of those years which condenses a lot of issues to become a significant, symbolic spectacle – a critical moment of moral effervescence. The actual period it signifies is much broader – possibly the late 1950s to the mid-1970s; and in reality the year exemplifies endless multiplicities, complexities and harbours no internal unity or linear logic of the kinds that analysts might like to claim. Gerard de Groot's (2008) view of the 1960s as a kaleidoscope comes closest to mine. I am very aware of the limitations of historicist and overly structural determinist accounts. The student politics of 1968 should then be seen both as one event in a stream of events and as part of a much broader period of time – contested maybe, but taking in much of the 1960s and the 1970s (and often linked to the period 1958–75: Marwick's 'cultural revolution').

'1968' is an overloaded, over-determined and maybe by now even over-theorized symbol; but its events are so multiple and contingent that it is dangerous I think to look for any big story. My stance cautions me of grand theory and over-generalization. Sociology needs a better way to handle multiplicities.

I want to suggest that once we start to examine the range of meanings, structures, situations – the full range of micro, meso and macrostructures in which '1968' was embedded – we have to notice at the very least the chaos behind it all. It is absolutely not cut from the same cloth. We need theory that has ambiguity, contingency, variability, plurality, complexity, contradiction, change, process and flow built into its heart at the local and the global levels. We need a theory of multiplicity and complexity (Urry 2003). Sociology is good at picking up on themes, but it really has very weak tools for approaching the total as a multiplicity like that I have located above, and as examining one year in the world – 1968 – has made me so aware.

1968: Generational subterranean worlds rising

If dominant cultures exist (I sometimes wonder if they actually do – I can never locate them as easily as some sociological work does), we must always see this in relation to what I would like to call 'subterranean cultures' and 'traditions'. In all societies there are what we might call *the deep traditions of the subterranean* to which sociologists often pay little focused attention: everywhere there are traditions that persistently work to minimally creatively react to and engage with whatever passes as a 'dominant culture': they negotiate it, play with it, subvert it. They reform it, rebel against it and revolutionize it. And at extremes, they aim to destroy it. All of social life is active and across the world people are always resisting, changing, modifying, denying and sometimes rejecting the realities they live in. Subterranean cultures display submerged and less visible patterns of culture which subvert, criticize, mock or distance themselves from the dominant culture. These are likely to have a lot of varieties, will have long histories and are quite likely to be found in most societies. Nobody agrees fully with any status quo and everybody negotiates their own space. Some of these will be directly confrontational and critical; many will be subversive; others will simply retreat from the dominant order (Matza 1961).

Dominant or hegemonic cultures, then, are never all there is – and ironically, they may not even be that dominant if we want to understand social life. I suspect all societies thrive not only on the ascendant but also on the descendant. There may even be an *imagined dominant world* that has to be resisted. There is a lot at work beneath the formal conventions, the orthodoxies. Societies generate subterranean traditions – whole worlds of values, meanings, practices that have little to do with these orthodoxies. Certainly, in much of the Western world since the late nineteenth century we can trace subterranean worlds evolving and mutating into various modern forms. Consider the following. Throughout all of the twentieth century, much of the nineteenth century and possibly a good part of the eighteenth century we could find a seething cauldron of bubbling differences: these are the social worlds of ethnicities (from the colonized, the slave, the refugee), gender and queer sexualities (women, men, gay, lesbian, bisexual, transgendered, sadomasochist, paedophiliac), political differences (of both extreme right and extreme left, and especially Marxist-left worlds, Anarchist-Situationist worlds, fascist worlds) environmental and back-to-nature worlds, peace and anti-war worlds, art and culture worlds, intellectual worlds, bohemian and outsider worlds, religious (evangelicals, reformers, millenarian movements), and of course class worlds and age worlds.

All of these work to break down and subvert any idea of any kind of consensus throughout recent history and most of them have acted as the basis of prototypical social movements of resistance and change. Table 3.1 suggests some of these. It is a major research project to follow all these through. But each one of these can be seen as a kind of contemporary social world in the making – some more strongly than others, some more political than others. Their roots dig back through the twentieth century, into the nineteenth century, and often into the eighteenth century. They all have quite long histories that are now well documented: none of them just appeared in 1968.

In a string of important books, the late Charles Tilly has documented the significant growth of social movements in the modern world at a global level. Social movements are a key factor in ordinary folks' participation in the running of their lives, and he links their rise and fall to the 'expansion and contraction of democratic possibilities' (Tilly 2004: 3). From their earliest days, such movements can be seen as arising in subterranean worlds where people are resisting dominant powerful forces. Under conditions often of stress and crisis, they engage in the stages of collective activity which produce claims and help frame arguments

Table 3.1 Generational subterranean traditions rising

Eighteenth–twentieth centuries: emergent 'subterranean worlds'	'1968' as symbol	Twenty-first-century social movements and tribes
1. Slave movements, the colonized, migrant and refugees' worlds		Black Power, anti-racism, postcolonial movements, the subaltern
2. Sexual emancipations – mollies, queers, transgender, sexual worlds		GLF/GBLT, trans, bisexual, poly-amorous, queer movements
3. Gender – women's worlds, suffragettes, etc.		35 varieties of second-wave and third-wave feminisms: radical, socialist, black, etc.
4. Political cultures – of both extreme right and extreme left: Marxist-inspired left worlds, Anarchist-Situationist worlds		All kinds of major and minor political parties, and their resistant break away groups: Multiple and many interconnections and schisms
5. Naturalist, conservation, pacifist, peace groups		Most did not exist 200 years ago. Environmental movement, anti-war protest, Green Parties: Greenpeace, etc.
6. Age stratification and generations, student cultures		Grey Power. Youth cultures, subcultures: Goths, punks, hippies and the rest
7. Bohemian worlds (becoming countercultures)		Hippies, countercultures, etc.
8. Art and culture worlds – expressionism, impressionism		Avant gardism, Dadaism, Surrealism, atonalism and the rest
9. Intellectual worlds – free thinkers outside of the conventional corpus		Postmodern, postcolonial, queer theory, etc.
10. Religious cultures – evangelicals, reformers, millenarian movements		The new religious movements, splits and fundamentalism
11. Class worlds – growth of working-class movements		Class-based politics and movements

about the nature of their lives and their problems. From this they work to get organized – to mobilize resources. Initially based on specific countries, by the nineteenth century they increasingly had become international. And by the time of 1968, such movements were almost global: certainly, as Todd Gitlin (1980) argued, 'the whole world was watching'.

At this time there is a spectacular growth of social movements. A range of movements existed before 1968 in relative isolation and quietness, but the furore of 1968 helped them find space to develop in the years between 1969 and 1975: for this is the time that we really get to see the growth of the Environmental Movement, the Women's Movement, the Gay/Lesbian and Queer Liberation Movements, and the spread of Anti-Race and Postcolonial Movements. These had all existed before for at least a century or more; but public awareness shifted around this time and made conditions more plausible for social movements to thrive publicly. Such movements are now firmly part of the modern world – and some such as Manuel Castells and Alan Touraine see them as absolutely central to it.

Although 1968 did not achieve any of its grander goals like the ending of capitalism, the collapse of modern technology, the ending of wars or even the creation of university cultures that were genuinely concerned with knowledge and ideas and not dominated by markets and managers, it could be claimed perhaps that it served as a marker event for a long historical trend to bring subterranean values more openly into the mainstream, and that the generation itself promulgated ideas of change, creativity and individualism that have often been manifested in the activities of a vast network of social movements and change agents. In my wider paper, I have tried to suggest that modern day movements – from the Women's Movement and Queer Movement to the Environment Movement and Postcolonial Movements – have long traditions back into the nineteenth (and in some cases eighteenth) century that were brought together at critical effervescent moments that occurred during the early 1960s and mid-1970s and which is symbolized by '1968'. Achieving little directly, it transformed the culture of expectations in which life has since been lived even if routinely contested. The importance of human rights across the world and the significance of individual lives across major differences – of living with and developing the differences – are now firmly on the agenda.

Subterranean traditions also have a clear generational dimension – in some ways generations get organized through their social movements. For me, it was the gay movement and my queer identity that has haunted my vision of the world all though my life.

III. 1968: Queer life and resisting cultures

I have used my own life – of gay rights and queer issues – as one clear and simple example of all this. In the Western world, queer life has been radically re-organized over the past 40 years. New generations can hardly comprehend how the new world has been won (for them?). Indeed, I can hardly grasp it. There back in the 1960s homosexuality was a crime, a sickness, a huge secret. It was not easy to be gay then or indeed for centuries before. And it is still not easy in much of the global world, as the battle becomes a worldwide one. But the transformations that took place during this period have established the agenda: human rights for all gays is now a reality in many places. Life is still hard for most, but for many millions a world has arrived which was inconceivable before. We must therefore be wary of analysing society and its changes too negatively. In many subterranean worlds of life once downtrodden and excluded, we have seen real change. It is in part the spirit of 1968 which has helped in this, as it has many movements.

The same story can be told over and over again. Societies here can be documented not as hegemonic structures, but as multiple strands of resisting cultures. A. C. Grayling has recently (2007) documented: 'five hundred years of struggles for liberty and rights that made the modern West'. In a sense this is a historical and philosophical guide to the gradual development of modern social movements that engage daily to enhance freedom and protect rights. He is rightly concerned that we can easily lose these rights: that the struggles and high costs of the last 500 years can be easily lost. History is not inevitably on the side of progress. Events like 1968 help to consolidate and lead us towards utopian visions of human life.

Sociology has long been engaged with debates over values and politics. At one level it functions in a highly orthodox and professional fashion; at another it has its own underground of subterranean traditions. The debates in 1968 were notoriously part of this – they brought to the surface a large number of brooding tensions, described the world we wanted to live in, suggested the kind of studies that sociology should do, signposted the changes that were needed. We were naive perhaps, but unashamedly partisan. I came into sociology with a passion and anger about the understanding of homosexuality – I was angry about the long historical and wider cultural rejection and abuse of homosexuals. It was a fortunate contingency to be born an early baby boomer and find myself in a culture which dreamt of radical change: it was a culture where everything seemed possible. Although I had just missed the excitement of 1968, I was indeed in time for the Gay Liberation Front. And this, I know, has been a major defining fact of my life.

I have been publicly out as a gay man now for over 40 years – at home, at work and at play; and I can hardly imagine now what pains must exist if people stay in the closet. In my lifetime I have seen major changes and many of them for the better. There has been a major progress (see Weeks 2007; Robinson 2009). But my value and political baseline was actually very narrow; it was restricted to a neophyte queer imagination lodged in liberalism with Marxist aspirations. It served me very well at the time, but as I have aged, so my value and political baselines have broadened. My utopian dreaming has somehow never vanished. I am now what I call a 'critical humanist'.

Social life is always contingent, creative and contested. It is always incorrigibly plural. Values and politics touch everything we do, even when we do not want them to. And we had better come clean about it. In the vast multi-paradigm discipline that we have invented called sociology, we need to get our values up front and clear. Of course, we need objectivity, 'science', critical reasoning, edge: I am not arguing for any kind of postmodern relativism, but a knowledge that is grounded surely on where we want to go. Many of the old dreams of sociologists have been destroyed: we need to make our agendas clearer for the twenty-first century. Do we support the long-term search for human capabilities flourishing for all and is human rights the best mode for doing this? Do we wish to live in a world where the multiple patterns of inequality – from class to disability – are weakened? Do we wish ultimately to cultivate a humane and cosmopolitan attitude in global citizens? (Appiah 2006; Chhachhi and Nicholas 2006; Sznaider 2001). My affirmative answer to these questions provides my utopian dream: not a utopia which will ever arrive, but one which a humane sociology can help each generation rework and thus enable social life to flourish.

Notes

1. At the '1968 Conference', I presented an argument in four stages: a lyric, a slide show, an auto/ethnography and a paper. There was too much material to present on this occasion; and there is far too much to present in this chapter. I have chosen here, therefore, to provide the lyric, the auto/ethnography and a few comments. The slide show which accompanied the lyric (in PowerPoint) and the full paper (10,000 words) can be accessed on my website at www.kenplummerandeverardlongland.info.

Part II
Theoretical Engagements

4
From 1968 to 1951: How Habermas Transformed Marx into Parsons

John Holmwood

The 1960s marked a major shift in theoretical sensibilities within sociology, evident in the increasing criticism of what was perceived as an 'orthodox consensus' within the discipline (Atkinson 1971).[1] This orthodox consensus was associated with the structural functionalism of Talcott Parsons, which he had presented as the necessary framework for sociological analysis (Parsons 1954 [1950]), as well as at the 'abstract empiricism' of quantitative research (see Mills 1959; Willer and Willer 1973). What lay behind this shift in sensibilities, and grew in momentum, was the rise of new social movements to challenge the prevailing status quo, in particular the Civil Rights Movement in America and, waiting in the wings, second-wave feminism and the Gay Liberation Movement. Moreover, the USA – what Parsons (1966) had called the new 'lead society' – was embroiled in the Vietnam War and opposition to it was growing, while, in Europe, the events of 1968 appeared to be dramatic harbingers of radical social change.

It seemed that after a period of social conformity and conservatism in the 1950s, Western societies, far from being characterized by an 'end of ideology' (Bell 1960), were entering a new 'noisy ideological age' (Baltzell 1972). Parsons's structural-functionalism was the main sociological approach that explicitly addressed macrosocial process, but with its emphasis on social integration, rather than conflict, and on the social system, rather than agency, it was widely seen as deficient in precisely those areas of understanding that were now most pressing. From this moment, there was a move within sociological theory away from the Parsonsian problematic to embrace issues of agency, conflict and change.

This shift in the social context of social theory coincided with Jürgen Habermas's first engagements with sociological theory, largely conducted through the modified Marxism of the Frankfurt School. If, initially, his criticism of Parsons was less than systematic – in common with others, he regarded the deficiencies of structural-functionalism as mostly self-evident – the development of his own position brought him to an understanding of Parsons's theory as something that needed to be addressed more fundamentally. Thus, by 1981, Habermas was writing that 'any theoretical work in sociology today that failed to take account of Talcott Parsons could not be taken seriously' (1981: 174).

The sociological substance of Habermas's theory – broadly, as developed between the early article on 'Technology and science as ideology' (1971 [1968]) and his magnum opus, two-volume *Theory of Communicative Action* (1984 [1981]; 1987 [1981]) – is a sustained bringing together of Marx (mediated by Weber) and Parsons. However, while the 'dialogue' begins strongly in the voice of Marx, it concludes with that of Parsons being dominant. In the process, Parsons's categories live on in the work of Habermas, but, rather than transcending their flaws, Habermas reproduces them. In this chapter, I shall suggest that this convergence is indicative of wider problems in attempts to recuperate Marxism within sociological theory, problems that have given rise to an impasse and are a continuing legacy of 1968 for sociological theory.

I

Parsons, himself, intended his first major work, *The Structure of Social Action* (*TSofSA*) (1937), to delineate a shift in sociological theory. In the process, he identified the elements of a general frame of reference that he argued would unify hitherto conflicting forms of social analysis derived from positivist and idealist traditions of social thought. He identified convergent tendencies towards this common framework from within each tradition, and he illustrated this convergence in a detailed treatment of the work of Max Weber, Emile Durkheim, Vilfredo Pareto and Alfred Marshall. His account of this '1890–1920 generation' of social theorists of economy and society represented them as a transitional generation presaging a synthesis that would establish the foundations of future scientific endeavours (Parsons 1937). Marx is notable by his absence. The 1890–1920 generation, for Parsons, was a 'transitional' generation, because it was also located in a transition in the institutional development of capitalism itself, a transition that was becoming ever more evident. Developments in capitalism, and not just in the social sciences, were contributing to the declining salience of Marx's arguments.

In the period between writing *TSofSA* (1937) and *The Social System* (1951), Parsons elaborated these arguments in a range of other books (many co-authored) and articles. The latter book articulated a 'structural-functional' account of society and the relations among the disciplines. In effect, the object of sociology came to be interpreted by Parsons as 'the theory of the social system in its sociologically relevant aspect' (1954 [1950]: 5). The social system was characterized by Parsons in terms of coordinating mechanisms that are generative of tendencies towards perfect integration, considered analytically as an asymptote of the system. 'Environmental' contingencies occur as 'strains' and 'disturbances' that are accommodated to the coordinating mechanisms of action systems (which include the 'rationalization' of their action by actors as integral to the generation of the mechanisms of systems).

The core of these arguments remained in all of Parsons's subsequent works, which can be regarded as their elaboration, rather than a fundamental transformation, as Alexander (1984) proposes. In particular, he went on to develop a conception of coordinating mechanisms in terms of four functional imperatives (goal attainment, adaptation, integration and pattern maintenance) and divided the social system accordingly into four subsystems (polity, economy, societal community and latency subsystems). These further developments did nothing to allay the unease of critics, an unease that was initially focused on *The Social System* and grew throughout the subsequent decade. Moreover, the rising tide of criticism was in stark contrast to Parsons's claims about the foundational role of his general theory, which was to serve an integrative function for the activities of the sociological community itself.

The problems were twofold. One was the emphasis on the integration of the 'total action system'. Parsons frequently argued that this was an *analytical* assumption, rather than a *concrete* description, but while this is a qualification of fundamental importance, it does not eliminate the issue of the problematic empirical reference of the analytical theory. The latter is intended to refer to concrete circumstances, but reference is in terms of the mechanisms identified through the idea of functions. These identify tendencies towards integration as a property of concrete systems of action, *in so far as they can be analysed as systems*. The second issue was that of how the empirical reference of the scheme bears upon its adequacy. Any lack of integration in concrete systems of action is, for

Parsons, precisely that, *concrete*, lacking any *equivalent* theorization to that of integration in terms of the scheme and its analytical categories.

What also appeared crucial to his critics was that precisely what was identified by Parsons as 'mere' empirical phenomena, namely conflict, contradiction and transformative social change, were all issues that came to the fore in the changed social circumstances of the 1960s (see, for example, Dahrendorf 1958; Gouldner 1970; Lockwood 1956, 1964; Rex 1961). Moreover, although the scheme was described, analytically, as containing no concrete data that can be 'thought away', it seemed to embody the circumstances of late capitalism (its separations of economy and polity, etc.) as the 'end point' of history. It was, then, a developmental scheme in which no further fundamental transformations were conceivable, except as regression or de-differentiation (Holmwood 1996).

II

As already suggested in the introduction, the 1960s initially presaged a major change in theoretical sensibility and, to many commentators, an apparent shift in the focus of conceptualization as significant as that claimed by Parsons for the 1890–1920 generation. Parsons's neglect of Marx, alongside the claimed convergence of Durkheim and Weber, two sociologists frequently seen as offering radically distinct approaches, was something that came to the fore with critics seeking alternative readings of the 'classics' that would open up the dimensions of conflict and change apparently neglected by Parsons (see Pope *et al.* 1975; Warner 1978).

While Marx, especially, was seen to have contributed to those areas where Parsons's theory was perceived as deficient, on closer examination, this response also frequently conceded the same point that Parsons (1967) had made, and that had led to his dismissal of Marx, namely that Weber incorporated the important insights of Marx, but did so in a way more appropriate to the development of systematic sociological theory (Habermas 1987 [1981]; Lockwood 1964; Rex 1961). Not the least of the reasons for this preference for a Weber-inflected version of Marx was that Parsons was seen to have shifted from an action frame of reference to a systems approach in which 'external structures' dominated over actors. Critics frequently perceived a problem of structural determinism in Marx too, albeit a determinism directed towards the production of change. In this context, Weber was seen to be superior to Marx, just in so far as he addressed action as a fundamental category of social theory. At the same time, he seemed to share Marx's concern with power and social change, which is not to say that Weber's writings were not themselves argued to be imbued with other problems.

Habermas (1971), writing from the perspective of the Frankfurt School, published a series of essays that continued their theme of the tendency of 'politics' to be reduced to 'administration' and the public sphere to be dominated by 'expertise'. To some extent, Weber represented an antidote with his appreciation of value-rational action alongside instrumentally rational action. However, for Habermas, Weber did not develop this framework sufficiently, and so remained captured by a 'subjective' conception of action that did not develop the implications of systems of purposive rationality *and* intersubjective meanings (1971 [1968]: 91). Habermas proposed to do this through the dimension of 'work' and 'interaction', or what he would later call 'system' and 'lifeworld'.

Initially, Habermas barely referenced Parsons, except to state that he shared Weber's 'subjectivism', implying a failure to transcend the individualistic means – end framework of the latter. Significantly, however, when Habermas specified the substance of the two dimensions of work and interaction they appear remarkably similar to what Parsons himself had proposed. Thus, he writes, 'Purposive-rational action realizes defined goals under given conditions. But while instrumental action organizes means that are appropriate or inappropriate according to criteria of an effective control of reality, strategic action depends only on the correct evaluation of possible alternative choices, which results from calculations supplemented by values and maxims' (1971 [1968]: 92). In contrast, he writes, 'by "interaction", on the other hand, I understand *communicative action*, symbolic interaction. It is governed by binding *consensual norms*, which define reciprocal expectations about behaviour and which must be understood and recognized by at least two acting subjects. Social norms are enforced through sanctions' (1971 [1968]: 92).

What is striking is that Habermas also follows Parsons in terms of how he attributes violations of order to contingency. In the case of purposive action, violation has the form of incompetence, while in the case of the violation of norms, it has the form of 'deviance'. In the former, violation elicits failure, or lack of success, as intrinsic to the action, while in the latter case it elicits sanctions from others. He states further that 'learned rules of purposive-rational action supply us with *skills*, internalized norms with *personality structures*. Skills put us in a position to solve problems; motivations allow us to follow norms' (1971 [1968]: 92).

It is perhaps a little too soon to claim that these have a similar elaboration to that found in Parsons, where coordinating mechanisms of interaction serve to secure the integration necessary to their character as systems. At least initially, Habermas distanced his account from that of Parsons by attaching it to another critique, that of David Lockwood's (1964) discussion of 'system integration' and 'social integration'. Habermas treated these as equivalent to his own categories of 'system' and 'lifeworld'. However, I shall suggest that these terms play a different role for Lockwood than they do for Habermas. An examination of their role in Lockwood will indicate the way in which a very specific Marxist concern with contradiction begins to be displaced in Habermas's treatment.

We have seen that criticisms of Parsons tend to focus around issues of conflict and social change. At the same time, the distinction between the social system conceived *analytically* in terms of its integration and *concrete* systems which are less than fully integrated was also seen implicitly to be a distinction between action in conformity with the system and action as *deviance*. In so far as Parsons was able to deal with conflict, it seemed to be only by regarding it as a form of deviance. At the same time, systematic processes are associated with mechanisms for securing the reproduction of systems against potential deviance. What is missing is an identification of systematic mechanisms producing deviance (or, more properly, since the very term 'deviance' implies its contingent, rather than systematic, character, *oppositional interests*). As already argued, the problem seems to point both to the lack of generality achieved by the Parsonsian scheme and to a limitation in its conception of action.

Drawing on Marx's analysis of capitalism, Lockwood suggested that what was missing, in functionalism and conflict theory alike, was a concept of *system contradiction*.[2] Simply put, Parsons had no place for the idea that the parts of a social system may contain tendencies towards malintegration. According to Lockwood, those tendencies may eventually come to the surface in the form of oppositional interests and conflicts among actors. These conflicts may, or may not, then be contained by the normative order. Thus, Lockwood proposes an independent role for the dimension of social integration in managing problems of system integration.

Rather than proposing two separate models of 'conflict' or 'consensus' as earlier conflict theorists such as Dahrendorf (1958) and Rex (1961) had done in response to *The Social System*, Lockwood argued that it was necessary to consider the question of cooperation, conflict and social change in terms of two distinct, but inter-related, sets of processes. One concerned normative processes of *social integration*, the other concerned material processes of *system integration*. The problem with Parsons was that he conflated the two and emphasized the mutual operation of both sets of processes; the task for Lockwood was to be more aware of the possibility of contradictions within the system and how they are managed at the level of social integration.

Lockwood's article was highly influential, but it was not clear what kind of further development he thought should follow from it – his own book-length study based on the article (Lockwood 1992) did not appear until very much later. He used Marx's account of the contradiction between forces and relations of production in capitalism as an example of a problem at the level of system integration, but he did not fully endorse the example as one that was correct in its own terms. Its purpose was to show a type of sociological argument that was outside the confines of Parsons's functionalism and, in this respect, the point was very effectively made. However, it is difficult to see that there could be a *general statement* of contradiction, rather than a series of substantive analyses of specific contradictions, each difficult to accommodate to the Parsonsian treatment on integrative tendencies (see Holmwood 1996).[3]

While others also took up Lockwood's categories and sought to develop them as part of a systematic framework, in particular Giddens (1984), Archer (1988) and Mouzelis (1995), Habermas is particularly interesting because of his own background in Marxism. Ironically, this involved turning around the significance that Lockwood had drawn from Marx's analysis of the contradictions of capitalism. From a Marxist perspective, given the continuity of capitalism, it must appear that system contradictions have been successfully managed at the level of social integration. If Lockwood perceived the problem in Parsons's work to be the absence of a concept of system contradiction, the problem in Marx's work potentially appeared to be an inadequate account of mechanisms of social integration. At the same time that Habermas adopted the categories of system and social integration from Lockwood, then, he shifted the focus back towards mechanisms of social integration, in particular considered from the perspective of supplying a missing 'normative' dimension.

It is this that explains certain peculiarities of Habermas's (1981) first sustained critique of Parsons. Habermas associates the dimensions of system and social integration with two distinct approaches to the coordination of action. Each offers a paradigm of action, but, while the mechanisms of social integration are directly based on action orientations, the mechanisms of system integration operate through the consequences of action.[4] Thus, he writes that in the former case, action is integrated through conscious mutuality in the action orientations of the parties concerned. In the latter case, action is integrated through a functional coupling of the consequences of action to each other, consequences that may remain latent or beyond the conscious horizon of the action orientations of the actors involved.

(1981: 175)

According to Habermas, the task for social theory is how to synthesize the two approaches and how to prevent their 'bifurcation' (in which one dimension comes to be over-emphasized at the expense of the other), something he believes occurs both in Marx and, more importantly for our purposes, in Parsons (although, even here, his criticism is ambivalent because he has to recognize that the latter's four-function paradigm has two sets of functions each specified in relation to what Habermas identified as the dimensions of system and social integration; the bifurcation is, in fact, better expressed as a problematic elision of the fundamental difference between them).

The critical literature on Parsons had developed since Lockwood had written, and Habermas accepts many of the interpretations that had become standard, especially those of Scott (1963) and Martindale (1971). Thus, he identifies phases in the development of Parsons's theory that have him beginning from an appropriate recognition of 'action' in *TSofSA* and tipping over into a 'systems' approach that displaces 'action'. The consequence, however, is that, unlike Lockwood, he criticizes Parsons for an overemphasis on system integration at the cost of a properly worked out conception of social integration as its complement.

In setting out this account of Parsons's theoretical development, Habermas makes the argument familiar from his earlier essay on science and technology that, in Parsons's early writing, 'in the last analysis the single unit act of an isolated actor remains the critical building block' (1981: 179). For Habermas, this emphasis on the 'monadic actor' means that coordination mechanisms operating through the unintended consequences of action receive greater theoretical emphasis than those that derive from actions oriented to mutual understanding and, therefore, 'with the concept of values as an already intersubjectively shared culture' (1981: 180). As Habermas puts it, 'if one first treats action-oriented decisions as *an emergent of the private arbitrariness of isolated actors*, as Parsons did then one deprives oneself of a mechanism that could explain the emergence of a system of action out of unit acts' (1981: 180). These, of course, are significant misrepresentations of Parsons's work. Indeed, Habermas's own account contains the very specification provided by Parsons in *The Social System*.[5]

Significantly, Habermas believes that Parsons came closer to an adequate approach in his later work when he elaborates his conception of different systems, namely personality system, social system and culture system. However, the linking of these three systems is inadequate, he believes, precisely because Parsons lacks an appropriate development of the subjective aspect of action, as is found in phenomenological or hermeneutic schools of thought. Yet, the basic architecture of the theoretical framework appears to be very similar to the one advocated by Habermas. In part, this is because Habermas fails to comprehend that the different phases in the development of Parsons's theory are driven by the attempt to overcome the dualism of two paradigms within a single frame of reference. Indeed, Habermas comes to criticize Parsons for failing to recognize the intermediation of culture, society and personality, writing that 'Parsons abandoned trying to explain in action-theoretical terms the notion that cultural values enter society and personality via institutionalization and internalization, respectively. Instead a model of mutually interpenetrating but analytically separate systems gains a central position on his theoretical stage' (1981: 183).[6]

Yet Habermas's formal scheme of categories is also convergent with that of Parsons, in the sense that he comes to accept that the two paradigms of system and lifeworld each operates in terms of two functional imperatives (see, Habermas 1984). Indeed, when he addresses the issue that any scheme of functional imperatives tends to overemphasize integration, he has recourse to the idea that functional imperatives can operate autonomously as well as interdependently.

At the same time, Habermas confirms Parsons's account of structural differentiation that is derived from the analysis of functional imperatives, as a *description* of modern societies. However, his own interpretation of the critical resources integral to the paradigm of the lifeworld suggests to him that this can also be represented as a form of alienation. Here, Habermas apparently draws on Marx, but, once again, his critique is different from that of Lockwood. Where the latter had drawn on the idea of the contradiction between forces and relations of production within the processes of system integration, Habermas draws on Marx's idea of an alienated lifeworld, separated from economic and political subsystems and subordinated to them, and thereby deformed. The problem, Habermas suggests, is that the steering mechanisms of system integration continue to require legitimation, but the lifeworld may lack the capacity to do so because of its deformation.

Given that Habermas fails to identify any substantive problems of system integration, the problem of social integration that he identifies is essentially that of *anomie* – loss of meaning – rather than alienation. What drops away is the specific idea of system contradiction as discussed by Lockwood (as an issue *within* the system and not simply *between* it and the dimension of social integration).

Habermas is critical of Marx precisely because he fails to recognize that structural differentiation is a necessary feature of modern society. Habermas specifically represents the creation of differentiated subsystems as a process of societal learning by resolving system problems that represent evolutionary challenges (1987 [1981]: 305). The creation of separate 'media-steered' subsystems is not itself the problem for Habermas. He writes,

> Marx conceives of capitalist society so strongly as a totality that he fails to recognize the *intrinsic* evolutionary *value* that media-steered subsystems possess. He does not see that the differentiation of the state apparatus and the economy *also* represents a higher level of system differentiation, which simultaneously opens up new steering possibilities *and* forces a reorganization of the old, feudal class relationships. The significance of this level of integration goes beyond the institutionalization of a new class relationship.
> (1987 [1981]: 339)

Nor is the 'new' class relationship the same as that set out by Marx. With the rise of the welfare state has come an 'institutionalization of class conflict' in the sociological sense, where 'the social antagonism bred by private disposition over the means of producing social wealth increasingly loses its structure-forming power for the life world of social groups, although it does remain constitutive for the structure of the economic system' (1987 [1981]: 348).

Given that Habermas accepts that the social antagonism contained within the economic subsystem does not operate within the lifeworld, it is difficult to know what remains of its substance as contradictory (in either Marx's or Lockwood's sense). Moreover, when Habermas identifies pathologies of capitalist modernity, these are associated with the 'fragmentation' of the lifeworld and its 'colonization' by systems of purposive rationality. Even where the system dominates over the lifeworld this, apparently, does not bring social antagonism into the lifeworld, but is part of a process of masking contradiction!

At this point, Habermas is operating within the same problematic theoretical context as Parsons. On the one hand, general theory sets out the general requirements of systems of interaction as practical systems and as systems of communicative action. Both dimensions are defined by the requirements of integration. Obviously, Habermas presents an apparently more radical approach than Parsons, suggesting that the logic of practical systems can dominate over the lifeworld. However, his own theoretical approach suggests that there is an overarching logic, which is expressed in the four-function paradigm that each shares, and describes a balance in the operation of functional imperatives as the optimal state of a system of interaction.

In this context, it is somewhat surprising that Habermas declares that Parsons lacks the theoretical resources to address the resistance to colonization that the lifeworld can engender, since the resources that Habermas is identifying are derived from the theoretical categories they have in common. Indeed, part of the misunderstanding is that they disagree in their description of the concrete systems of capitalist modernity to which they apply their theories. What Habermas describes as the colonization of the lifeworld in late modernity, Parsons describes as a relatively healthy societal community (Parsons 2007).

However, Parsons's and Habermas's presentations of general theory are not without problems that bear upon the issue of its logical consistency, even in its own terms. In the case of Parsons, this is the presentation of a system of action in the context of untheorized and contingent deviance. Second, and more importantly, it appears that general theory *presents the analytical form of a generalized action system as without problems*. The integrated form of the generalized action system is, for Parsons, as Alexander (1985) says, a 'possibility' – in terms both of the 'valid knowledge' and of the 'values' that it expresses. It would, therefore, be impossible to associate problem-solving activity with the substance of social life, since a 'possible' solution is already available in the facilities integral to the theoretical form of the system to which concrete actions asymptotically tend. In so far as Habermas also sets out the characteristics of systems and their coordinating mechanisms, he reproduces this formulation. Notwithstanding any wish to argue that the 'logic' of systems can give rise to the 'colonization' of the lifeworld, any resources for resistance are given in its corresponding (and, apparently, countervailing) logic.

Ironically, it would seem that, from the perspective of Habermas, late modern lifeworlds do lack resources to ward off the colonizing tendencies of systems of purposive rationality, while for Parsons the transition from early to mature capitalism is to be characterized by a deepening of the structures of the societal community. However, in representing the colonization of the lifeworld in terms of the expansion of subsystems of economic and political rationality that are otherwise to be recognized as positive, it seems to be Habermas that lacks the resources for their critique. Certainly, the Marxist account of their contradictory character no longer supplies the substance of that critique and remains only as a rhetorical shell.

The problem for Habermas is that he entered the terrain of Parsons and accepted that a general theoretical framework is a necessary precondition for social enquiry and that it can be grounded in terms of a generalized problem of social order. Thus, Habermas writes, 'naturally even the simplest action systems cannot function without a certain amount of *generalized* action assumptions. Every society has to face the basic problem of coordinating action: how does ego get alter to continue action in the desired way? How does he avoid conflicts that interrupt the sequence of action?' (1987 [1981]: 179). Any general statement of the problem of order begs the question of a general solution, for it sets order not against particular problems, as did Marx, but against a general threat of chaos, where, according to Habermas, 'the fundamental function of world-maintaining interpretive systems is the avoidance of chaos, that is, overcoming of contingency' (1976: 118).

With statements like this, Habermas's convergence with Parsons is complete. At the same time, the implication must be that the problems of such schemes are not contingent to a particular writer – either Parsons or Habermas – but are intrinsic to the very project of general theory (see Holmwood 1996). Adding Marx does little to transform the scheme, but rather gives rise to the systematic evacuation of precisely those concerns with agency, conflict and change that led to calls for his incorporation into the synthesis of classical social theory held to be the necessary foundation for social enquiry.

On the one hand, the profound and sweeping nature of Marx's theoretical scheme reinforced the idea that it would be compatible with the project of general theory. On the other hand, Marx's focus on the particularity of social contradictions – that they are always specific and substantive, requiring solution in their own terms, and never general – suggests an alternative approach to that of general theory. The legacy of 1968 in social theory has primarily been in the development of general theory leading to the impasse described in this chapter. This impasse has been recognized, but frequently, as in the case of postmodern theory, leading only to the embrace of the very contingency that is part of the impasse. Indeed, this is itself part of the emphasis on 'agential disruption' brought in the wake of the social movements of the 1960s. What has been tried less frequently is the address of substantive social contradictions – contradictions other than those identified by Marx – as the object of social theory.

Notes

1. This is an edited version of a paper that first appeared in *the Czech Sociological Review* 44(5), 2008. Thanks to the editors for permission to reproduce it here.
2. He also offered an illustration drawn from Weber of the contradiction of patrimonial bureaucracy in a near-subsistence economy.
3. In fact, in Lockwood's own later work he seems to come implicitly to this conclusion. Much like Burger (1977), he suggests that the problem of order – of the relation between normative and non-normative influences on behaviour – is better addressed in a series of substantive studies than it has been in terms of general theory. He writes, 'this is another reason for thinking that the search for grand theory, whether by way of synthesis or contestation, may be misdirected' (1992: 395).
4. This corresponds with Lockwood's statement that the distinction between 'system integration' and 'social integration' is a 'wholly artificial one' (1964: 245), implying that they are two perspectives on a single system of action.
5. Thus, Habermas writes, 'I shall speak of communicative action whenever the actions of the agent involved are coordinated not through egocentric calculations of success but through acts of reaching understanding. In communicative action participants are not primarily oriented to their own individual successes; they pursue their individual goals under the condition that they can harmonize their plans of action on the basis of common situation definitions. In this respect the negotiation of definitions of the situation is an essential element of the interpretive accomplishments required for communicative action' (1984 [1981]: 285–6). This is mirrored in Parsons's statement that 'the most important single implication of this generalization [of symbol systems] is perhaps the possibility of communication, because the situation of two actors are *never* identical and without the capacity to abstract meanings from the most particular situations communication would be impossible. But in turn this stability of a symbol system, a stability which must extend between individuals and over time, could probably not be maintained unless it functioned in a communication process in the interaction of a plurality of actors. It is such a shared symbolic system which functions in the interaction of a plurality of actors which will here be called a *cultural tradition*' (1951: 11).
6. It should be clear that Parsons does have a clear view of 'interpenetration' operating through processes of institutionalization and internalization. Indeed, Lockwood's criticism of him was precisely that these were the primary processes within his account. Habermas's criticism is more effective against Parsons's German student Niklas Luhmann's idea of autopoietic social systems (Luhmann 1995 [1984]). The latter does propose a form of general systems functionalism that is hostile to the 'humanistic' orientation of a theory

of communicative action. According to Luhmann, self-regulating social systems construct themselves self-referentially as social relationships made up of differentiated subsystems. These subsystems interact, but have their own relatively autonomous logics, and are not limited by a pre-given set of functions. However, this is not what Parsons is arguing. Since he explicitly sets out four functional imperatives with a similar substance as that identified by Habermas, it is hard to accept that he gives over the functions of 'integration' and 'latency' to self-steering systems of purposive rationality.

5
Critical Theory and Crisis Diagnosis: Key Exchanges Between Reason and Revolution after 1968

Tracey Skillington

I. Introduction

In its reflections on the great paradox of rationalization or the correlations between instrumentalist reasoning, western imperialist expansion, and the humiliation of servitude under a capitalist regime, 1968 was an important turning point for critical theory. Not only did the events of 1968 revive interest in the Hegelian-Marxist, Weberian, and Freudian traditions of thought, they also compelled critical theory to revisit certain philosophical accounts of modernity's capacities for insurrection. Prior to this period, critical theory had all but resigned itself to the belief that the objectified world would never be fully negated by a critical praxis. As the twentieth century progressed and the rebel component of the working classes seemed to disband, critical theory increasingly felt compelled to convert its normative critique of society into one of 'transcendence'. This conscious shift from the 'real' to the 'ideal' basis of critique was necessitated by the perceived 'fallen nature of modern man' (Adorno and Horkheimer 1972: xiv) whose gradual descent into silence had precipitated a premature 'end of reason' (Horkheimer 1982) and seemed to confirm the absence of any societal crisis that could have a revolutionary outcome.

Almost in defiance of such negativity, a crisis would dramatically unfold in 1968 across various university campuses in Europe and the US. Tensions had been mounting from the mid-1960s when domestic and international opposition to America's involvement in the Vietnam War began to gather momentum. Atrocities like the My Lai Massacre of 1968 were constructed as evidence that America was also a perpetuator of genocide against innocent people, a far cry from its symbolic representation as the great liberator after the Second World War. Within a few years, critical impulses in Western civil society were gaining a degree of influence over value orientations. Critical theory now had to find a way of accounting for tensions between modernity's powerful capacity to integrate and pacify 'the dutiful child of modern civilization' (Adorno and Horkheimer 1972: xiv) and, at the same time, consider those opportunities for resistance created by newly discovered 'structural leaks' (Offe 1968) within the repressive rational order.

In an effort to address these central issues, a number of 'second-generation' critical theorists set out to change the dominant perspective of the critical paradigm. Such theorists would begin by realigning critical social theory's explanatory-diagnostic dimension with a neo-Kantian utopian impulse towards future transformation. Critical theory would now return to an analysis of the field of tension between the 'real' and the 'possible' by pointing to the limitations of any Frankfurt School critique of the present societal order that had not considered the potential for future change.

Second, such critical theorists drew from the collective events of 1968 an appreciation for the need to recast interpretations of reason and its relationship to revolutionary praxis in a more socio-historically sensitive fashion. Although at times a thesis of despair seemed to cast a long shadow over the critical project of hope for a more egalitarian future (for instance, Adorno 1974), at no point did critical theory ever relinquish its commitments to the sanctity of reason and autonomy. Hegel (1929) identified the first step towards a true conception of reason as a negative one, entailing a critical rejection of both enduring categories of common sense and of the world selected by them. Critical theory would now add to Hegel's insights a complementary focus on future transformation through human praxis. In so doing, it continued to embrace the Hegelian interpretation of dialectical reason as a 'critical tribunal' (Marcuse 1968) through which new emancipatory currents flow (see McCarthy 1991; Habermas 2008), but would now also attempt to document the precise manner in which reason becomes 'detranscendentalized' (Habermas 2008) through the interpretive practices of the social actor operating on the ground. Critical social theory's re-orientation towards praxis in the post-1968 period would entail a more practical illustration of the way reason continues to act as a guide for social critique, yet also performs a vital norm-setting function that makes such critique possible in the first place (Habermas 2003).

Overall, 1968 saw an awakening of critical theory's interest in that social actor whose revolutionary impulses encompass a broader array of 'knowledge interests' than mere class interests (Habermas 1972). In its explorations of the new 'cultural interests' of such actor types, critical theory now turned its attention to a socially decentred use of reason. A focus on the latter became the primary means through which critical theory could restore the socio-political relevance of its critique of instrumental reasoning and reconnect its normative project for social change with those 'crisis tendencies' now occurring more generally in 'post-material' Western democracies (Inglehart 1990). Crucial to this change in orientation were a number of social theorists including Alain Touraine. Touraine would illustrate how, for example, tensions between the ideal and the real entered into the social reality of the situated interactions and meaning-making practices of the student radicals of 1968 in their explorations of issues of exploitation, manipulation, and authoritarianism at the hands of a hierarchical university system. In forming militant 'truth squads' and 'free assemblies', student protesters appealed to the idealizations of rational accountability, justice, democracy, and, crucially, notions of 'truth' on what was really happening in the university's corridors of power, in Western societies more generally, as well as in the killing fields of Vietnam and elsewhere. Indeed, it was the increasing distance between reason as a concept and the institutionalized reality of technocracy that energized the often violent clashes between security forces and those student radicals purporting to stand on the side of freedom and equality. New countercultural practices of self-determination brought tensions between the subjective consciousness of aggrieved protesters and the objective spirit of democracy to a head in a dramatic style, fuelling a mass international appeal for social justice and democratic accountability. It was only when the democratic spirit became liberated from bureaucratic constraints, inter-subjectively diffused in the situated contexts of various protest events, and animated through the protesters' radical projects for reform, that reason could effectively be transformed from 'substance to subject'. In moments of conflict such as these, the democratic spirit manages to avoid becoming over-entangled in the limited horizons of subjective interpretation and preserves its idealized status as a guide for social action (Touraine 2000).

For theorists like Touraine, the protest events of 1968 were a critical opportunity for learning how the socio-cultural elaboration of justice and truth ought to be theoretically and, indeed, methodologically accounted for (as reflected in the proliferation of a cultural studies paradigm from the 1970s onwards). '1968' laid bare the fact that reason continues to be 'detranscendentalized' (McCarthy 1991; Habermas 2008) through the meaning-making practices of that protest actor who cultivates an intimate relationship with the democratic spirit (Touraine 2000). Especially with the introduction of his theoretical insights on historicity, Touraine (1988) would illustrate how democracy, justice, and accountability are not just idealizations towards which society aspires, but also act as crucial components of self-identity in moments of social conflict. In this instance, historical forms of protest action and justification become varied dimensions of a symbolic embodiment of reason and a conscious internalization of the meaning of democracy, as it is mediated by language, recognition, memory, and experience. Modernity's democratic spirit facilitates this re-conceptualization of individuals as 'free subjects who produce their own history and whose actions can reconcile the universalism of reason with the particularism of a personal or collective identity' (Touraine 1997:186). Touraine (2000: 295) acknowledges the historical significance of this process when he argues: 'The freedom that we defend today means recognition of the social and cultural rights of minorities and, therefore, defending diversity and the right of each individual to be themselves and reconcile their values and their forms of action with the instruments of historical action.'

'1968' saw a symbolic embodiment of democratic reason develop around modernity's culture of human rights in a manner that creatively blended a universal civic solidarity with both the particular (situated contexts of action) and individual (self-actualization) dimensions of democratic reason. Touraine interprets the interplay between these various aspects of democracy as collectively enhancing the ability of the subject, both individual and collective, to intervene and shape the nature of public life. In the process, reason comes to be conceptualized as the essential component binding the individual, society, and historical change together.

An emphasis on the dual character of reason as both idealization and as situated thought emerging after the events of this historical period led another key critical theorist associated with this reformulation of the relationship between reason and revolution, Jűrgen Habermas, to revise elements of Weber's diagnosis of societal rationalization and situate the neo-Kantian notion of reason in the communicative potentials of the present critical juncture. Habermas abandoned what he intuited to be the extreme negativity of Adorno and Horkheimer's (1972) interpretation of the process of rationalization in favour of the theory of communicative rationality. To this day, Habermas continues to illustrate how the ongoing critique of political economy involves the activation of norms of communicative rationality, freedom, equality, and justice – all prominent in the self-understanding of Western democratic societies. By grounding his construction of reason in the inter-subjective contexts of daily linguistic life, Habermas distinguishes himself from Adorno who believed that the only protection offered to reason against the spread of instrumental rationality was in the aesthetic realm. Reason, Habermas argues, does not need to make such a retreat from the 'administered world', but rather needs to communicatively engage with this world in order to demonstrate the extreme social relevance of its various principles and ideals.

Habermas was thus able to show how the formal rationality associated with modernity's rational administrative order, in spite of frequent problems in regenerating its own legitimacy, had not destroyed norms of fairness, equality, accountability, and justice. From this critical perspective, any erosion of meaning arising from instrumental rationality in modern culture could not be interpreted as equivalent to a loss of reason, and while evidence of a destruction of meaning is everywhere today, there also continues to be an active commitment to a communicative reason and to norms of freedom and equality. The critique of today's global capitalist order offered by the international human rights organization, Global Exchange, embodies ideas of reason that are both immanent in being grounded in the trials of everyday life but that are also transcendental in that they embrace universal norms of democracy. As Global Exchange (2008) explain, 'We trust in democracy' and 'defend universal rights'. While such critical actors' normative perspective on the continuing ethical-political relevance of the culture of democracy and rights draws inspiration from the imagination of the present and current diagnoses of crises, it is always firmly focused on transforming the future of capitalist society. Just as the protest actors of 1968 had concentrated on the dream of a better future 'amid the confusion of the present' (Touraine 1971: 26), today's global justice movement proclaims that another world is possible if only we could see that 'this is the moment' in which alternative futures can be born. Implicit in such actors' thinking is the assumption that Western democracy is an incomplete social truth whose attained results thus far in the form of constitutional rights eagerly await further elaboration. Like the May Movement radicals before them, today's global anti-capitalist protest actors construct the contemporary, new millennium project of emancipation as the realization of the underlining, if frustrated democratic potential of the present societal order.

II. A critical diagnostics of the contemporary administrative order: Return of the (anti-capitalist protest) actor

Within the critical research paradigm, the 'critique of instrumental reason' has in recent years been realigned with an empirical consciousness of the activities of today's international protest actors. The latter's critical reflections on the social forces currently shaping the 'new spirit of capitalism' (Boltanski and Chiapello 2005) internationally inspire a degree of reconciliation between reason and revolution. Of particular interest to the critical research paradigm is the contemporary global justice movement's defetishizing critique of capitalism. Movement affiliates, such as Fifty Years is Enough, Mobilization for Social Justice, Global Exchange, Public Citizens' Global Trade Watch, or Action Aid, demonstrate how the transnational social reality of global capitalism often presents itself to the actor as a social fact with law-like objectivity. In disclosing the constructed nature of this vision of contemporary capitalism, the critical actor re-appropriates social reality and contributes to a critique of the doctrines of structural adjustment and 'best practice' models in social policy, advocated by the three international pillars of neo-liberalism – the International Monetary Fund (IMF), the World Bank, and the World Trade Organization (WTO). The latter continue to bring pressure to bear on governments internationally to open their social welfare programmes up to greater labour market flexibility, reduce public spending, and introduce further public management reforms. What is at stake here in the conflict between citizens who oppose these initiatives and those who support them is the interpretation of social services as an endowment of 'social' citizenship and, therefore, as a democratic entitlement. Already a more intense application of the commodity form to social service provisions across the Western world is generating certain structural and economic dysfunctionalities, and a 'lived crisis' (Benhabib 1984) in the quality of health care, transport, education, employment, and security currently being provided to citizens. The attempt to establish an abstract equivalence between qualitatively different things such as commodities, human relations of care, responsibility, and services, by means of their equivalence to money, has been on the basis of a profoundly damaging abstraction from ethical and substantive considerations in the interests of profit and efficiency.

A greater emphasis on a 'market order of worth' over and above a 'civic order of worth' (Boltanski and Thevenot 1991) is leading to the current administrative order's inability to regenerate its own legitimacy both for its publics and, increasingly also, those professionals working within the system as, for instance, those who voice discontent with various government policies and hospital management practices in the healthcare sector. Collectively, such critical publics enter into interpersonal relationships based on mutual understanding and diagnosis of crisis. They continue to share communicative experiences of institutional neglect (e.g., cases of misdiagnosis, hospital-acquired infections, death through patient neglect, etc.) with each other and with observing media publics against the background of inter-subjectively shared lifeworld experiences. Even in the face of such administrative crisis, government continues to use the language of function, efficiency, and 'sound economics' to insulate itself from an over-engagement with discourses of human suffering and general crises syndromes.

Nowhere is this alienation arising from an over-commodification of the individual's relation to a social felt more deeply than in the everyday lifeworld, where a 'social dynamics of disrespect' (Honneth 1999) and the individual's experience of 'moral injury' at the hands of an administrative order that 'doesn't care' are encouraging a new elaboration and dissemination of ideas of democracy and justice across the Western world. It is here that we see active attempts to bridge ideals of freedom, accountability, and security with the everyday reality of inadequate housing, schooling, or access to healthcare by new citizens' initiatives. Yet again, it is this desire to understand and communicate grievance, as well as discover new ways to re-invigorate the sense of social justice that preserves modernity's human rights culture. The latter continues to form an essential 'normative common ground' (Brunkhorst 2005) on which an endless interlacing of particular and universal constructs of social justice can occur. Reason, therefore, in finding embodiment in modernity's culture of human rights, maintains its function as a critical hearing (Marcuse 1968) before which the various consequences arising from a global imposition of strict neo-liberal economic policies and restricted opportunities for autonomous policy-making, can be normatively assessed.

Highest on the agenda of those transnational activists involved in Jubilee 2000 – one of the largest transnational protest networks in recent years – was the desire to reverse the fate of humanity when capitalism's desire to make money triumphs over its historical sense of duty and obligation to care for the 'other'. The growing relevance of this issue today in the light of experiences of state neglect and indifference to the needs of society's vulnerable, marginalized, and disadvantaged, or the level of disrespect shown towards immigrants, asylum seekers, or those 'praying to foreign gods' (Offe 2005: 162), prompts critical theorists like

Bryan Turner (2006) to call for a conscious effort to protect the ethical viewpoint against the dehumanizing effects of global markets and the populist political entrepreneurship of anti-immigrationists. Turner promotes what he calls 'cosmopolitan virtue' or a 'cosmopolitan ethics of care' and a critical recognition theory that re-contemporizes critical theory's emancipatory project in the light of current international processes of economic, social, and political change. In its explorations of various democratizing currents and transnational networks of communication fighting for social justice beyond the boundaries of the nation state, post-1968 critical theory does, indeed, attempt to fulfil the intentions of a critical theory with emancipatory intent.

Today, critical theory's focus remains on those liberationist interests which not only bridge multiple experiences of moral injury within lifeworld contexts with a wider societal critique of the dynamics of global capitalism, but also target those whose activities are in breach of internationally binding norms of justice, equality, accountability, and human rights (e.g., Our World Is Not For Sale). In evoking such a system of reference, the global protester juxtaposes the norms of current society, including those of justice, equality, and responsibility, with the bleak actuality of unequal social relations. In so doing, the critical actor calls attention to the practical principle of procedural duty, institutionally embedded discourses on rights of freedom of expression and assembly, as well as obligations to citizens worldwide. For instance, the European Charter of Patients Rights, developed originally by the Italian Active Citizenship Network, sets out 14 basic rights of patients worldwide, including the right to information and free choice, as well as the right to avoid unnecessary suffering. In linking the suffering of individuals with expressions of human rights, this protest actor graphically illustrates the abilities and inclinations of the modern subject to become a social actor. Criticality here acts as a safeguard against any attempts to purge Europe's welfare legacy of its normative content and extend a market logic and capitalist commercialization into ever more spheres of life. Failure on the part of the administrative order to address this emphatic normative critique of the growing integration of capitalism's economic structures on the one hand with its administrative structures on the other, and make a genuine commitment to dialogue, accountability, and communication with its publics, is due largely to its overarching desire to preserve the logic of capitalist production.

Contemporary critical theory's interest in those crisis tendencies inspired by the global spread of neo-liberal policies of marketization and a calculist mentality, is on the basis of the opportunities they create for a conflict-led collective moral learning. The emphasis in this instance is on the real needs and motives of publics (for instance, the need for empathy, understanding, dialogue, solidarity, etc.), as opposed to those created by the often mystifying power of capitalism (see Offe 1997; Habermas 2001; Miller 2005). Channels of resistance emerge across the globe in response to crisis. The communicative turn that accompanies such developments ignites a greater reciprocal interpenetration of social worlds on the basis of a more intense degree of public communication about definitions of the common good and a deep desire to understand the nature of such social problems. Reason moves from the ideal to praxis in conflict scenarios when the struggle for recognition (Honneth 1999) of one's interests evolves into a struggle over the interpretation of collectively shared rights (consumer rights or market rights versus human rights). The enduring validity of democratic norms stems from the recognition they continue to enjoy internationally and the ongoing willingness of social actors to evoke them in dispute.

This leads to the question of how present relations of communication allows those contemporary subjects who have been harmed by disrespect, neglect, or marginalization the opportunity to articulate their experiences of suffering and align the particularities of such experiences with more general societal norms of justice and equality in a democratic public sphere. It is to this issue that I will now turn.

III. Using the investigative gaze of the media as a protest weapon against the international violation of human rights

Accompanying the current globalization of the purposive-rational functional media of administrative power and monetary capital is the globalization of the mass communications media. The student radicals of 1968 took full advantage of the re-invigoration of investigative reporting during the era of the Civil Rights Movement and the Vietnam War when the search for truth and the disclosure of inequality and corruption became paramount (Thompson 2005). The 'politics of trust', arising from this newly politicized culture of investigative journalism, helped to radicalize the social function of reason as a kind of absent high court judge because the conditions underwriting the credibility of the scrutinized government official in this instance centred chiefly on their underlying allegiance to truth and justice.

As a media-inflected moment of transnational resistance to repressive regimes around the world, 1968 set an important precedent for an internationally based solidarity with globally dispersed 'others'. Students in New York, Berkeley, Paris, London, Berlin, and so on, developed a strong sense of solidarity with the Vietnamese fighting the imperialist domination of a power whose influence was also felt in the Western world. Identification with the global 'other', forged on the basis of common cultural and political interests opposing a unified system of power and domination (Touraine 1968:34), was greatly enhanced by the presence of mass media technologies. The latter not only helped document various atrocities against the Vietnamese people, but also accounted for such violence alongside incidents of police brutality against students closer to home in Berkeley or Paris. The students of 1968 were amongst the first protesters to take full advantage of the mass media's 'space-time compression of the modern world' and its 'de-spatialized visibility' (Thompson 2005) to highlight our common vulnerability to global capitalist corruption and the potential for human suffering. Students blended the media's morality of exposure with such anti-capitalist ideologies as anarchism, feminism, pacifism, and environmentalism in the hope of making those aspects of the global face of capitalist corruption more transparent to the wider social imagination.

In terms of its engagements with the protest politics from the sixties onwards, the mass media has not only transformed modern culture and identity, but has also fundamentally altered the shape of public consciousness, creating an instantaneous global transmission of information and spectacular scenes of exploitation, poverty, and human rights violations in China, Asia, or South America. In so doing, the media has not only dismantled the immediacy of the lifeworld, but also allowed for a far greater acquisition of non-local knowledge by extending cognitive horizons on human rights abuse into distant worlds. Inadvertently, this process has also facilitated the human rights monitoring efforts of protest networks like the Seattle to Brussels Network or the much larger OWINFS (Our World Is Not For Sale) Network, which campaign tirelessly against the exploitative practices of transnational corporations in the Free Trade Areas of the Americas, Western militarism and occupation, and the systematic denial of the rights of immigrants, amongst other things.

Today's global anti-capitalist protesters, like the students' movement of 1968 and the environmental and peace movements before them, use media technologies to disseminate symbolic messages that challenge the legitimacy of the current power order and extend modernity's fields of vision to include a critical perspective on the living conditions of the distant 'other'. In this way, protesters like Global Exchange hope to stimulate a critical interpretation and understanding of mutual suffering around the world by emphasizing our common humanity and the need 'to feel deeply about injustice against anyone, always in the world' (Global Exchange 2008). Solidarity with the 'other' on the basis of our shared commitment to international standards of human rights thus continues to be forged through the human relation to suffering. For instance, growing public awareness of the contemporary suffering of banana plantation workers in Guatemala, their appalling work and living conditions, and the level of state violence targeting union leaders and social activists. In cases like Guatemala or Nicaragua, cyber-activists like NicaNet or the Guatemala Solidarity Network use a multi-media inflected critical diagnostics to lay bare the interconnections between the suffering of the 'other' and the suffering of the self in an increasingly interconnected global capitalist order.

In a similar vein, protest actors like Action Aid, campaigning on behalf of child labourers working in the sweatshops of New Delhi, attempt to communicate an understanding of how the distant and familiar subject realities of global capitalist exploitation are linked in their failures to respect the international culture of human rights. The distant suffering of globally distributed 'others' and the familiar suffering attached to life under a Western capitalist regime, such as the growing sense of alienation, frustration, and feeling of relative deprivation, are construed as related components in a circular system of global capitalist exploitation.

Instead of feeling overwhelmed by the passivity of both distant and familiar suffering, however, mass campaigners like the Third World Network advocate a policy of fighting back. For instance, campaigns to boycott certain food companies for selling Israeli oranges or South American bananas. In this way, the protest actor not only defetishizes the global might and supposed infallibility of the corporate world, but also manages to illustrate how contemporary practices of the self and practices of the 'other' are intricately inter-related, even in a global context. The anti-capitalist protester threatens the global power of a multinational when it publicly reveals how more ethical purchasing practices in the West can have a profound impact on the working conditions and life chances of workers in the developing world. By threatening to expose the 'true' nature of working conditions in factories in India or Pakistan producing garments for Western high street chains, such actors direct processes of justification towards 'the highest court of reason' (Habermas 2008: 35), that is, truth, and in the process force such companies to abide by the rules of the Ethical Trading Initiative and protect the rights of poor and under-aged workers, or face public exposure as violators of modernity's shared norms of equality, justice, and freedom.

IV. Conclusion

In bringing such regulative ideals as freedom and accountability to bear on knowledge of international suffering, transnationally organized protest actors single themselves out as new cognitive agents exposing the counterfactual realities of global capitalism. Politically, such knowledge becomes especially operative in the margins of difference between the imaginary and real conditions of global production and exchange. Such knowledge, in turn, becomes the empirical basis of actors' demands for justice, human rights, fair trade, and accountability. In the context of current transnational discourses on human rights, modernity's principles of democracy are socially activated through new globally significant practices of 'networking', where experience, action, and discursive justification are brought together by internationally dispersed protesters who, for instance, regularly gather to form counter-summits that run in parallel with various meetings of states, including the G7/G8, the World Economic Forum, and the Organization for Economic Cooperation and Development. Attracting anything from one thousand to one hundred thousand participants, such gatherings prove to be strategic opportunities for a democratic expression of collective opposition to worldwide neo-liberal imperialism, the disappearance of diversity, and the tyranny of corporate agriculture. Indeed, it is modernity's long suffering 'utopia of freedom' which prompted the 1968 protester, as it does the more contemporary anti-capitalist protester of today, to attempt to realize Enlightenment freedom again and again, regardless of powerful obstacles in its way or its propensity to collide with the limits of the bureaucratic world. Modernity's ongoing commitment to principles of freedom, justice, and accountability consistently proves to be the primary motivational force for successive waves of social movements' engagement in a transformative praxis.

Such human praxis promises a stronger public sphere in the making (Brunkhorst 2005), one that relies heavily on the new digital technologies and the Internet to create a sense of intimacy in a public sphere freed from the constraints of co-presence. The information disseminating capacities and de-spatialized visibility of the Internet prove to be indispensable to protesters' efforts at stimulating the level of cyber-activism needed worldwide to force governments, the WTO, the IMF, and the World Bank to take notice of their demands for justice. For example, the global petition signed by 24 million people in 2000 in support of a 'Jubilee year' of debt elimination. Reitan (2007) discusses the role of this campaign in spearheading the agreement amongst the G7 governments and major banks that year to write off $110 billion in Third World debts. Like the May Movement radicals, today's global activists set out to unmask their adversary by simultaneously revealing the universal nature of inequality and exploitation. Just like their historical predecessor, today's activists 'destroy the illusion of a society united by growth and prosperity' (Touraine 1971: 32), by substituting the myth of social modernization with graphic illustrations of modernity's struggles and contradictions. In this sense, the cultural radicalism of 1968 was a crucial forerunner to the kind of expressive politics and critical exchanges with the media adopted by today's anti-capitalist protesters. Organizations like Global Exchange, the International Forum on Globalization, Jobs with Justice, Mobilization for Social Justice, or Action Aid depend heavily upon new media technologies to uncover capitalism's hidden arenas of action and communicate an intensely visual message of protest around the world.

The link between media technology, consciousness of suffering, solidarity, learning, reason, and democratization continues to be explored by various social theorists today, including Beck (2005), Thompson (2005), and Habermas (2001). Habermas (2001) points to the emerging global sense of civic solidarity amongst a postnational democratic constellation with a shared sense of responsibility and commitment to inclusion. Beck highlights the symbolic and political significance of the protest endeavours of new transnational movements and their role as a counterbalance to the growing competitiveness and ruthlessness of the global market economy. The level of 'transnational conflict', evoked by today's movements of world citizens fighting for a democratization of 'worlds of capitalism' (for instance, the Fair Trade Initiative), prevents the disappearance of norms of justice, equality, and truth. Beck stresses the importance of the protest actor in stimulating cosmopolitan sympathies towards globally impoverished 'others'. Such actors strategically use the media to promote a greater sense of mutuality between Western self and non-Western 'other'. Solidarity in this instance arises chiefly from a growing feeling of global interdependence amongst communities of risk and 'networks of shared fate' (Habermas 2001: 55).

Critical theory preserves a strong imaginative, even utopian dimension to its thinking on the interrelationship between reason and a principle of reform which transcends the current institutional limits of democracy. Its critique of the contemporary face of instrumental reasoning and the practical necessity of efforts to align such a critique with an imminent critique of life conditions under the new global capitalist order continue to draw its attention back to collective efforts to socially activate democratic reason. Human rights principles of reason still provide the critical actor with the necessary tools to pierce the hard core of formal rationality and explore the vulnerabilities of humanity that lie beneath. The global justice movement of today digs deep to find modernity's 'utopian momentum' (Brunkhorst 1997) and shows how its spirit of democracy has not yet been fully exhausted. This transnational actor promotes a project of egalitarian solidarity amongst global strangers whose vulnerabilities to abuse and exploitation are measured against denationalized legal norms on human rights.

In its anticipations of the future of modernity, critical theory has routinely added the pretext 'revolution' to various accounts of the role reason plays in resolving the incongruities of modern rationalization. What remains constant in a neo-Kantian critical project is the understanding that the greatest 'adventures of the dialectic' (both past and future) are those that allow the autonomous subject to realize the self through the universal and re-affirm modernity's democratic spirit.

6
On Totalitarianism: The Continuing Relevance of Herbert Marcuse

Sarah Hornstein[1]

I. Introduction

The late sixties, particularly 1968, was a time of heightened political awareness and social unrest not only in France, but all over the world as well. In the United States, Herbert Marcuse's books, especially *Eros and Civilization* (1955) and *One Dimensional Man* (1964), resonated with members of the student movement and he was frequently asked to give lectures at universities and demonstrations. Indeed, it was through this 'sudden popularity' that his work and, as a consequence, that of the Frankfurt School more generally, became so influential to the development of both the American and the international New Left (Jay 1973: 5,284). Herbert Marcuse is therefore, at the very least, an important historical figure. And yet, his work deserves to be treated not just as historically influential, but rather as *prescient*; Marcuse's work is perhaps even more relevant today than it was when he first wrote it.

The protestors of the 1960s were concerned with putting an end to war, with workers' rights, with social justice, and with the development of an anti-colonial solidarity with the developing world; theirs was, generally speaking, an explicitly anti-totalitarian ethos. Yet today, 40 years later, we find ourselves again at war, still witnessing the imperialist exploitation of 'third world' labour at the hands of the 'developed' nations, and again observing what to many appears to be the revival of fascism (or, at the very least, 'neo-fascism') in the West. Given all of this, I suggest that Marcuse still has something to teach us and that his legacy is an understanding of the totalitarianism of advanced capitalist society that we can, in the current climate, ill afford to do without.

Marcuse's engagement with the issue of totalitarianism relies on the understanding of the transformation of reason and for him this transformation is exemplified by the emergence of positivism as the dominant means of making sense of the world. He argues that the totalitarian character of advanced industrial society and its concomitant 'totalitarian rationality' (Marcuse 2001 [1961]: 52, 55) have specific, potentially devastating, consequences for the members of that society. Most important here are what Marcuse conceptualizes as 'matter-of-factness', 'psychological neutrality', and 'repressive desublimation'. I begin, then, by discussing the emergence of technological rationality in some detail before moving on to Marcuse's understanding of totalitarianism, its repercussions for the individual, and the possibilities for resistance and social change.

II. The development of technological rationality

Throughout his work, though especially in *One Dimensional Man* (1964) and 'Some Social Implications of Modern Technology' (1998 [1941]), Marcuse argues that in the course of the development of the prevailing social order a 'new' form of rationality has emerged. This rationality can be distinguished from 'traditional', 'pre-technological' rationality in several ways; most importantly, it is characterized by the transformation of negative, two-dimensional into positive, one-dimensional thought. The reason that had informed the Western tradition was, for Marcuse, characterized by its fundamentally dialectical nature. Its logic was 'the mode of thought appropriate for comprehending the real as rational' and its primary concern was the discovery of truth (Marcuse 1964: 123, 125). Crucially, however, the delineation of the true versus the false reflected 'the experience of a world antagonistic in itself' due to the fact that philosophy, and thinking more generally, was traditionally concerned with the difference between 'appearance and reality' (Marcuse 1964: 125). Things cannot be taken as they immediately appear and pre-technological, negative rationality understood this fact. Indeed, characteristic of two-dimensional thought is its ability to think through the difference between 'essential' and 'apparent' truths, between how things are and how things should be (Marcuse 1964: 135, 132; see also 133 n.3, 140–2, 167). The importance of this cannot be overstated, for to understand that despite how things *are* they perhaps *ought to be different* involves 'critical judgment' and this judgment is inherent in two-dimensional thinking itself. Indeed 'is' and 'ought' *are* the two dimensions of this mode of thought. In being able to think alternatives, in recognizing that what appears to be true could be the manifestation of a deeper truth (if not something else entirely), dialectical thinking is intrinsically subversive; this is its negative quality (see Marcuse 1964: 123–43, 171).

The dialectical character of two-dimensional thinking, its ability to (at least attempt to) think through both the immediate and the potential reality, requires a certain degree of abstraction. Marcuse (1964: 134) argues that abstraction in and of itself is not a 'bad' thing; indeed, '[a]bstractness is the very life of thought'. However, there are 'false and true abstractions' due to the fact that abstraction 'is a historical event in a historical continuum. It proceeds on historical grounds, and it remains related to the very basis from which it moves away: the established societal universe' (Marcuse 1964: 134). As negative rationality emerged in the socio-historical context of a widespread separation between intellectual and manual labour, its philosophy was not concerned with those 'who bore the brunt of the untrue reality and who, therefore, seemed to be most in need of attaining its subversion... It abstracted from them and continued to abstract from them. In this sense "idealism" was germane to philosophic thought' (Marcuse 1964: 134, 135, 139). We have here the beginning of the transition from negative to positive, one-dimensional thinking. With the idealist turn in philosophy the stage was set for the emergence of formal logic.

Formal logic is, for Marcuse, connected to the desire to 'understand', order, and control the world in an eminently 'reasonable' way. What is false about the abstraction required by formal logic, and positive, technological thinking more generally, is that in it '... the conflict between essence and appearance is expendable if not meaningless; the material content is neutralized; the principle of identity is separated from the principle of contradiction... Well defined in their scope and function, concepts become instruments of prediction and control' (Marcuse 1964: 137). Though discussion of the specific details of the development of formal into symbolic and mathematical logic is beyond the scope of this chapter, what is crucial here is that these modes of thought 'share the radical opposition to dialectical logic' (Marcuse 1964: 139). If what sets *truly* dialectical thought apart is the fact that it critically judges and therefore subverts the prevailing order, and that it understands this order as fundamentally antagonistic, then opposition to this comes to mean conformity with and justification for the world as immediately given, for the 'is' (Marcuse 1964: 140–1; see also Marcuse 1998 [1941]: 49–50). Two-dimensional thought is opposed both to an idealism that fails to grasp the material reality and to a science or way of thinking that fails to see beyond that reality, for the latter finds its 'truth' in the 'concreteness of immediate experience' and fails to free itself 'from the deceptive objectivity which conceals the factors behind the facts' (Marcuse 1964: 141, 182). This is indeed the defining characteristic of one-dimensional thinking and is a major contributor to its 'totalitarian' quality. It is to more explicit discussion of this aspect of essentially affirmative thought that we now turn.

III. The totalitarian quality of technological rationality

Positive, one-dimensional thinking is characterized by the 'radical acceptance of the empirical' and, according to Marcuse (1964), this in fact 'violates the empirical, for in it speaks the mutilated, "abstract" individual who experiences (and expresses) only that which is *given* to him (given in a literal sense), who has only the facts and not the factors, whose behaviour is one-dimensional and manipulated.... [T]he positivist cleaning of the mind brings the mind in line with the restricted experience' (182 [original emphasis]). We see here that one-dimensional thinking is reflective of one-dimensional existence and vice versa. What makes this rationality and this existence totalitarian is the fact that in both cases, 'Subjection to the established facts is total' (1964: 178; see also Marcuse 2001 [1961]: 55); positive thinking, and its manifestation in positivism proper, mathematization, standardization, and scientific method, seeks exactness and calculability (1964: 184). Positive thinking is always concerned with liquidating anything it views as 'unscientific', 'incalculable', *qualitative*, which it sees as mere mystification. Yet, as Marcuse argues, it is this rationality itself that is truly and *completely* mystifying (1964: 189–90). For Marcuse, as for the Frankfurt School more generally, the emergence of this one-dimensional rationality is clearly related to the mode of production upon which society is organized. The two inform, perpetuate, and solidify each other. In Marcuse's work, the focus in articulating this connection is centred, to a large extent, on the understanding of our social order as a 'technological society'. Indeed, positive, technological thinking arose 'in the course of the technological process' (Marcuse 1998 [1941]: 42) and with it new forms of individuality and experience also emerged.

Marcuse differentiates between 'technics' and 'technology' arguing that while the former refers to the 'technical apparatus of industry, communication, transportation', the latter is the social process in which 'technics is but a partial factor' (Marcuse 1998 [1941]: 41; see also Marcuse 2001 [1961]: 45). The mode of production operating in advanced capitalist society is a *technological* mode of production (ibid.), requiring efficiency, standardization, and mechanization on a mass scale (1998: 63; Marcuse 1998a: 73-7). While the technological achievements of the prevailing social order could perhaps be used to combat both toil and scarcity (i.e., to fundamentally change the prevailing social relationships), in the contemporary period, for the most part, technology instead is 'a manifestation of prevalent thought and behaviour patterns, an instrument for control and domination' (1998: 41; see also 47-9). As the prevailing form of thinking in our technological society is one-dimensional and therefore essentially affirmative in nature, the technology itself manifests this both in its organization and in its use. In fact, both positive, technological rationality and the technological apparatus that it produces require conformity and compliance from individuals. Indeed, in Marcuse's view, this is due to the fact that technological rationality itself has a specific *political* character and 'operates as political rationality' (2001 [1961]: 47). The three major factors that contribute to this political character *in general* are: (1) the fact that advanced capitalist society maintains and reproduces itself through mass production; (2) the fact that its technical apparatus 'consists not only of the machinery employed in material production but also of that which fills the offices and stores and streets and, not least, the private homes and apartments' (2001 [1961]: 48); and (3) the fact that 'in the functioning of the productive and distributive apparatus, technical and political operations, technical and political controls are inexorably intertwined' (2001 [1961]: 49). The mass production of goods requires a concomitant system of mass distribution and consumption and this demands the extensive coordination of all realms of social life.

This two-fold integration of the technical apparatus and technological rationality into not just every realm of social life but also into the actual psyches of each individual is precisely its totalitarian element. Therefore, what separates the overtly fascist from the democratic society is not so much that the former is totalitarian while the latter is not. In fact, Marcuse is clear that in any case,

> [b]y virtue of the way in which it has organized its technological base, contemporary industrial society tends to be totalitarian. For totalitarian is not only a terroristic political co-ordination of society, but also a non-terroristic economic-technical co-ordination which operates through the manipulation of needs by vested interests and thus precludes the emergence of an effective opposition against the whole organized by these interests. Not only a specific form of government

or party rule makes for totalitarianism, but also a specific system of production and distribution which may well be compatible with 'pluralism' of parties, newspapers, 'countervailing' forces, etc. In the contemporary period, political power asserts itself through the power of the machine process, which moves the technical ensemble of the productive apparatus. The government of advanced and advancing industrial societies can maintain and secure itself only when it succeeds in mobilizing, organizing, and exploiting the technical, scientific, and mechanical productivity available to industrial civilization – and this productivity tends to involve society as a whole, above and beyond any particular individual or group interests.
(2001 [1961]: 50–1)

In a certain sense, then, what separates the 'democratic' from the fascist regime is that the former is a non-terroristic technocracy while the latter is a terroristic one (Marcuse 1998 [1941]: 42) and that consequently in the one case a non-terroristic 'unfreedom' prevails while in the other this unfreedom takes an openly terroristic form (see Marcuse 2001 [1965]: 88–9; Marcuse 2001 [1961]: 37, 43, 52; Marcuse 1998a; Marcuse 1998b). In other words, the advanced industrial organization of both fascist and 'democratic' systems is ruled by the same technological rationality; under fascism, however, the totalitarian element finds its extreme manifestation. The crucial distinction is whether the totalitarianism of a given social order is terroristic or not and this obviously has consequences for the ways in which technocratic organization manifests itself.

IV. Terroristic and non-terroristic technocracies

Under National Socialism (the terroristic technocracy *par excellence*) the focus on efficiency, calculability, standardization, and the like is taken to its most extreme point; technological rationality, with its governing 'principle of efficiency' (Marcuse 1998a: 73–7), is here 'in the total service of imperialist expansion' (1998a: 77; see also 72–3, 78–80, 92) and this desire for expansion is absolutely uncompromising. Everything, all of the horror, is committed in its name. As a consequence of this, the terror that holds this society together is 'not only that of the concentration camps, prisons and pogroms; it is not only the terror of lawlessness, but also the less conspicuous though no less efficient legalized terror of bureaucratization' (1998a: 77), which aims to assist in the abolishment of the separation between state and society and between society and individual (1998a: 70, 75–6, 78). Insofar as the latter is concerned, this is achieved in two ways: first, by releasing the forces of competitive self-interest, the regime facilitates the organization of individuals into a mass (1998a: 80). Second, the regime relaxed and in some cases completely removed prevalent taboos, such as those on privacy, chastity, monogamy, and the sanctity of the family (1998a: 83–6, 90). The abolition of the taboo on privacy, under which these other taboos fall, was most disastrous insofar as the status of the individual's relationship to the social order is concerned due to the fact that in one's private, leisure time one 'may come to *think*, [one's] impulses, feelings and thoughts may be driven into regions which are foreign and inimical to the prevailing order' (1998a: 89 [original emphasis]). Furthermore, these taboos 'tended... to aggravate the antagonism between individual satisfaction and social frustration; the former was kept apart from society and, by this very fact, retained elements of a freedom and happiness which were alien to the social reality' (1998a: 83). The removal of these taboos therefore has a repressive rather than truly liberatory function (1998a: 90) despite appearance to the contrary. Indeed, the abolition of taboos and the emergence of the mass, particularly when connected with 'the drives and impulses directed against the chosen enemies of the Third Reich' (1998a: 86), result in the (almost) total identification of the individual with her society (1998a: 87). The terror of the National Socialist order is tolerated because individuals come to see themselves as *compensated* for it; the identification is so strong that they, as the privileged members of the 'German race', see themselves as the new masters instead of as the ones who are mastered by the National Socialist constellation of industry, party, and army (1998a: 86–7).

Now, while it is certainly the case that many contemporary 'democratic' societies are also rabidly imperialistic, highly bureaucratized, and also to a certain extent organize individuals into a 'mass', these societies have not (d)evolved into an openly terroristic technocracy due in large part to the fact that in this case liberal values (such as liberty, self-determination, civil rights, and rule of law) are at least formally and ideologically upheld (see Marcuse 1998a: 71–2; Marcuse 1964: 51) and in many cases were an integral part of the history of their state-formation.[2] Nonetheless, Marcuse argues that 'Democracy would appear to be the most efficient system of domination' (1964: 52) *due to the very fact that its unfreedom is non-terroristic in nature*. Under these circumstances unfreedom in fact appears, and is indeed experienced, as freedom (Marcuse 2001 [1965]: 86; Marcuse 2001 [1961]: 37). 'Democratic' advanced capitalist societies are particularly good at liquidating, containing, and/or integrating threats to the self-preservation of the status quo; indeed, the 'irrational in this society appears as rational because people indeed have more comforts, and more fun. Domination appears as freedom because people indeed have the choice of prefabricated goods and prefabricated candidates. Behind the technological veil domination of man by man continues as it did before, and operates within the conception and context of free individuals' (Marcuse 2001 [1965]: 86; see also Marcuse 2001 [1961]: 38, 40, 49–50; Marcuse 1964). The efficacy of this domination-through-integration is especially clear if we look at its manifestation in the very psyches of the individuals living in these societies. The most important of these are what Marcuse terms 'matter-of-factness', 'psychological neutrality', and 'repressive desublimation'.

The matter-of-fact, or technological, attitude is part and parcel of what Marcuse calls an overall 'psychological neutrality'. With the emergence and development of technological rationality, the individual has found herself in a situation in which unquestioning, obedient adjustment to the prevailing social order is not only required but almost a matter of *reflex*. The technological attitude, as the outcome of the totalizing force of technological rationality, is characterized by (sometimes extreme) rationalization on the part of the individual. Wars, scarcity, toil – injustices of all kinds – are seen as reasonable and/or pragmatic, and this leads to a standpoint of detachment and resignation (Marcuse 2001 [1961]: 49; Marcuse 1998b: 187–8; Marcuse 1998 [1941]: 44–8). Marcuse (1998b: 187) argues, 'The pragmatic matter-of-factness of every day life which characterizes the behaviour of men [*sic*] in the technological era tends to interpret the concrete issues, the fate of every single individual which is actually at stake, in terms of objective forces, machines, and institutions', and this tendency itself becomes an integral part of the 'mechanics of conformity' in technological society (Marcuse 1998 [1941]: 48). The result is not only that the attitude serves the self-preservation of the whole but, perhaps even more troubling, it becomes perceived by the individuals themselves as necessary to their own survival (1998: 44–8).

One of the clearest symptoms of the technological attitude is repressive desublimation; indeed, the two reinforce each other. While sublimation in general occurs when libidinal energy is diverted from its overtly sexual aim to a related, but non-sexual (what Freud terms 'social' or 'higher') one instead (Freud 2001 [1916–1917]: 345), 'desublimation' is characterized by the replacement of '…mediated by immediate gratification' (Marcuse 1955: 72). In its non-repressive form, the libido is free to find this gratification and the object it chooses for said gratification is freely chosen. In contrast, the immediate gratification experienced through repressive desublimation is '... "practised from a position of strength" on the part of society... sexuality is liberated (or rather liberalized) in socially constructive forms.... [I]t operates as the by-product of the social controls of technological reality, which extend liberty while intensifying domination' (Marcuse 1955: 72). Repressive desublimation bears the mark of the repressive society in which it operates. It is institutionalized, adjusted, and controlled desublimation and it works in the service of 'social cohesion and contentment' (Marcuse 1955: 72, 74–5, 77, 79). While people may feel as though they are freely choosing the objects which satisfy their desires, the reality is that these desires have been preconditioned; individuals have been trained to seek their gratification in particular objects (commodities) at particular times in particular ways. Furthermore, sexuality itself has been commodified; in this way, non-terroristic technocracies, like terroristic ones, also relax taboos around sexuality and sexual life and do so towards a repressive end. In both terroristic and non-terroristic industrial societies repressive desublimation operates as a means of promoting 'satisfaction' and this satisfaction, be it the 'privilege' of belonging to the 'master race' or that of being able to watch 'Sex and the City' or 'Desperate Housewives', to sit behind the wheel of a Honda or a Cadillac, only serves the self-preservation of the entire order which produces and assimilates such 'freedom'. In other words, both of these technocratic orders provide many opportunities for desublimation, yet it is always desublimation on their own terms, in service of their own aims, however monstrous or apparently benign those aims may be. This is what makes the desublimation not only repressive but dangerous. Repressive desublimation is a powerful tool of domination: it can be used to bolster not only the 'democratic' capitalist order but also the more openly terroristic brand of socio-political organization and psychological compliance discussed in relation to National Socialism above.

There is no doubt that Marcuse's work in particular, and that of the first-generation Frankfurt School in general, continues to influence contemporary social theory. Not only does this thought itself continue to be an object of study, but it also impacts upon the work produced in such areas as media and cultural studies (e.g., Kellner 2003, 2005; Postman 1993), the sociology of consumption and leisure, and in the continuing engagement with the problem of methodology in the social sciences (e.g., Aronowitz and Ausch 2000). In these areas, Marcuse's analysis of technology, the critique of positivism, and the development of the concept of 'repressive desublimation' have been especially important. For example, Kellner is clear that his aim is to develop a 'critical theory of the contemporary moment' (2003: 10; 1989: 177). In this vein, both he and others have argued that current advertising and media techniques, by consciously appropriating elements from sub- and counter-cultural movements, have absorbed and therefore 'desublimated' their oppositional power. Similarly, Neil Postman (1993) has emphasized the ongoing relevance of the positivist dispute in his critique of the 'scientism' of technological rationality, which he terms 'Technopoly'. We are reminded of Marcuse's understanding of what is at stake in this dispute when Postman argues,

> [b]y Scientism, I mean three interrelated ideas that, taken together, stand as one of the pillars of Technopoly... The first and indispensable idea is... that the methods of the natural sciences can be applied to the study of human behavior. This idea is the backbone of much of psychology and sociology as practised in America.... The second idea is... that social science generates specific principles which can be used to organize society on a rational and humane basis. This implies that technical means – mostly 'invisible technologies' supervised by experts – can be designed to control human behavior and set it on the proper course.... The third idea is that faith in science can serve as a comprehensive belief system that gives meaning to life, as well as a sense of well-being, morality and even immorality.
>
> (1955: 147)

The influence of Marcusean themes, particularly the ideological function of repressive desublimation, is also apparent in Judith Schor's (1999; 2004) work on the sociology of consumption in the United States. This is particularly clear in her analysis of the pacifying effects of the absorption of commercial culture by children and adolescents (see Schor 2004: 37, 173–5 *cf.* Walsh 2008: 254). These scholars have, in a certain sense, perhaps gone beyond Marcuse and other first-generation members of the Frankfurt School insofar as they have attempted to develop concrete, critical programmes for resisting the stultifying effects of modern cultural and media techniques – namely a 'critical media studies' in the case of Kellner (2003; 2005) and what Postman calls a 'media ecology' (1993: 19, 198). Nonetheless, their works do not have the historical sweep or philosophical justifications that characterize Marcuse's own perspective.

Furthermore, despite the clear influence Marcuse continues to exert in these diverse areas, the importance of the Frankfurt School's engagement with the issue of totalitarianism has often been (and continues to be) neglected, misunderstood, or simply written off as 'dated' or exaggeration (Jones 1999). Yet, perhaps one of the most significant lessons we have to learn from Marcuse's analysis of the totalitarian tendencies of advanced industrial societies is that fascism and democracy (as we know it) do not sit at two opposite ends of the political spectrum. Fascism is not simply imposed on a society from without; rather, the potential for fascism is present even in 'democratic' systems from the beginning. As long as positive, instrumental reason dominates, as long as society and individual experience are organized according to the principle of exchange, the potential for the re-emergence of a truly terroristic order persists. Any analysis of fascism, or even of totalitarianism, that locates it as a phenomenon 'out there', or explains it in terms of 'isolated' events, commits a dangerous error. Under the current conditions, when the matter-of-fact, technological attitude towards the status quo, towards 'business as usual', is as apparent as ever in 'politics', homes, offices, and classrooms, we must not complacently believe that liberal democracy as such is all the protection we need. The distance between resignation, or even satisfied acceptance, and the readiness to be unquestioningly compliant even in the face of atrocity, is not great at all. At the same time, however, we would be missing the point if we were to argue that Marcuse's thought is *only* warning us of what *could* happen if we stay on our current path. His argument is also more direct than that. His is a call to understand that despite a higher standard of living, despite the 'luxury' of (what appears to be) more options than ever before, ours is a mutilated reality and a mutilated experience. The barbarism of everyday life can be seen in the fact that we live in a world where alienation has become almost total; we live subjected to an order in which we are blind to our subjection and our unfreedom appears as freedom.

V. Conclusion

Under these circumstances, the possibilities for resistance and emancipation may appear particularly bleak. However, the tension running throughout Marcuse's work is actually that of the simultaneous impossibility and *possibility* of freedom (Marcuse 1964: xlvii). Where does this possibility lie? Marcuse (2001 [1965]: 93) argues that the reactivation of critique, and of critical thinking more generally, offers the best hope for 'unless the recognition of what is being done and what is being prevented subverts the consciousness and the behavior of man [sic], not even a catastrophe will bring about...change' (Marcuse 1964: xlvii). This requires the recuperation of two-dimensional thought and of its ability to recognize history as a 'hidden dimension of meaning' in the dominant discourses of society. According to Marcuse (1964: 181), such recognition 'shatters the natural and reified form in which the given universe of discourse first appears'. Furthermore, the reactivation of two-dimensional, negative thinking would also be the re-emergence of the critical judgement, which could at least challenge, if not destroy, the technological attitude due to the fact that this form of judgement not only imagines and articulates how things *ought* to be but is also, therefore, explicitly *political* (1964: 123f). Marcuse sees the development of a philosophy that is immanently critical (e.g., the Frankfurt School's own 'Critical Theory') as one of the main means of reactivating critical thought. He argues,

> The unscientific, speculative character of critical theory derives from the specific character of its concepts, which designate and define the irrational in the rational, the mystification in the reality. Their mythological quality reflects the mystifying quality of the given facts – the deceptive harmonization of the societal conditions.
> (1964: 189; see also 140–1)

Therefore,

> In the totalitarian era, the therapeutic task of philosophy would be a political task, since the established universe of ordinary language tends to coagulate into a totally manipulated and indoctrinated universe. The politics would appear in philosophy, not as a special discipline or object of analysis, nor as a special political philosophy, but as the intent of its concepts to comprehend the unmutilated reality.
> (1964: 199)

Of course, as we have seen in the earlier discussion of the transformation of negative into positive thinking, critical thought, even when active, is capable of being contained and absorbed by the prevailing social order. Indeed, this form of thought has become increasingly 'socially impotent' as a result both of the 'growth of the industrial apparatus' and the resulting coordination of 'all spheres of life' and as an outcome of the assimilation of historically oppositional elements, such as labour and art, into the apparatus itself (Marcuse 1998 [1941]: 51–2). Nonetheless, Marcuse argues that we must continue to develop this critique, in both thought and action (e.g., activism, pedagogy), in an effort to find ways of keeping it from losing its 'edge' and becoming 'merge[d] with the old and familiar' (1998: 51). Otherwise, we run the risk of becoming completely incapable of escaping a truly pervasive and destructive totalitarianism, one that covers not only all of society but the mind and body as well.

Notes

1. I would like to express my gratitude to Dr Philip Walsh for his support, insight, and guidance in the development of this chapter. My appreciation also to Trish MacMillan, Liz Rondinelli, and Dr Henry Hornstein for their encouraging and helpful comments on an earlier version.
2. The argument can of course be made that especially in the current climate these values are, at the very least, under threat if not protected in name only. Yet even if this is the case, this only underlines Marcuse's point that democracy (as we know it) is not fundamentally incompatible with the development of an openly fascist order. Again, given that technological rationality dominates both systems, the question is not whether it is *possible* for a democratic state like the United States, England, or Canada to become fascist but rather what provides for the most effective resistance *against* such a possibility. Put differently, the question is how to keep countries like these from becoming so. As Marcuse (1998a: 190) argues, 'Certain groups among the population of the democratic countries are all too readily inclined to marvel at the efficiency of the Nazi machine in dealing with internal problems (labour trouble, rationalization, overall control of production, distribution and consumption, elimination of waste and subversive activities, etc.). They may be tempted to seize upon any opportunity to contrast these German "achievements" with the conditions of their own country, and to draw the conclusion that, after all, Nazism did some useful things.' It may not be ridiculous to argue that these words are perhaps as true today as they were when Marcuse first wrote them and Marx's famous dictum that history repeats itself, 'the first time as tragedy, the second time as farce', seems an especially prescient caution.

7
Everyone Longs for a Master: Lacan and 1968

Stephen Frosh

The Paris events of 1968 were observed sympathetically by Jacques Lacan, who had a longstanding commitment to refusing to accept any pregiven order, and whose own son-in-law/heir (Jacques-Alain Miller) and daughter became members of the Maoist Gauche prolétarienne. However, the role he took up is described by Elisabeth Roudinesco as that of the 'stern father' who always knew better, in a way that might be construed as authoritarian, than did the revolutionaries themselves. 'As revolutionaries, what you long for is a master,' he told them; 'You'll get one...' More importantly, perhaps, Lacan distinguished between totalitarian revolutionary movements – in which he included Maoism – and the truly revolutionary movement of Freudianism (at least as refracted by Lacan). The key issue here was that of the *'pas-tout* (not-whole)': the Freudian revolution is that which has no ambitions to total knowledge, but allows for the fallen, divided subject. Without this *pas-tout*, there will always be demand for a master. Hence the parallel (failed?) Lacanian revolution of the time: the *passe* or famous 'self-authorizing' procedure for becoming a psychoanalyst. This chapter looks at Lacan's actions and arguments of the time and examines these relationships between posturing, mastery, and radical reconfiguration.

Lacan's famous comment to the students at Vincennes in December 1969, included at the end of Seminar XVII, 'The Other Side of Psychoanalysis' (Lacan 1991), is worth reminiscing over. The immediate context was a fraught moment of teaching. Following the 1968 revolts, a new 'experimental' university, the Université de Paris VIII, had been opened at Vincennes, and within it (under the general umbrella of Michel Foucault's Department of Philosophy) was the first Department of Psychoanalysis in the French university system, chaired by the Lacanian Serge Leclaire. Clemens and Grigg (2006: 1) comment that

'The department itself boasted an impressive list of a new breed of philosophers, including Gilles Deleuze, Jacques Rancière, Alain Badiou, and Jean-François Lyotard.' The wider Department of Philosophy also cataclysmically contained Lacan's daughter, Judith Miller, who in 1970 provoked its official Governmental disaccreditation by handing out course credits to someone she met on a bus, and subsequently publicly declaring in a radio interview that the university was a capitalist institution, and that she would do everything she could to make it run as badly as possible. This gesture was well in tune with the times, but as we shall see probably fell foul of her father's strictures on the limitations of politically revolutionary activities.

As Clemens and Grigg point out, the issues raised by the apparent institutionalization of psychoanalysis in the university, as a marginal entity apparently brought to the centre of power, were significant, as they still are: should psychoanalysis, conceptualized as a practice that *disrupts* the apparently smooth surface of academic knowledge, be contained by, contaminated by, the discourse of the university? Freud had started the debate, arguing that there would be benefits for the 'medical student' if 'he' was taught psychoanalysis in the university, though these would be limited: 'for the purposes we have in view,' he wrote, 'it will be enough if he learns something *about* psychoanalysis and something *from* it' (1919: 173). Nowadays the issue is often framed as a tension between demands for academic 'rigour' and the essentially experiential mode of learning characteristic of psychoanalysis and other psychotherapies, the special nature of which psychotherapeutic training institutions often fear will be lost in the bookishness and the obsessional writing and auditing requirements that pervade university life. From the other side, the academy is suspicious of the mysterious and anti-egalitarian principles of psychoanalytic training, which operates by apprenticeship or even discipleship, with its quasi-priestly 'laying on of hands' procedure for the accreditation of analysts – that one is approved as an analyst through a process that requires bowing one's head to authority, rather than developing a critical perspective. Which is which here, one might ask? Is it psychoanalysis that is the authoritarian practice, the inscription into a religious order, and academic learning that is critical and independent? Or is it the other way around: the university is the site of the ordering and normalizing of knowledge, and psychoanalysis attests to the continuing waywardness of all such sites? In the immediate aftermath of 1968, it seemed to be more the latter than the former; that is, psychoanalysis was the radical outsider to a bureaucratized system, brought in to enliven it and to speak of freedom to its frustrated subjects. This, however, raised the usual worry for self-styled or real revolutionaries, whose critical perspective arises precisely from being on the margins, as psychoanalysis had always been, and who find themselves given a platform in the heart of the system. Once inside the university, is one still able to speak of its fractures and contradictions, or is the process of acceptance actually one of political containment?

For Lacan, entering amongst the rebellious students of Vincennes who were themselves challenging the nature of learning and the relevance of the university, the question of what constitutes knowledge and how to preserve the radical nature of psychoanalysis was of considerable moment. 'Psychoanalysis is not something that can be transmitted like other forms of knowledge,' he told the students (1991: 198), 'The psychoanalyst has a position that sometimes manages to be that of a discourse. He doesn't thereby transmit a body of knowledge, not that there is nothing for him to know, contrary to what is foolishly asserted. This is what is called into question – the function in society of a certain form of knowledge, the one that is conveyed to you. It exists.' Psychoanalysis constitutes its own mode of challenge to what is taken to be knowledge, a challenge that had been worked on by Lacan all year long in this seminar that dealt with the famous 'four discourses,' those of the Master, the Hysteric, the University and the Analyst. In this scheme, the discourse of the university is that of knowledge as flattened and bureaucratized; in Žižek's (2006: 109) extravagant version of this it is 'the expert-rule of bureaucracy that culminates in the biopolitics of reducing the population to a collection of *homo sacer* (what Heidegger called "enframing," Adorno "the administered world," Foucault the society of "discipline and punish").' Knowledge loses its capacity to radicalize; psychoanalysis, Lacan claims, calls this kind of knowledge into question. Hence, psychoanalysis cannot be transmitted in the university, or at least not through the discourse of the university; if it is, then it is reduced precisely to 'knowledge' rather than knowing *something* – as the analyst does: it is not the case that the analyst 'has nothing to know,' only that such knowledge cannot be taught by such structures, in such places, with such physical and intellectual premises. 'It exists,' said Lacan, perhaps referring to the discourse of the analyst, or perhaps to the burden of university discourse that gets carried around by all its inhabitants, including its rebellious students.

So what happens 'in' the university is at odds with psychoanalysis, even when psychoanalysis appears in the university itself, and even when what happens in the university is a rebellion against the university. The students challenged Lacan, as he stood there (and everyone knows how laboured his speech could be):

> *Lacan, we have been waiting for over an hour now for what you have been stating obliquely, a critique of psychoanalysis. That's why we are silent, because this would also be your own self-criticism.*

To which Lacan answered,

> You are the product of the university, and you prove that you are the surplus value, even if only in this respect – which you not only consent to, but which you also applaud – and I see no reason to object – which is that you leave here, yourselves equivalent to more or fewer credit points. You come here to gain credit points for yourself. You leave here stamped, 'credit points.'
>
> (1991: 200–1)

The students are 'stamped' when they leave; that is, what they learn is neither here nor there, for the university is not a place to gain real knowledge, which psychoanalysts do know something about, but rather to be processed, valued, accredited. Is this just the bad-tempered behaviour of a supposed revolutionary, who feels undervalued and misunderstood, in his specific case made less significant than the other intellectual hero Sartre, and even inferior to Mao, a Chinese peasant who could not appreciate Chinese culture in the way Lacan could? Roudinesco describes how the Maoist tendency of the young Lacanians in 1968 was 'a disaster' for Lacan, as it took away from him those on whom he had founded his hopes for the renewal of the psychoanalytic project. Mixed in with this, according to Roudinesco (1994: 338), was an affront to his pride:

> he found it insufferable that he, a 'man of culture' in terms of Chinese language and thought, should see the maxims of a proletarian helmsman preferred to his own teachings. That is why, when Alain Geismar approached him for money to help the GP [the Maoist Gauche prolétarienne, of which Jacques-Alain and Judith Miller were members], he answered, in substance, 'The revolution, c'est moi [I am the revolution.] I don't see why I should subsidize you. You are making my revolution impossible and taking away my disciples.'

Telling the students that they were part of the system even when they thought they were rebelling against it was perhaps part of Lacan's arrogance born of frustration, his sense that the only revolutionary practice was psychoanalysis, because only through this could the subjection of the subject to the signifier be revealed; but also because he could see, simply, the symmetrical nature of what was happening, the actions of the students as the subtext of the administrative apparatus of the university itself. Lacan was in some respects nostalgic for the traditions of the university, and had a keen understanding of how the apparent democratization of the university system could mean the death-knell of its situation as a place of learning. The old-style authoritarian structures were explicitly based on a master–subject, teacher–pupil relationship including all its fantasy dimensions, thus producing the possibility of material confrontation between one and the other, positive and negative transferences of a psychoanalytic kind, Oedipal conflicts and identifications that might constitute embodied, erotically inspired learning. The new university is more distant, everyone has their say, is a consumer of the knowledge it fabricates; there is something anodyne and impartial, something unreal about its presence in the lives of its subjects. Roudinesco (1994: 347) comments that when Lacan framed the university discourse as one of flattened and meaningless 'communication' that could also be understood as the dominant mode of regulation visible in the Soviet Union, 'he couldn't have spoken a truer word: it is clear today that the revolution of the barricades was one of the key stages in the university's replacement of intellectuals by technocrats.'

Perhaps reflecting idealization of 'real' knowledge, or maybe out of sheer outrage at what can become of a university when it turns itself into a processing-factory, Lacan revealed his irritation with the straightforward ignorance of the students. In response to a long intervention from a student on the need to be outside the university in order to agitate for its destruction, Lacan commented that it is not possible to be *outside*, because once one has been within the university one carries it with one, one speaks from within that discourse, it pervades the social world. 'Because when you leave here you become aphasic?' he asks rhetorically, to which comes the brilliant response, a response which, if it were not so clearly unintended, might have been that of the analyst who vacates the place of knowledge: '*I don't know what aphasic is.*' Lacan is scandalized: 'You don't know what aphasic is? That's extremely revolting. You don't know what an aphasic is? There is a minimum one has to know, nevertheless' (Lacan 1991: 205–6). Lacan is not in role as disappointed analysand here, expecting the students to have answers and instead finding that they occupy the place of the fool – as he himself did (a 'clown,' one calls him), and as certain contemporary Lacanians still like to do. He is, it seems, simply shocked, in a *Daily Mail* kind of way: these students, they know nothing. The Lacanian idea that the transference is resolved when the analysand discovers that the analyst is not the 'one who knows' describes a moment of breakthrough, in which illusions fall away; Lacan had no such illusions about the students, but this still seems to be a moment in which the utter limitation of their revolt came into focus – all because of a lack of knowledge of Greek words. '*I am not at the university twenty-four hours a day*,' says the student, which is hardly the point, as Lacan is arguing that no amount of being in or out will make much difference. This revolution is part of the game, and Lacan will have nothing to do with it, not because he is on one side or the other, but because he holds that without the kind of knowledge supplied by psychoanalysis, the act of revolution – and of revolutionary enlightenment – is part of the same process of administered truth that it is rebelling against. Only psychoanalysis, with its 'pas-tout,' its opposition to totalizing systems and instead its focus on the schisms or gaps in the system, could offer the kind of leverage necessary for truth. Without that, revolutionary display is just that, display; and its function is not to produce change, but to act as a kind of warning to the others as if to say, 'this is what rebellion leads to, this ignorance and destruction of culture.' Lacan makes no claims for himself here, but he does situate psychoanalysis as the discourse that can reveal the hidden movement of power.

> I am, like everybody is, liberal only to the extent that I am antiprogressive. With the caveat that I am caught up in a movement that deserves to be called progressive, since it is progressive to see the psychoanalytic discourse founded, insofar as the latter completes the circle that could perhaps enable you to locate what it is exactly that you are rebelling against – which doesn't stop that thing from continuing incredibly well. And the first to collaborate with this, right here at Vincennes, are you, for you fulfil the role of helots of this regime. You don't know what that means either? The regime is putting you on display. It says, 'Look at them enjoying!'
> (1991: 208)

And so to the moment of exasperation or truth: in obeying the hidden dictates of the system, in being processed by the credits of the university, the students are caught up in a hysterical discourse which is a consequence of the breakdown of the master's discourse *exactly parallel* to that of the university, as Žižek (2006: 109) explains: 'Hysterical discourse and university discourse then deploy two outcomes of the direct reign of the master...' The university totalizes discourse; Parker (2008: 378) identifies as one of the strands of Seminar XVII an opposition to what Lacan describes as a 'spherical' conception of the world, 'a conception... of total unified knowledge, as if the whole world has become one gigantic university.' This search for unity produces totalitarianism in the form of a master – and in hunting for revolutionary upheaval in the way that they do, that is where the students will end up.

> If you had a bit of patience, and if you really wanted our impromptus to continue, I would tell you that, always, the revolutionary aspiration has only a single possible outcome – of ending up as the master's discourse. This is what experience has proved. What you aspire to as revolutionaries is a master. You will get one.
>
> (Lacan 1991: 207)

Lacan was known as the 'Master,' ironically perhaps but also truthfully; his living and dead hand weighed heavily on the various movements which he joined or founded. But here he is not positing himself, nor even psychoanalysis, as the students' master; he is warning, upbraiding, patronizing, diagnosing – and in many ways he was right. The capacity of an administered society to absorb dissent and make it part of its own – the ineluctable drive of capitalism, in other words, which produces commodities even out of its contradictions – is nowhere more visible than in the consequences of the 1968 revolts. Lacan's diagnosis here relies on the idea that it is the *Freudian* revolution, as the revolution which has no ambitions to total knowledge but allows for the divided subject, that opposes totalization and hence exerts a brake on the search for total solutions and idealized knowledge. Without this *pas-tout*, there will always be an imaginary fantasy of 'a subject who knows'; that is, there will always be a demand for a master.

There is an obvious idealization of psychoanalysis in this suggestion that it is the only true revolutionary activity, and as many commentators have pointed out, Lacan disrupts this too in his seminar and in his broader work. Parker (2008) describes belief in the progressive possibilities of psychoanalysis as one of the 'lures' or 'temptations of pedagogery' that Lacan unmasks in Seminar XVII: 'I am not a man of the left,' asserts Lacan (1991: 114). The *problematic* status of psychoanalysis here can be seen in some of the manoeuvrings with which Lacan was preoccupied at around this time of the late 1960s, which recast the questions of mastery and, famously, 'self-authorizing' as something with which psychoanalysis cannot actually deal. It is worth noting that Lacan's attitude to the 1968 rebellion was not wholly cynical, whatever he may have said to the Vincennes crowd. At the time, he was rather more favourably disposed to the students than to his own followers, as accounts of his contact with them show. On the day after the demonstrations of 13 May, Lacan asked to meet with some of the students and that evening, Daniel Cohn-Bendit and others came to his flat. Roudinesco (1994: 336) describes the scene:

> Cohn-Bendit and his friends tried to explain the aims of their own movement, while the analysts really just wanted to listen to some protesters. So the two parties hadn't much to say to one another... After this exchange, the psychoanalysts gave the students some money. The students then went and had dinner at La Coupole, where they met their benefactors doing the same.

The analysts, apparently, were affronted to find their watering-hole so polluted, but Lacan was impressed with the demonstrators and took his irritation out on his own followers the next day. He interrupted his seminar, in compliance with a strike notice issued by the lecturers' union, praised Cohn-Bendit and commented, ' "I half-kill myself telling psychoanalysts they ought to expect something from the insurrection. And some of them reply: 'And pray, what does the insurrection expect of us?' Then the insurrection answers: 'What we expect from you is help in throwing cobblestones when the occasion arises.' " Then Lacan said that cobblestones and tear-gas canisters performed the function of object *a*, the object of desire' (Roudinesco 1994: 336). It is hard to know if Lacan was serious in his last comment, but what is clearly evident is his restlessness and disappointment in his own movement, which he was already seeing as sclerotic and unable to withstand the drift towards normalization that characterized (and characterizes) the psychoanalytic movement as a whole – a normalization that may have protected it when under attack, but which was now turning into an exclusionary mode of practice in which the marginals and non-conformists were increasingly being victimized (Roudinesco 1986: 447). Placed in the ambiguous position of both master and insurrectionist, Lacan was especially alert to the dangers of rigidification, and contemporaneously with the student revolts was looking for a way of dealing with this.

The issues came to a head in the famous controversy over the mode of accreditation of psychoanalysts of the Lacanian school, 'la passe.' The École Freudienne de Paris (EFP) had been formed by Lacan in 1964 and provided an opportunity, or perhaps even an imperative, to think through what might be involved in being a 'non-orthodox' psychoanalytic institution. As had been the case with the earlier exclusion of the Lacanians from the International Psychoanalytic Association, the key issues centred on training. What claim can psychoanalysis have to be a unique practice and revolutionary form of knowledge if its training regime is dependent on either or both of formal academic training or professional scrutiny of a kind that acts to regulate rather than to provoke; that, in the terms of Lacan's 1969 seminar, buys in from the start to the discourse of the university? Roudinesco (1986: 443) sets the scene:

> All the companions in arms were agreed on at least one point: they did not want to reproduce the kind of instruction and hierarchy in effect in the societies affiliated with the IPA.... In brief, they refused a bureaucratized form of psychoanalytic training that they regarded as contrary to the manifestation of an authentic desire to be an analyst. They all wanted to found a Freudian republic that did not resemble an association of notables and functionaries. But they did not know how to make the transition from an organization whose failings they knew to one that would better conform to true Freudian doctrine.

The correspondence with the students of 1968 is fairly exact here: the desire for something non-authoritarian and non-bureaucratized accompanied by a lack of vision as to what this could be, with the danger of resulting re-absorption into the bureaucratic way of being. In the case of the EFP, Lacan's capacity to resist this was a powerful driver for change, for continuing disruption of fixed structures; but this potential for subversive practice was undermined by the cult of Lacan-the-Master, which stifled the creativity of those who followed him as they constantly looked out for the nods and winks that would tell them they were on the right track.

The key question here was, what is the necessary 'qualification' whereby the status of psychoanalyst can be attained by a candidate? By the autumn of 1967, Lacan was convinced that the only truly Freudian criterion would be one separated from any requirements of academic discipline or clinical practice, the standard accrediting procedures of the normalized psychiatric and psychological professions. Rather, what is at the heart of the psychoanalytic enterprise is the capacity to speak the truth of the experience of analysis itself – that is, to be able to articulate one's own psychoanalytic encounter in such a way as to bring it to a close, by making a statement of what the Lacanians call 'the desire of the analyst.' The implications of this were in some ways orthodox, in that the training analysis had long been seen as central to induction into the psychoanalytic community; but whereas the success of the training analysis was normally measured in terms of length of time and combined with other assessment, here it would be testimony to the quality of the experience – or, more accurately, quality testimony to the experience – that would matter. In his 'Proposition' of 9 October 1967 on the topic, Lacan (1967) wrote, 'Our only selection lies in facing the truth or in the ridicule of our knowledge. The shadow that covers the merge I hereby consider, that in which the psychoanalysand turns into a psychoanalyst, is what our school can unveil.' The procedure here, known as '*la passe*' and spelt out in laborious and confusing detail in the 'Proposition,' was for candidates for acceptance to present themselves to a panel and to speak to it of their analysis; the panel would then report on this to a *jury d'agrément* who would decide on the *passant*'s fate. Roudinesco (1986: 448) summarizes,

> The purpose of the testimony which was thus conveyed was to clarify the specific act transforming a psychoanalysand into a psychoanalyst. The jury would not judge the candidate's clinical experience...but an *en plus*, a supplementary dimension: the ability to theorize the training experience transmitted by way of the couch.

In principle, this was a deeply democratizing vision, making accreditation available to anyone who could speak of their personal analysis in such a way as to testify to its end ('After the barricades, Lacan would say that he had achieved in his school a May '68 before the fact' – Roudinesco 1986: 449), and for this reason it was opposed by many of the more 'senior' members of the EFP, those who had stuck with Lacan through the twists and turns of his institutional career but whose own standing was now threatened. The controversy centred in some ways on a famous, if misleading, statement of Lacan (misleading because it ignores the functioning of the judging panel): 'The psychoanalyst derives his authorization solely from himself' (ibid.). If this was to be the case, then what criteria could be applied to judging the authenticity of this self-authorization: can absolutely anyone who can speak *at all* of their analysis become an analyst? Or was this to be understood, as has subsequently been claimed, as a statement that has no real bearing on the institutional process of accreditation, but was a simple truth, in line with Lacan's Vincennes comment that psychoanalysis cannot be passed on like other forms of knowledge? In any event, this seems to have been part of the impasse that blocked *la passe*: no one could understand what was needed to qualify as a self-authorized psychoanalyst.

Roudinesco (1986) sees much of the difficulty associated with *la passe* as arising out of the conditions of its emergence and the way in which its apparent ultra-democratic, even 'Maoist' promise was undermined not only by organizational incompetence but also by the continuing presence of Lacan as master.[1] Building on the momentum generated by the students' revolt of May 1968 and the response to this, Lacan 'decided to let go of the dissidents and to seek support among the turbulent young in order to implement, at whatever price, his turbulent reform' (1986: 456). A revised version of the proposal for *la passe* was manoeuvred into place by Lacan in January 1969, leading to the resignation of some of his more experienced followers and the institution of a procedure that no one could fully master, but which became a source both of pride and of despair within the EFP. Roudinesco notes that the failure to specify clear methods of judgement led over a period of ten years to a situation in which the panels were swamped by applications, many of them outlandish, to which they could not respond, with the consequence that those few who were approved got through not on the basis of some new and systematic understanding about true speech, but rather by a kind of accident, or more likely a transference. This took a very familiar form:

> As the anonymous *passes* began to expand, appointments, in the course of time, followed an identical model: a virtually silent jury waiting beneath Lacan's omnipresent gaze; he then giving a nod or an interpretation allowing the others to reach an opinion...The functioning of *la passe* in the EFP had the effect of reducing the protagonists of the great Lacanian drama to the imaginary relation each entertained with a founding father.
>
> (1986: 462–3)

By 1977 and the suicide of Juliette Labin, a talented young Lacanian analyst who had waited over a year for the panel's decision, only to be turned down apparently because she was no longer in analysis and therefore could not testify to it, the system was in a state of collapse – as, indeed, was the EFP. At the end of a tumultuous set of accusations, meetings and debates consequent on Labin's suicide, Lacan commented, 'To be sure, it's a total failure, this *passe* business'

(Roudinesco 1986: 639). In fact, *la passe* continues in existence to this day, particularly in Jacques Alain Miller's World Association of Psychoanalysis, where it has been rethought and clarified, so perhaps Lacan was wrong; but the revolutionary fervour seems to have left it, even if it continues as a reminder that there is an alternative to the bureaucratization of desire that threatens to overcome the psychoanalytic movement as it has overcome so much else.

The fate of *la passe* can be seen as one aspect of the fate of 1968. For Lacan, the students' revolt was not a revolution, but the flip side of the accession to dominance of the bureaucratic regime of the university. Psychoanalysis could reveal this, but it could not be looked to for revolutionary activity, whatever it might do to consciousness. Lacan's attempt to introduce a genuinely democratic reform into the institutional practices of his branch of the psychoanalytic movement created a split, as all such reforms probably do, but was also chaotic both for contingent reasons (the difficulties of drafting rules, for example) and for thoroughly psychoanalytic reasons – put crudely, the impractical power of the transference. 'As revolutionaries, what you long for is a master,' he had said, and in the case of the EFP, where he might perhaps have been the only revolutionary, albeit an authoritarian one, this was precisely so. With all its talk of self-authorizing and of speaking the truth of the subject's desire, what is revealed again and again in psychoanalysis is the difficulty, perhaps the impossibility, of escaping the realms of authority – the interminability of the task, to adapt Freud's usage. Additionally, the 'not-all' that psychoanalysis aspires to, its recognition that no ideal solutions exist, acts against the utopianism of revolutionary action: every end state is either imaginary in the strict sense of a promise of something impossibly whole and sublime, or it is posited on its own collapse, its own blind spot or edginess that will bring it to failure. Indeed, contesting totalitarianism relies on this being the case – every move forward can only be a kind of staging post, its demolition inscribed within it. Is it better that the structures of authority should be evident, available for Oedipal dispute, and that there should be a killing of the father in line with Freud's own myth of the origins of culture? Is a master–student relationship better than an egalitarian one, if the price of the latter is that little can be learnt, that dissent is smoothed over in the interests of 'credit points'? Or is the lesson from this complicated tale that a revolutionary process does indeed depend on a master, even a wish for a master – but the master has to, at some point, if something is really to be gained, learn what it means to fail?

Note

1. Ian Parker (personal communication) has suggested that 'Lacan behaved exactly like Mao (stirring up his supporters to attack the bureaucracy and then backing off from them when it got out of hand); in some ways it would be possible to argue that Lacan's group was precisely the Maoist response to the decaying bureaucracy of the IPA' (email of 19 May 2008).

Part III
Other Voices

8
May 1968 and Algerian Immigrants in France: Trajectories of Mobilization and Encounter

Maud Anne Bracke

I. Introduction

In a comment that was to become famous, leftist intellectual Henri Lefèbvre stated that the fact that Nanterre students had to travel through one of the country's largest and poorest *bidonvilles* to reach their modernist university campus was a key vector of mobilization in 1968 (Ross 1996). Indeed, 1968 is usually understood as the moment at which French students and leftists 'discovered' the injustices done to immigrants by the French state and society. Yet very different views exist in the literature on the significance of the encounter between the North African immigrants on the one hand and the predominantly white student groups and *gauchistes* on the other. Abdallah (2000) depicts a rather harmonious picture of the relations between workers, students and immigrants, arguing that the events of May 1968 created the basis for new forms of solidarity. By contrast, Gastaut (1994) points out that while slogans such as 'French and foreign workers: all united' were ubiquitous, the reality behind these statements often remained unclear. An often-heard thesis in the literature on 'the 1968 years' in France is that it was characterized by a *prise de conscience* by a number of so-called minority groups, immigrants in the first instance (e.g., Benoit 1980: 177). This is in fact an older argument, articulated in 1978 by Régis Debray, who understood the main feature of '1968' to be the 'recognition of minorities and of the right to be different' (1978: 5). The reality is more complex. '1968' was a moment of formation of an immigrant consciousness, but, I will argue, in a complex way, increasing rather than decreasing tension between immigrant mobilization and other, white groups in French society.

This chapter aims to formulate a number of hypotheses regarding the significance of the 1968 events in the longer-term history of the formation of an Algerian immigrant politics in France. I propose that we can meaningfully identify a perspective on the May 1968 events that is one of Algerian immigrants as a group, despite the socio-economic, gender and cultural differences among them. May 1968 to this group meant the rise of a new form of political subjectivity, the articulation of a problematic regarding the (multiethnic) *condition immigrée*, and the paradoxical discovery of at once belonging and non-belonging to French society. '1968', from the immigrants' perspective, receives its meaning only within a series of moments of increased mobilization, flanked as it was by two episodes that were arguably more important, the Algerian War of Independence (1954–62) and the immigrant actions of the early 1970s, which evidenced the emergence of a new political subject. It was through the 1968 strikes that politicized sections of the immigrant workforce became aware of the need to organize on the basis of a *specific* immigrant identity, and that it re-situated this with regard to the organizations and institutions of the traditional and the new left.

The 1968 experience of immigrant workers in France has until recent years received little attention in academic debate, and it continues to be marginalized from commonplace representations of the 1968 years.[1] Yet, a simple indication of the fact that immigrant participation was significant in the strike movement is the fact that it were those plants where foreign workers formed a majority or substantial section of the workforce, where participation in May–June was near-complete and which formed the backbone of the strike movement; for example, in the car factories Renault-Flins and Renault-Billancourt 66 per cent of the unskilled workers originated from the Maghreb countries, and at Citroen-Nanterre 65 per cent of the workers originated from Southern Europe and the Maghreb (Vigna 2007: 45). It is only in recent years that a strand of literature has emerged which looks at the role of immigrant workers and foreign students in the strike and protest movements of 1968 (Abdallah 2000; Gastaut 1994; Gordon 2003). Roughly, these analyses have taken the following approach: first, tracing immigrants' level of participation, hereby attempting to dispel a longstanding belief that their involvement was minimal; second, explaining the reasons why their participation was limited when and where it was, by looking mainly at state repression which specifically targeted foreigners;[2] and third, looking at the attitudes of various actors of the new left and the radical left groups (*gauchistes*) as well as the student movements *vis-à-vis* immigrant workers, and the emergence of the first campaigns of solidarity with them. However, the perspective taken by most of these analyses is one which is based on a supposedly well-established narrative of the 1968 events, and tries to fit immigrant workers into it.[3] Much of the literature continues to be limited by its focus on non-immigrant, white activists and their attitudes with regard to immigrants. I propose to turn the analysis on its head, by focusing on the perspective and experience of immigrants themselves, their organizations and actions. This means investigating what the '1968 years' may have meant to them, how it affected their consciousness and identity, how it can be located in the history of their political and social trajectories, which is a history of staggered immigration, complex relations between generations, and multiple spheres of belonging. In the next section I reconstruct some of the life and work conditions of Algerian immigrants on the eve of the 1968 events.

II. Algerian immigrants in France in the 1950s–1960s

Immigration from Algeria between the 1940s and the 1970s was regulated only to a limited degree by the French state, the employers' organizations having a major influence over immigration entry. Up to Algerian independence in 1962, Algerians could officially travel freely between the two countries, though in practice they needed a work permit to be allowed into France. After 1962, Algerian workers had to apply for work and residence permits, which were issued on a temporary basis for usually three years. In the context of debates on the 'uncontrollable' nature of North African immigration, as of 1964, entry from Algeria was gradually restricted. This led to an increasing number of Algerians either living without regular documents or working with a regular contract, but without having obtained state recognition of their status, which placed them in an ambiguous legal position (Granotier 1979: 59). In 1968, about 80 per cent of non-European Economic Community (EEC) immigrants had no legal status other than their work permit (Tripier 1990: 68). The living conditions of Algerian immigrants in France in this phase were characterized by, on the one hand, ghettoization, exclusion and discrimination and, on the other hand, the formation of an immigrant and in some cases ethnicity-based identity and community. According to the census of 1966, 75,346 immigrants lived in 225 *bidonvilles* across France, the regions of Paris, Marseille, Toulon and Lille having the highest concentrations. The major North African *bidonville* was Nanterre near Paris, with, according to the same census, 9737 inhabitants. A law of 1964 decreed the gradual elimination of the *bidonvilles*, and although a few, much-publicized, actions were taken, these had little impact on actual population numbers as, until the early 1970s, the number of inhabitants in the *bidonvilles* overall increased (Benoit 1980: 196). As of the mid-1960s the material conditions further deteriorated, due mainly to rising unemployment among male adolescents. Ghettoization was, to some extent and implicitly, helped by the attitude of the first waves of Algerian immigrants, the 'zoufris'. As argued by Boubeker (2003: 192–196), they never saw themselves as permanently settled in France and protected themselves from racism by withdrawing from the public sphere.

Between 1945 and 1949, the majority of Algerian immigrants corresponded to the classic immigrant profile of a single, young or middle-aged man from a rural background. In 1954 only 6.5 per cent of Algerian immigrants were women (Tripier 1990: 58). Those who Sayad (1999: 71–2) identifies as the second wave of immigrants arrived roughly between 1950 and 1962 and already had, to some degree, been 'de-ruralized' in Algeria. They were generally younger, and were more expectant of being considered full members of French society. Although the 'in transit' attitude still prevailed, this second group of immigrants shed the earlier immigrants' reflexes of self-segregation. This phase also saw the start of family migration: women migrated in large numbers during the first years of the Algerian War of Independence, and even more so afterwards. The arrival of families, although still not regarded by immigrants themselves, by French society or by the Algerian state, as a permanent form of settlement, did lead France to relate in a fundamentally new way to the immigrants, who were now required to 'become French'. It was at this stage that the notion of assimilation emerged in French state and public discourses, creating a context where cultural hostility against immigrants was intensified.

To this generation of immigrants, the Algerian War of Independence was of central importance in their socialization in France. It, on the one hand, transformed the way they related to their homeland and politicized them on the issues of national independence, pan-Arabism and anti-imperialism, and, on the other hand, negatively influenced their relation to France. During the war, the French state suspected Algerian workers and students of being a so-called 'fifth column' for the *Front de libération nationale* (FLN).[4] A first sign of the extent to which Algerian immigrants in France were involved with the war appeared in 1957, when the FLN's call for an eight-day strike in France in favour of independence was widely supported (Benoit 1980: 98–9). Thousands of Algerians participated in the street demonstration in favour of Algerian independence in Paris on 17 October 1961, a date that became fundamental to the collective memory and consciousness of Algerians in France. The massacre of 17 October, as it became known, saw the killing of over 300 Algerians by the Paris police,[5] and tens of bodies were dumped in the Seine. The march had been a peaceful one, although it had been held in defiance of the curfew imposed specifically on Algerians. In February 1962, another case of extreme police repression occurred, this time following a peaceful but illegal rally in favour of Algerian independence and against the actions of the *Organisation de l'Armée secrète* (OAS), and called for by the communist party, *Parti communiste français* (PCF), and other organizations of the left. The remembering of these events was, as Rioux (1990) and Ross (1996) have suggested, of central importance to the creation of Muslim, Arab and North African identities in France, and served as vehicles of anti-racist mobilization in the 1970s and 1980s. It was thus, crucially, through and with their activism for decolonization that Algerians in France became politicized on issues of discrimination in their everyday lives. A factor of mobilization linked to this, for sections of the Arab communities in France, was the situation in the Middle East, the Palestinian cause, and the Six Days War of 1967, as becomes clear from testimonies of activists such as Said Bouziri.[6] However, this did not yet give rise to a mass immigrant movement, the majority of Algerian immigrants choosing not to expose themselves to state suspicion and police repression (Giudice 1992: 75).

While their housing situation, state repression and international politics were factors of exclusion from French society, their situation in the workplace, although characterized by grim forms of exploitation, was, as argued by Tripier (1990) and Vigna (2007), often a factor of integration with the multinational workforce. Especially before the outbreak of the Algerian War of Independence, relatively high degrees of integration existed among workers, particularly in the major industrial plants with a multinational workforce such as Renault-Billancourt. In these workplaces, informal bonds of co-operation and solidarity were established during these years between workers of various national and ethnic backgrounds, which were to be of longer-term significance. The Algerian War generally had a detrimental effect on intra-racial relations in the factories (Tripier 1990: 159), which were further rendered difficult by forms of institutionalized racism. The majority of North African workers had the status of *ouvrier specialisé* ('OS'), a Fordist category euphemistically denoting unskilled workers. As pointed out by Vigna (2007: 175), North African workers were routinely employed in the lowest category (OS3), while French workers without experience usually started in the second-lowest category (OS2). Union rights were restricted as, until the early 1970s, non-French workers were not entitled to vote for union delegates or present themselves as candidates. Social rights and benefits were restricted, too: non-French workers could not receive benefits for children not living in France, and could not get medical assistance until they had lived in France for three months. They were entitled to unemployment pay only for the duration of their work permit, which in practice meant they hardly ever benefited from it (Granotier 1979: 130). Thus, in an era where citizenship came to include a set of social and welfare rights, a substantial section of the workforce was effectively excluded from it. The immigrants' situation painfully evidenced the limitations of social citizenship and meritocracy which made up the discursive façade of French modernization during the *trente glorieuses*, and, thus, revealed a wider crisis of this modernization project.[7] It was this modernization project and its discourses that came under fire in 1968, and the 'immigrant condition' evidenced most clearly its structural limits.

III. Immigrants and the left in 1968

As stated, '1968' as a moment of encounter between immigrant communities and young radicals was largely a problematic one. The key dilemma of the student and leftist movements of solidarity with immigrant workers, I propose, was the question of nationality. In their attempts to improve the socio-economic, legal and political status of immigrant workers, the non-immigrant campaigns suffered from an evident, although not thematized, contradiction between the right to difference on the one hand, often accompanied with Orientalist, romanticized views regarding this difference, and the urgent need for integration on the other, often translated into the equally naive demand for universal French citizenship. The new left and the student movements, while in no way resolving these issues and in fact often adding to the confusion surrounding the immigrants' identities and needs, did at least attempt to engage with questions of cultural difference, where the traditional left had failed to do so.

Already before 1968, a number of campaigns had been set up by French students and intellectuals attempting to reach out to the often-unknown immigrants. The most successful one was *Droit et Liberté*, which, since the early 1960s, campaigned for the improvement of the legal and political status of immigrant workers. Importantly, it argued in favour of the 'right to be a foreigner' rather than the naturalization of immigrant workers. Its vision to end marginalization and discrimination rejected notions of integration through assimilation and included advocating for anti-racist legislation. The group presented a series of drafts of anti-racist laws to the National Assembly in 1959, 1963 and again in 1967; however, the government parties as well as the left opposition failed to follow these through (Granotier 1979: 223–4).[8] During the 1968 protests and strikes there was a proliferation of initiatives in solidarity with immigrants. However, these were often motivated by the wish simply to bring immigrant struggles into the wider mobilization in the streets and factories. Generally, this approach was taken by the *Comité d'action des travailleurs étrangers* (CATE), which aimed to 'educate foreigners to strike', and the *Comité du droit des étrangers*, set up in June 1968 and dedicated to the struggle against what started to be referred to commonly as the 'super exploitation' (*surexploitation*) of immigrant workers. The latter notion was understood as a particular condition of capitalist exploitation, which considered immigrants as the most precarious section of the working class, but was often not, as suggested by Gastaut (1994), cognizant of the immigrants' specific culture or background. Some of these actions were mixed with utopian, universalist visions of a world without frontiers. This was the case for groups such as the *Comité des trois continents*, which aimed to offer practical help to immigrants, but also claimed that 'we are not Africans or Asians; we must overcome all nationalisms' (Abdallah 2000: 21). The *Comité d'action bidonvilles*, set up in June 1968, aimed to end discrimination through granting French citizenship to all immigrants.[9]

It was from the traditional left that some of these groups inherited the denial of socio-cultural specificity and a naive view that was both Eurocentric and universalist. The traditional left was largely unable to conceive the working class in terms of what it had actually become, a multicultural entity made up of subjects with differing living conditions and needs. The two major parties of the left, PCF and the *Section française de l'Internationale socialiste* (SFIO), up to the 1960s, devoted little attention to the specific needs of immigrant workers or indeed to the phenomenon of immigration generally. In the trade unions – the communist-dominated *Confédération générale du travail* (CGT) and the Catholic *Confédération Française Democratique du Travail* (CFDT) – there existed a widespread fear that immigrants would undercut French workers. Moreover, the two major trade unions displayed little initiative in lobbying for the expansion of the union and the social rights of immigrant workers, or even in pursuing recruitment campaigns among those communities. Unionization among Algerian workers never reached above seven per cent between 1945 and 1968.[10] The CGT did not display signs of awareness of the issue until 1967, when it started recruiting among foreign OS workers and its programme featured, for the first time, a separate chapter with immigrant-specific demands. The most progressive of the points listed here were, first, the demand that all immigrant workers receive the same social benefits as French workers did, even if their families lived abroad, and second, the abolition of all temporary contracts and the guarantee of permanent work after 15 working days (Tripier 1990: 173). Nonetheless, most of these immigrant concerns, as formulated by the CGT, were no more than the recognition that immigrants should be treated on a par with French workers and that they currently were not.

On the other hand, and in contrast to the traditional workers' organizations, many of the student and *gauchiste* groups displayed naive admiration for the immigrant workers, projecting onto them images of the *bon sauvage* hero of unorganized social struggles or of the radical fighters in Third World liberation wars. Algerians specifically were loaded with symbolic significance, in memory of the Algerian independence struggle. The students' often-heroic representation of (Algerian) immigrants can be seen as a reaction against the universalism of the traditional left, in that their cultural difference was exalted, as well as reflecting deeply rooted cultural stereotypes which were not yet problematized. The difficulties with which encounters between students and immigrant families were established can be seen from a number of incidents taking place at Nanterre in March–May 1968. As investigated by Lemire (2008), what dominated discussions among the immigrant families of the *bidonville* was not the student uprising, but the fact that a Tunisian worker had died on the building site of the university campus. Tensions were aggravated when a student group offered a load of potatoes for free to the immigrant families. The initiative provoked outright anger among the immigrants who were weary of this type of charity. However, while there was often disinterest for and even resentment against the student actions ('their demonstrations do not help us', as put by one inhabitant of Nanterre; quoted in Lemire 2008: 141), there seems also to have been meaningful encounters on the micro-level, for example, cases of female student activists providing shelter for an Algerian women escaping a situation of domestic violence (Lemire 2008: 139).

It was in this context that Algerian workers became involved in the strikes of May 1968 and were led towards setting up separate initiatives, outwith the trade union structures, and in most cases (though not always) on a multinational basis. Relations between immigrant workers' organizations and the major trade unions deteriorated throughout May–June 1968, as immigrant workers became acutely aware of the persistence of racist attitudes. Their experience of participation in the strike led them to conclude that their silence had lasted too long, not only *vis-à-vis* the French state and the employers, but also with regard to trade union paternalism. Two important nationwide initiatives in this regard were the *Comité du droit des immigrés* and the *Comité de liaison des organisations de travailleurs immigrés de France* (CLOTIF), an organization set up by Algerians (Granotier 1979: 248). At Renault-Billancourt, immigrants, encountering implicit racism from the CGT, set up their own *Plate-forme de combats des ouvriers immigrés*. The tracts, written by immigrant workers, included demands such as the abolition of temporary contracts, the end of discrimination in the workplace, the granting of full trade union and representative rights to non-French workers, and full social benefits for families living abroad.[11] Though relatively small, this was an important initiative as it reflected the emergence of a *multinational* immigrant identity and the discovery of cross-national immigrant concerns, as distinct from French workers' issues. Initiated by Algerians, it brought together African, Portuguese and Italian workers, both unionized and not. While the CGT refused to support the initiative, the CFDT in some instances helped by promoting it among French workers (Pitti, quoted in Zancarini-Fournel 2002: 3).[12] A crucial feature of the immigrants' activism was their denunciation of institutionalized racism in the workplace through which they, more concretely than any other group, challenged hierarchies in the factory, a key theme of the 1968 strikes more generally.

IV. Immigrant actions in the 1970s

The short-term outcome of the general strike of May 1968 was particularly poor for non-French workers. The trade union leaderships did not take the demands of the ad hoc immigrant committees to the negotiating table, and there was no mention of immigrant concerns in the Grenelle agreement.[13] As a result, Grenelle did not demobilize immigrant workers – quite to the contrary. As analysed by Vigna (2007: 135–6), in most of the major plants that had been on strike in May 1968 – Billancourt, Flins, Citroen-Nanterre, Coder-Marseille and Caterpillar-Grenoble – informal, non-trade union committees of immigrant workers were set up in the following months. They led a number of wildcat actions, often in reaction to the many sackings of activist immigrant workers that occurred in this phase. Immigrant action and mobilization reflected the need for new forms of mobilization – first, the understanding that there was a need for *autonomous* immigrant organizations, independent from political parties and trade unions and even from non-immigrant social movements; second, new forms of action were tried out, such as the hunger strike, which were not among the traditional methods of the workers' movement; and third, labour issues came to be linked to legal, political and social problems, particularly housing and residence permits. Yet if issues were broadened, the factory and the workplace remained key spaces of mobilization. This can be illustrated, for example, with the strikes at the harbour workshops of La Ciotat near Marseille in 1971. Over 1500 workers went on strike over an issue that was not directly related to working conditions, namely the wave of racist attacks on North African immigrants in the region (Vigna 2007: 128).

One theme that was to become central to immigrant politicization in the 1970s was the problem of rights of immigrants without legal documents, or *sans-papiers*. The many campaigns to obtain residence and work permits took place in a context of tighter immigration legislation. Through a bilateral French-Algerian agreement of December 1968, the number of annual entries into France was limited to 35,000; it was in 1971 further limited to 25,000, and a full stop to non-European immigration was introduced in 1974.[14] In 1972–73 the government seized the occasion of intensified social unrest to initiate a wave of expulsions of North African workers. The Marcellin-Fontanet ministerial letter of 1972 was an attempt to 'regulate' the ambiguous legal situation of non-EEC workers, effectively making 83 per cent of them illegal. It provoked widespread panic among these communities and a wave of spontaneous strikes ensued, among which was a three-day action at Margoline-Nanterre (Vigna 2007: 129). The actions in favour of *sans-papiers* mobilized new groups of immigrant workers and, especially, their families. The introduction of new modes of action such as the hunger strike was initially met with suspicion by the parties and trade unions of the left, but had a much wider impact on the post-1968 'new social movements' (Trappo 1990).

The widening of issues was accompanied by a preference for immigrant-specific action. Immigrant-specific strikes took place at the Pennaroya mines near Lyon in January 1972, in an action that was to become emblematic. Algerian and Moroccan OS workers were on strike for over a month, following a workplace accident in which one of their workmates had died. While the factory management attempted to cover up the circumstances of the accident, ad hoc collectives of immigrant-dominated workers publically denounced the fact that the accident was caused by poor safety standards (Benoit 1980: 238–9). The action was supported by sections of the radical and intellectual left, such as the *Cahiers de mai* journal and the Maoist *gauche prolétarienne*. At the end of the strike, nearly all demands were met by the employers (Artières 2008; Zancarini-Fournel 2002). Immigrant-specific mobilization continued, in many cases, to be multinational and multiethnic, thus giving rise to a discourse on the *condition immigrée* (Tripier 1990: 189).

Another action that provoked mobilization across the country was a non-union strike at the Girosteel factory in Bourget, where the majority of the 150 workers on strike were immigrants. The flyers reflected the predominance of immigrant-specific issues ('An immigrant worker will never become a skilled worker, while for the same work a French worker will be in the P1/2 category') as well as calling for unity of all workers ('the bosses give more benefits to the French workers to undermine our unity').[15] Apart from the revision of the system of labour qualifications, demands included basic health and safety issues and the abolition of six-month contracts. These actions were responses not only to racism in the wider society, but also to racism in the workplace. In the context of an economic crisis, rising unemployment and reflecting the anti-immigration policies of the state, working-class racism increasingly became a problem. North Africans, especially, were victims of racism among workers; some of the radical leftist groups active in the factories, such as the Maoist ones and increasingly also the CFDT, denounced this.

Anti-racism continued to be closely linked to international issues, and Arab identity became a source of mobilization, as was reflected in the *Mouvement des travailleurs arabes* (MTA), active as of 1972. Its founding members were politicized crucially on the issues of Palestine and anti-imperialism, and many of them were former activists of the *Comités palestiniennes*. A core of the older generation of anti-imperialist activists allied themselves in the 1970s with younger immigrant students and workers.[16] MTA's membership was made up mostly of Arab workers and students, although also non-Arab immigrant workers, students and intellectuals adhered to the loosely organized movement. Its aims included fighting racism and inequality at work as well as building a 'national Arab consciousness'. Whether a degree of tension existed between the emphasis on Arab identity of organizations such as MTA and the multiethnic character of other immigrant campaigns remains disputed in the literature. What seems clear, as argued also by Tripier (1990: 190–2), is that the emphasis on specific ethnicities did not undermine the by now well-established pockets of multinational immigrant activism in the factories. In fact, the rise of Arab consciousness may have helped the emergence of a pan-immigrant political identity and subjectivity. This can be seen from the mobilization at Renault-Billancourt in January–February 1972 following the sacking of the activist Saddok Ben Mabrouk, who proclaimed, 'Je suis licencié parce que je suis combatif et arabe'.[17] Wildcat actions and additional sackings of militants ensued, following which Ben Mabrouk and others initiated a hunger strike. One month into their action, activists from MTA and other immigrant organizations called for a major demonstration at Charonne tube station, in solidarity with Mabrouk and to commemorate the 1962 repression. In what was the start of an escalation of violence, Renault worker and *Gauche prolétarienne* activist Pierre Overney was killed by a member of the security personnel at Renault. His funeral became a political event, attended by over 200,000 people. New organizations emerged in the wake of the Overney killing at Renault and elsewhere in the Paris area. Strikes were organized by ad hoc committees throughout 1972–73, in a distinctly anti-hierarchical sphere, once more evidencing the emergence of the political subjectivity of the immigrant workers beyond national lines, as well as solidarity with them among small groups of the radical left (Abdallah 2000: 23–6).

Immigrant workers often bypassed the established system of elected union representatives as they were in many cases unable to vote or stand for such elections, but also because generally they preferred a situation where decisions were taken in a plenary assembly of all workers, unionized and not. The CFDT accepted this in some cases; the CGT never did (Zancarini-Fournel 2002: 6). The right of non-French workers to become trade union representatives was extended to immigrants from Algeria and some African countries in December 1968, and in 1972 to all foreigners. It was evident that the trade unions were willing to grant these rights only in response to continued and widespread grass-roots pressure, both from the de facto immigrant organizations and from the *gauchiste* groups.[18] It was also clear that the approach taken by especially the CGT continued to be one that aimed to integrate immigrants and their concerns into overall trade union strategy, without however understanding that this would necessitate a major transformation of the trade union itself, either with regard to strategy, matters of internal democracy, or with regard to the active promotion of non-French workers to leadership positions.

Frustration over the unions' dealings with immigrant problems was exacerbated in the debates surrounding the first general strike against racism in September 1973. The strike was called for by a platform of immigrant organizations in response to the escalation of racially motivated violence against especially North African immigrants, and to the acute rise of racist discourse in the context of the economic crisis (Zancarini-Fournel 2008: 269). It was supported by leftist groups such as *Gauche prolétarienne* and renowned intellectuals such as Michel Foucault. During 1971-1973, a number of assaults and killings occurred, first in Marseille and then spreading to other parts of the country, and were in most cases carried out by members of far right organizations such as *Ordre nouveau*.[19] The two events that sparked immediate mobilization were the killing of Djalili Ben Ali in October 1971 by a French citizen and the killing of Behar Tehala by the police in November of that year. The marches held in Marseille and elsewhere throughout 1972 amounted to the largest mobilization of immigrants since the police repression of 1961-62. The general strike of 1973 involved up to 30,000 workers in the Marseille area alone. The movement grew nationwide: in Paris gatherings were held in front of mosques, where thousands of North Africans and other immigrants were joined by students and French sympathizers. The CGT remained sceptical of the actions, declaring that it was not 'a true strike' because of its 'non-conventional' character and demands (Abdallah 2000: 30).

Around 1976, following the demise of most of the *gauchiste* organizations and a new wave of police repression, most of the militants of MTA and other radical immigrant organizations dispersed, choosing various forms of cultural activism such as local radio stations and theatre, instead of trying to influence 'high politics' via more traditional channels. This change of strategy was a wider phenomenon of the late 1970s, and general disillusionment, specifically with the parties of the left and the trade unions, can be seen as an important cause behind it. It would, however, be a mistake to understand this as a long-term move away from politics: as analysed by Boubeker (2003: 207-8), it were these *milieux* of grass-roots cultural-political activism which preserved the degree of consciousness and collective identity that had been achieved through the social struggles of the late 1960s and early 1970s, and which lay at the basis of the, apparently sudden, emergence of the *Beur* movement in the late 1970s.[20]

V. Concluding remarks

While research on '1968' from the perspective of immigrant communities has barely made a start, I have attempted in this chapter to present some provisional findings with regard to how '1968' can be situated in a longer-term narrative of Algerian immigrant politicization in France. The 1968 events were only one moment of increased political awareness; the Algerian War of Independence was at least as important. '1968' was an ambivalent moment in the development of a form of immigrant collective subjectivity. While, on the one hand, the factory strikes of 1968–73 helped create both a pan-immigrant and a more specific North African/Arab political identity, on the other hand, immigrant activists and workers had to deal with various forms of prejudice and incomprehension, the sometimes naive universalism and *tiersmondisme* of the students, and above all the unwillingness of the traditional left to come to terms with cultural difference within the working class. This led the more radical sections of the Algerian and North African immigrant communities, in the wake of 1968, to focus on immigrant-specific actions and goals. This mobilization took on highly original and innovative shapes, particularly in the systematic linking of workplace activism on labour issues with broader, non-work-related questions such as racism, housing and legal status.

'1968', thus, meant France's definite shift to postcoloniality. While de-colonization had started earlier, it was only in 1968 and its aftermath that French society became aware of the *permanent* presence of postcolonial immigrants. '1968' was the opening of the Pandora's box that contained the complex, explosive cluster of problems related to multicultural society. With their contradictory attitudes, the new left and the student movements in 1968 prefigured the failure of French society and the state in the decades to come, to engage with postcolonial immigrants as at once full and equal members of society and communities with distinct cultures and identities.

Notes

1. Partly, this is to do with the fact that in France and elsewhere the workers' strikes have received relatively little attention when compared to the student uprising. This should be understood in the context of hegemonic interpretations of '1968' which favours a cultural over a political analysis of the events (Zancarini-Fournel 2008: 84–91).
2. On 20 June 1968, *Le Monde* reported that 161 foreign workers and students had been expelled since the start of May (Abdallah 2000: 14).
3. Abdallah (2000) and Pitti (1994, 2006) are useful exceptions. There is also a strand of sociological literature focusing on the rise of immigrant, anti-racist activism (e.g., Boubeker 2003), which, however, remains partly disconnected from the historiographic debates on 1968.

4. In fact, the situation was far more complex. Divergent loyalties existed within the Algerian community, a majority actively or passively supporting the *Fédération de France* of the FLN, and a minority supporting the *Mouvement national Algérien* (MNA), which was to some degree manipulated by the French state in order to divide Algerians. MNA and FLN fought each other both in Algeria and France.
5. The Prefect of the Paris Police at the time was Maurice Papon, much hated among Algerians for his involvement in the repression in Algeria during the war of independence.
6. Interview with Bouziri in Trappo (1990). Bouziri was one of the leading figures of the hunger strikes of the early 1970s (on which more is discussed in the chapter) and later on was a founding member of the Paris-based immigration studies research institute *Génériques*. On the importance of the Palestinian question, see also Mamarbachi (2008).
7. In a similar vein, Prevost and Kadri (2008: 426) have argued that the emergence of a broad and radical immigrant movement in the 1980s testified to the failure of the system of nationally based welfare.
8. Further, there was the Gisti (*Groupe d'information*), which focused on gathering and promoting information on the immigrants' conditions; in 1962 the first ASTI (*Association de solidarité avec les travailleurs immigrés*) was set up, which was to become part of an important network in the 1970s (Abdallah 2000: 16).
9. 'Comité d'action bidonvilles', various tracts, May 1968, reproduced in Granotier (1979: 134).
10. This against a general figure of up to 25 per cent of industrial workers unionized in the same period (Granotier 1979: 250).
11. 'Voeux immigrés Renault' (tract), quoted in Vigna (2007: 46).
12. On the other hand, there were factories where specific groups worked on a national basis and found themselves more isolated from both French workers and other immigrants. This was the case, for example, for the Portuguese workers at the Perrier factory in Paris (Zancarini-Fournel 2002: 12).
13. This agreement was signed by the representatives from the government, the employers' organizations and the major trade unions on 27 May 1968 and was meant to end the strike movement. It stipulated an overall wage increase and the legal anchoring of the major unions in the factories. Despite pressure from CGT leaders, workers at Renault-Billancourt rejected the agreement.
14. Algeria had already in 1973 suspended all migration to France, in the context of escalating violence against Algerians in France. In addition, restrictions were introduced in these years on the issuing of residence permits to families (Benoit 1980: 100).
15. 'Texte collectif des travailleurs en grève de Girosteel Le Bourget', 14 February 1971, [translation by the author], quoted in Vigna (2007: 123).
16. Said Bouziri, for example, has testified to the importance of the Palestinian question to the general mobilization of North African workers and students during the early 1970s (Trappo 1990). See also Hajjat (2006a: 76–85, 2006b: 74–92).
17. 'I have been fired because I am an activist and an Arab'.
18. This new trade union approach was linked to an implicit agreement between them and the state, as in the context of the Marcellin-Fontanet circular

trade unions obtained a say in the regulation of immigrant entry into France (Abdallah 2000: 27–8).
19. Between June 1973, the start of *Ordre nouveau*'s public calls to 'Stop uncontrolled immigration', and September 1973, 11 North Africans had been killed in Marseille. For an extensive list of assaults against North Africans in the 1970s, see (Giudice 1992).
20. This movement of second-generation North African youngsters was involved in mass mobilization against racism in France in the 1980s.

9
Turning to Africa: Politics and Student Resistance in Africa since 1968

Leo Zeilig

The year 1968 was the high-point of student unrest and politics for more than one continent. Despite a few honourable exceptions one of the problems with the huge amount of literature that poured out of the social movements in the late 1960s and 1970s was its significant Eurocentrism. The decade was also, in many ways, as important for student activists in Africa as it was in Europe and North America. Similarly, 1968 was a crucial year for student revolutionaries on the continent. In Senegal, in events that some have claimed predated the upheavals in France, students were central to the worst political crisis the president, Leopold Senghor, had faced since independence eight years previously. Forcing him to flee the capital and call in the French army to restore order, after only eight years of independence. This chapter looks explicitly at the nature of the student revolts in Africa in the late 1960s and 1970s. The chapter seeks to pull our attention away from Europe and North America, the privileged sites for discussing 1968, to focus on other voices that began to craft a new politics that year. The chapter argues that students at independence were pampered members of a privileged group who could expect state employment in the formal sectors after graduation, but the conditions of higher education on the continent changed quickly. It considers the nature of the student as a privileged political actor in the transformation of the modern world.

I. Students and intellectuals

There are three vital and related aspects to the immediate pre-independence period in much of Africa.[1] The first is that, contrary to much of the ideological and political rhetoric of the time, it was not, largely speaking, a working class and trade union leadership that led the struggles for independence (Seddon 2002). Although in many cases it was labour mobilizations after the Second World War which were crucial sparks to the nationalist movements, generally speaking it was another social group who took up the leading positions in the movements that were to oust colonial powers. Second, the group that did assume the responsibility for leading nationalist struggles was what has been called the 'intelligentsia'. This was made up largely of colonial staff, trade union bureaucrats and university students and graduates who had often been educated abroad on colonial scholarships and who had been immersed in a left-wing (frequently communist) milieu in American, British and French universities in the 1930s, 1940s and 1950s.[2] The third central factor during this period was the attraction among this 'student-intelligentsia' of the Soviet model of development (Davidson 1992). The Soviet Union was regarded as offering the 'intelligentsia' of the Third World the option of 'raising' their countries to a level of technological development equal to the advanced West. This project was often seen in terms of a radical project of socialist transformation, where the levers of state control could be wielded in the interests of the newly independent nation.

Many future leaders in Africa developed their politics in student groups (Diané 1990). One organization stands out: the West African Student Union (WASU), formed in 1925 in London, was regarded as the 'training ground for Nigerian nationalists' (Federici 2000: 90; see also Hanna and Hanna 1975). WASU welcomed students from West Africa who found themselves in London, however briefly, often providing them with accommodation and support. However, WASU was not principally a welfare service, but a political and campaigning union: it denounced colonial racism, forced labour, the expropriation of land and the unequal relationship linking the colonial metropoles with their African dependencies. Far from limiting its agenda to student issues, WASU sought to 'agitate for and emphasize the needs of the future "United West Africa"' (Adi 1998: 34).

Similar, and similarly radical, political organizations of Francophone African students were active in Paris: the *Association des Etudiants Sénégalais* (AES) and the *Fédération des Etudiants d'Afrique Noire en France* (FEANF) were seen as crucial to the emergence of students as a distinct social group (Diané 1990; Diaw 1993; Diop 1993). Marcel-Eloi Chambrier Rahandi (1990) a former activist and leading member of FEANF explained that the organization ensured the political formation of a generation of soon-to-be African leaders, and crucially the union instilled an ideological coherence among the disparate communities of African students studying in France.[3] Rahandi (1990: 16) describes these processes:

> one learnt to live, to think and to act together, FEANF was a school where we took our first political lessons. It was within FEANF that African students formed a concept of African nationalism... Through the practice and theory of the union they forged an idea of freedom.[4]

The list of those who were transformed by the metropolitan university and by their *luttes syndicales* in these countries testifies to the importance of the student-intelligentsia: Amilcar Cabral in Portugal, Leopold Senghor in France and Kwame Nkrumah in the United States and Britain. The role students were going to play was never underestimated. Leopold Senghor, Senegal's first president, addressed students in 1956: 'you are the elite of the elite, the best elements of our people' (quoted in Cissé 2001: 36) and it was believed that the next generation from the university would continue to play a leading role in post-colonial Africa.

Some of the more Eurocentric literature on student politics suggests that it was the influence of Western education on a group of Africans that instilled in them the desire for freedom, democracy and independence (Hanna 1975). Undoubtedly, one of the *unintended consequences* of the experience was to expose students to radical and left-wing ideas. A key factor was the intellectual hegemony of Marxism in left-wing politics in European universities in the 1930s and 1940s. Along with these influences was the role played by Black Marxists in political struggles in the United States and Europe (Georgakas and Surkin 1998). It is clear that student militants and intellectuals achieved an intellectual and organizational hegemony that was unparalleled in colonial Africa.

Evidence for this has emerged in documents released by the Public Records Office in the UK (March 2003) describing the emergence of radical and communist ideas in 'Negro organizations' during the Second World War. Although the files concentrate on the consequences for the West Indian colonies, they betray the paranoia of the British Secret Services at the growth of a Black consciousness linked to an embryonic civil rights movement in the United States. The documents stress the growing radicalization among groups of West African students studying in America. In a prolonged correspondence with the Colonial Office, staff at the British embassy in Washington reported with growing anxiety the activity of West African students studying in the United States. In 1944 they were particularly concerned about two Nigerians, Nwafor Orizu and

Ozumba Mbadiwe, who were to go on to play a prominent role on the radical wing of Nigerian nationalism.[5] A Colonial Office letter on the 3 January 1944 noted, 'We have had a certain amount of correspondence with various Departments over the unsatisfactory position that tends to develop in the cases of many West Africans who have gone to America as students.' Quoting another letter received the previous year on the alarming state of African students 'permitted' to study in the United States,

> between 20 and 30 students from west African [sic] have been permitted to come to this country, supported by the promise of profoundly inadequate allowances from their relatives at home. A few are all right, quiet, industrious and serious; others are anything but. They get into debt; they flit from one soft-hearted university to the next, piling unfinished course upon unfinished course. Gradually they learn there is a market value attached to the pose of the exploited victim of British imperialism; they write books and they address meetings and they get taken up and used by groups whose interest is not at all any improvement to African conditions.[6]

The letter continued that Orizu and Mbadiwe are clearly from the latter category of unsavoury characters mixing with dangerous (presumably left-wing) elements. The conclusion was often that these problems could be solved from the 'financial angle' ensuring that West African students do not find themselves without resources and so resort to the 'temptation to play to the anti-British gallery'.[7]

The independence settlements compelled the student-intelligentsia who had led the anti-colonial struggles to consolidate control in the existing state machinery. Many saw their role as liberators, taking their 'backward' societies into the modern (and frequently socialist) world (Adi 1998). For Nkrumah, Senghor and Nyerere (the leaders of Ghanaian, Senegalese and Tanzanian independence, respectively) 'socialism' was embodied in the state, and in the state they felt themselves 'above class antagonism generally' (Marx 1984: 45). As antagonism had no place in their 'newly' founded societies, a classless discourse became a necessity in state control. The state in newly independent Africa became the means of carrying out state-capitalist development (Cliff 1963). So, in the case of Ghana, once independence had been achieved, the movements that had been mobilized in the anti-colonial struggles (and these had been considerable) were abandoned (Davidson 1992). This left the state as the only lever of power. After the first decade of independence (the 1960s), First argued that the process of decolonization had been a 'bargaining process with co-operative African elites... The former colonial government guarded its options and... the careerist heirs to independence preoccupied themselves with an "Africanization" of the administration' (1970: 57–8).

Students were among the first to champion independence and question the political direction of self-appointed leaders of that independence. Still, as much of the literature cautions, student activism on the continent during the 1940s and 1950s was limited. Inevitably so, as Silvia Federici (2000: 90) explains, 'Africa had only a handful of secondary schools and universities; thus those who made it to a college were an absolute minority, who in most cases had to study abroad, often spending many years away from their countries' (see also Rodney 1981: 238–61). Charles Diané (1990: 38) makes the same point, noting that after more than 50 years of French colonialism in 1946 not a single university had been created in French West Africa. In Guinea, with a population of three million, only 48 school students took entry exams to proceed to graduation.

The politically privileged position of students in much of the continent was linked to their 'exaggerated' role in the movements for independence (Boren 2001). To be a student at the time was to be alienated from the social world many had emerged from. The sense of exclusion became the *raison d'être* of the student movement in the first decade of independence (Bathily 1992). It was a key element to their politically privileged status. They saw themselves as the harbingers of European development, destined to bring about modernization.[8] These ideas formed the backbone of much of the political and theoretical thinking in the immediate aftermath of the first wave of independence in Africa (Fanon 1963; Cabral 1969). Students inherited a politically privileged role after independence that derived from their direct experience in the nationalist struggle and their subsequent role as a 'transitory' group in the post-colonial state. Their world oscillated between visions of workers and peasants and urban privilege, contradictions which help to determine the nature of their activism in the first decade of independence.

II. The university at independence

As discussed above, students were a central element to the struggle to end colonialism, advocating and inspiring independence struggles from the 1930s. The university – the handful of higher education colleges and technical institutes that existed – became the contested ground where political leaders and democratic struggles found their voice. After independence both the student and university were transformed, often slowly and reluctantly, into national bodies with 'national responsibilities'. Students could not continue to be part of a political vanguard contesting state authority; rather they had to become part of the project of reconstruction and development. The universities had to produce the 'elites' that could power development (Mamdani 1994).

The university at independence in Africa was, in the words of one commentator, an 'implanted institution with largely expatriate staffs, metropole courses of study, and substantial political independence' (Hanna 1975: 11). For ten years it was at the centre of various attempts to Africanize the state, to disentangle the academy from its colonial past and engage it with what were regarded as African realities. It was also the crucial training centre for very limited sections of society dedicated to the needs of a tiny proportion of the population: in the Congo in 1960 the entire university population was only 2000 (Caffentzis 2000). Student enrolment was only just hovering above one per cent of the age-cohort in the mid-1960s; it was going to reach three per cent by the late 1990s (World Bank 2000).

Campus life for many students of the new universities was privileged. University students enjoyed generous grants, lived easily in subsidized accommodation and ate like kings. As one student remembered about the 'payout' (grant), at the University of Zimbabwe,

> Materially we never had any issues, we had disagreements here and there about payouts but by and large there was enough food. Actually it was excessive, in the Halls of Residence. We used to throw away bread. We used to call it, 'Christmas every day'. When you go to Varsity it is Christmas every day. In the rural areas, Christmas Day would be when you had rice and chicken. But at Varsity you would have rice and chicken everyday.
> (Arthur Mutambara, interview, 10 July 2003)

The university was a rarefied space of material privilege and political debate. In Zimbabwe during the 1980s these payouts allowed students to build houses for their parents in the rural areas. This picture of campus comfort was repeated across much of the continent.

In the immediate post-colonial period these prerogatives were to demarcate the parameters of student activity. Though some commentators have perhaps overstated the 'elitism' of early student activism

(O'Brien 1996). Pascal Bianchini (2004) argues in the case of Senegal that a 'real' student movement did not emerge until after 1966, and Federici (2000: 91) states that for much of the 1960s and 1970s student politics was limited in scope by the need for students 'to fill the empty spaces left by departing expatriates, and saw the expansion of higher education as a key condition for economic development'. However, close attention needs to be paid to the processes at work. It was both the breakdown of the anti-colonial consensus and the disintegration of economic and political development of the new nation that saw student resistance escalate. These tensions gave way to a fractious relationship between the state and the university and impacted on the nature of political unrest on the campus and on the identity of the post-colonial students (Hanna and Hanna: 1975).

In the first decade of independence, writers have described a social pact between students and the state, seen as an implicit guarantee that had ensured employment in the formal economy for university graduates. The state had been able to create a certain degree of solidarity between the institutions of the state and students, but this 'solidarity' was premised on the reward of graduate employment (Foucher 2002). It is also true that students were optimistic about the future social order. Inevitably, this resulted in a certain symmetry of interests between the newborn state and student identity. Although these factors had an important impact on student activism, they did not prevent the emergence of oppositional politics on the campus across Africa in the 1960s and 1970s (Hanna 1975). Federici argues that in Tanzania in 1966 students defended their elitism against President Nyerere on the question of their participation in national service. He argues that similar confrontations were witnessed in Ghana and Mozambique (Barkan 1975; Frederici 2000: 105).

Indeed, despite the alleged 'social pact', student activism was a persistent (and irritating) feature of political life in the early period of decolonization, prompting a number of important investigations into the subject (Hanna and Hanna 1975). In Côte d'Ivoire students contested Houphouet-Boigny's vocal support for the Algerian War while pan-Africanist protests demonstrated the political consciousness of student groups. In Senegal students demonstrated outside the American embassy after Nkrumah was deposed in 1966, a factor that made their role in the revolt in 1968 possible (Bianchini 2002, 2004). But in Ghana student activists celebrated the country's first coup against Nkrumah. While many of the early demonstrations were concerned with the end of minority rule in Africa, in South Africa and Rhodesia the issue of educational reform was also key. The Africanization of the university administration that had been dominated by white professors and lecturers became an important demand (Bathily 1992).

The expansion of student numbers, small though it was, meant that universities were no longer simply the training ground of the ruling classes. While the majority of the highest state functionaries and professors were still part and parcel of the post-colonial ruling elite, increasingly many students (and their parents) were not. However, the university had not become 'proletarianized', and universities for at least the first decade and a half of independence (from 1960 to 1975) were largely privileged institutions (Hanna 1975; Frederic 2000). The overwhelming majority of students were from 'professional and managerial' families, a section of the population which, at that time, had lifestyles and opportunities far superior to the great majority (Frederic 2000). '1968' was the year when many student movements on the continent broke with the social pact made with the state. Even if students had 'lifestyles' cut-off from the majority of the population, they increasingly saw themselves as societal watchdogs, guarding against a new and alien governing class. '1968', across much of the continent, saw the explosive convergence of left-wing ideas and the frustrations at the failures of independence.

III. Other voices in 1968: Congo-Zaire and Senegal

University students had been consistent and vocal critics of Joseph Mobutu's regime since the 1960s. During the first two years after Mobutu's 1965 coup, student groups supported his programme of nationalization and Africanization, the national student body *Union Générale des Étudients du Congo* (UGEC) – though cautious – took his radical rhetoric at face value. This relationship is easy to dismiss today, but as we have seen Mobutu was speaking from a radical script, condemning tribalism and calling for a new nationalism that would return the Congo to its African roots. The renaming of cities, towns and provinces and later the insistence that European names be replaced by 'authentic' African ones was confirmation to the student body of Mobutu's sincerity. Mobutu also saw the co-option of the student body – and principally its main representative body, the UGEC – as a key element in his control of potentially the most important opposition group in society. Taking the lead of the UGEC the new government even recognized the Congo's first murdered prime minister, Patrice Lumumba, as a national hero.

The student movement, then, was regarded as a vital element in Mobutu's attempt to conquer civil society. Was the regime exaggerating the threat from students? The organizational and political coherence of student groups – in the national union and university affiliates – was far greater than other groups in civil society. Mobutu was desperate to control his unruly students, and to convince them of his national project. As with much of the continent, however, this 'pact' could not hold.

The tension between the regime and students was graphically demonstrated on 4 January 1968. When the vice-president of the United States, Hubert H. Humphrey, attempted to lay a bouquet of flowers at the Lumumba memorial in Kinshasa, students from Lovanium University who had turned up for the occasion pelted the vice-president with eggs and tomatoes. A UGEC communiqué stated that the protest had been called to prevent 'a profanation by the same people who had yesterday done everything [so that] the great fighter for Congo's and Africa's freedom disappear[ed]' (Nzongola-Ntalaja 2002: 177). The event caused the regime obvious embarrassment, but also clarified the reality of Mobutu's fake anti-imperialism. The definitive rupture came later in 1968 when the regime banned the UGEC following the arrest of its President André N'Kanza-Dulumingu and student protests in Lubumbashi, Kinshasa and Kisangani.

Mobutu's strategy of co-opting the student leadership of UGEC eventually won out. Apart from the national President N'Kanza-Dulumingu, who refused co-optation for years, other leaders caved in. The *Mouvement Populaire de la Revolution* (MPR) would not tolerate an independent voice of student organization, instead the ruling party created the *Jeunesse du Mouvement populaire de la Révolution* (JMPR), whose leadership saw their political futures tied to a blind loyalty to the regime. The co-optation by the regime of the now-banned UGEC did not, however, silence student activism. The next years were marked by violent demonstrations and strikes across the country. In 1969, 60 students from the University of Kinshasa were killed. In what was to become a familiar gesture of solidarity, students in Lubumbashi marched through the city bare-footed and bare-chested in support of their fallen comrades in the capital almost 2000 miles away. Other universities came out in support, and hundreds of activists and student leaders were expelled (see Nzongola-Ntalaja 2002: 173–9).

Similar processes were at work in West Africa. By the end of the 1960s the situation in Senegal had begun to deteriorate. The French abolished the price guarantees on oil seed in 1967 and Senegal experienced the worse cycle of drought since independence between 1968 and 1969. The political calm was finally destroyed in 1968. The country faced economic difficulties. Between 1959 and 1968 the numbers of those out of work rose by 450 per cent, most of these job losses concentrated in Dakar. In addition, independence closed off political space. The main trade union federation was the *Union Nationale des travailleurs du Sénégal* (UNTS) formed in 1962. In the name of national unity it became tied to the state (Amin 1971: 46–7).

In 1968 students were among the first to question the government's political control. The radical *Parti Africain de l'Indépendence* (PAI) could fill the political vacuum on the campus. Nor was the movement simply a reflection of events in France. The first student strike in March started before events in France, although the two movements were very closely linked. A student strike in May 1968 was called to oppose the government's decision to reduce the amount of the student grant. But students came to express a general urban malaise.

On demonstrations the crowd declared, 'Power to the people: freedom for unions', 'We want work and rice' (*Le Soleil* 2001).[9] On 28 May a demonstration supporting the students was estimated to be between 20,000 and 30,000. With support for the strike spreading beyond the university, on 29 May police were sent into the campus. Students were viciously attacked. The official figures record 1 death and 80 injured. Incredibly, 600 students were interned in an army camp until 9 June, while foreign students were expelled from the country; 3500 were arrested. On 31 May the UNTS declared a general strike. One activist described the atmosphere: 'we had the impression that the government was vacant... ministers were confined to the administrative buildings... and the leaders of the Party and the State hid in their houses!' (Bathily 1992: 80).[10]

By early June, under a wave of repression, the government ordered the army to shoot demonstrators on sight. French troops intervened, occupying key installations in the town, the airport, the presidential palace. The university was closed, foreign students were sent home. Members of the national bureau of the UNTS and leaders of several independent unions were placed under house arrest. A state of emergency was declared in Dakar, forbidding any demonstration of more than five people. Meanwhile, the President gave his permission to the French Ambassador to plan his evacuation by helicopter from the *Palais* and then by plane to France. In increasingly hysterical tones Senghor blamed the movement on foreign influence: 'this insurrectional movement has come from Peking... We will resist until the end... The existence of

Senegal is at stake. If the opposition triumphs, the country will be plunged into catastrophe' (cited in Lo 1987: 39–40).

By 12 June the movement was largely defused. After the UNTS had been assured that their comrades would be released they entered into discussions with the government. But the eventual deal involved important concessions to both students and trade unionists. The minimum wage, the *Salaire minimum interprofessionnel garanti* (SMIG), was increased by 15 per cent, while privileges to parliamentarians were slashed. If it was not entirely a victory, it was certainly not a defeat. But the most significant result of the crisis was that the sense of the ruling party's invulnerability had been irrevocably shattered.

As one witness of the events recalled the main effect of the uprising for Senegalese society, 'May 1968 was the midwife of the "democratic opening"... Activists trained in the ranks of the PAI judiciously exploited this weakness and gave to the movement a radical orientation' (Thioub 1992: 281). Senegal now entered a period of political turmoil. There was also a proliferation of left-wing Maoist and communist groups. Militants attacked the cortege carrying the French President George Pompidou with Molotov cocktails during his official visit on 5 February 1971. Though Senghor managed to remain in power, Senegal would never be the same again.

'1968' was a turning point for both the Congo and Senegal, where privileged and co-opted university students broke dramatically with the regimes in place. Similar fissures were spreading out across Africa. Students may still have been privileged, but they no longer saw their political project and ambitions tied to those of the ruling parties.

IV. Students and the transition

With the onset of the international recession in the mid-1970s, Africa was plunged into a crisis that many parts of the continent have not recovered from. As commodity prices collapsed on international markets, higher education – the privileged recipient of state monies since independence – came under attack. With the introduction of structural adjustment programmes from the early 1980s, university funding was targeted for reorganization. Both the World Bank and the International Monetary Fund (IMF) insisted, through the 1980s, on massive and sustained cuts to higher education budgets. The effect was to plunge the continent's often renowned universities into a state of penury and collapse.

What happened to students? Some writers have asserted that with the collapse of the post-colonial 'social pact', student engagement has become 'corporatist', concerned only with issues of 'bread and butter'. In the case of Senegal, 'By the late 1970s Senegalese students saw themselves more modestly as symbols of the independent stalemate, of the political and economic failure of a regime which was unable to provide them with clear survival prospects.' Students, following this argument, have lost their status: 'from providers of modernity they became aid applicants' (Bathily et al 1995: 405). The respected scholar Cruise O'Brien makes a similar point about student protests in defence of their 'elite status': 'And students will riot for their privileges too... defending their "right" to better scholarship' (1996: 65).

The truth could not stand further from this analysis. From the late 1980s a wave of popular protest spread across the continent like a political hurricane. From 1989 political protests rose massively across sub-Saharan Africa. There had been approximately 20 annually recorded incidents of political unrest in the 1980s; in 1991 alone 86 major protest movements had taken place across 30 countries. By 1992, many African governments had been forced to introduce reforms, and in 1993, 14 countries held democratic elections. In a 4-year period from the start of the protests in 1990, a total of 35 regimes had been swept away by protest movements and strikes, and in elections that were often held for the first time in a generation. The continent was transformed by these protest movements. This explosion of popular protests – frequently led by university students – was hardly noticed in many parts of the world, but they were as far reaching as the changes that brought down the regimes of Eastern Europe and the Soviet Union. In the words of the long-standing president of Gabon, Omar Bongo, 'the winds from the East are shaking the coconut trees'.

Students acted, frequently as part of the 'convergence of forces', as the detonators to these dramatic transitions. Take one example. The students at the University of Kinshasa in Zaire were the first to initiate the protests that almost unseated Mobutu, and led to a largely urban protest movement and transition that lasted into the middle of the 1990s (Martins 2002; Renton et al. 2006). They demonstrated on 5 May 1990 asserting that the reforms announced by the dictator ten days previously were 'irrevocable'. The demonstration ended violently, after security forces attacked it. The students immediately issued an appeal for other universities and colleges across the country to rise up in solidarity: '[D]o not cross your arms. Follow our example. The dictatorship is finished. We cannot go back. Take on the state. Demonstrate! March!' (Nkongolo 2000: 182).

V. Restoring the neo-liberal tempo

The collapse into sectarian factionalism affected the student body when the transition was frustrated or after it had been achieved. Their role in the 'democratic transitions' was complex because it was inextricably tied to the liberalization of political space and the manipulations of these processes by incumbent governments and political parties. The 'success' of student activism was linked to the wider social forces that they could help animate and identify with; this was tied to their ability to 'converge' their struggles with broader popular forces. Mamdani (1994) is correct to recognize that when students were effective, they succeeded in 'forcing an opening up' even if they lacked an alternative strategy: 'Its possibilities depended far more on the character of forces that student action succeeded in mobilizing than its own internal energies' (Mamdani 1994: 259).

Popular mobilizations were a response to widespread disaffection with the policies of austerity and structural adjustment, yet these movements were responding in new ways. Class structures in sub-Saharan African had been transformed, and resistance did not simply take old forms. The processes of class alignment and resistance brought in new and heterogeneous forces (Harrison 2002; Seddon 2002; see also Seddon and Zeilig 2005). Seddon (2002) defines the role of the 'popular classes' in Africa, describing a shifting constellation of political forces that included the unemployed, informal sector traders and trade unionists. This chapter argues that students and unemployed graduates also formed an important part of the popular classes. Students are not 'free-floating' above the political and economic crisis, insulated as they had been from these concerns in the 1960s. The resulting hybridity of social groups in Africa has transformed their activism and identity and affected their ability to exercise political agency. We can say that students expressed their status as politically privileged actors in diverse forms during the political transitions, yet repeatedly they have sparked wider protests in a period that has seen the 'convergence of social forces'.

Higher education reforms, as we have seen, have transported student identity into the maelstrom of the structural crisis. Mamdani (1994: 258–9), in an important study on class and the intelligentsia, has seen these processes at work: 'previously a more or less guaranteed route to position and privilege, higher education seemed to lead more and more students to the heart of the economic and social crisis'. Students are no longer the 'transitory' social group waiting to be allotted government employment; on the contrary, they have become pauperized, converging more and more with the wider urban poor: social groups that they had historically regarded as their 'responsibility' to liberate.

This chapter has concentrated on the student revolt of the 1960s in Africa, but we have seen how this resistance was radically altered in the context of the neo-liberal assault on higher education from the late 1970s. One of the central factors influencing student politics was the ability to contest the ideological foundations of structural adjustment. If, in the 1960s and 1970s, students had access to a set of ideas from the international left, with the collapse of these alternatives in the 1990s, student activism was, to a certain extent, recast. The capacity of student organizations to confront the 'world view' presented by their governments (before and after the transitions) and the International Finance Institutions (IFIs) helped shape their political agency. But their ability to do this was influenced by wider political forces in society, and they were disabled by the lack of a coherent ideological alternative to neo-liberal reforms. Students found themselves buffeted together with the popular classes, by the resumption of a more or less unopposed politics of adjustment and austerity.

The status of 'student' – at university, as a graduate, as a 'cartouchard'[11] or part of the mass of unemployed – is not impermanent. The crisis for students in sub-Saharan Africa is precisely because they are not in 'transition' as they were in the 1960s and 1970s; on the contrary, they are increasingly permanent 'artefacts' in the post-colonial impasse. Their activism – always complex and contradictory – retreats into a routine of 'economic' and factional contestation when wider popular and democratic movements in society decline or are frustrated. The disillusionment that gripped student politics in dozens of campuses across sub-Saharan Africa as governments that had emerged from the 'transition' (re)committed themselves to implementing IMF and World Bank reforms. The predominance of neo-liberalism across the continent after the democratic transition ensured a quick death for the African renaissance and the movements that had heralded it.

VI. Conclusions

The first decade of independence on the African continent saw university students transformed from the privileged elite supporting post-colonial regimes to a critical and political opposition. This transformation – that blew apart the 'flag' independence of the early 1960s – took place for many movements in 1968, but not in isolation from the events in the North. The sense of a global movement of students and workers challenging the *ancien régimes* in Europe and America gave confidence to militants across Africa that year. In Senegal some student activists fought on the barricades in both the *Quartier latin* in Paris and on the streets of Dakar that year. For university students, impatient and angry with the slow and corrupt pace of change in nominally independent states, political challenges emerged to the new governments. These students tore up the 'agreements' made between students and ruling parties, that had for a moment guaranteed their loyalty to the government on the promise of formal sector jobs on graduation.

The voices that were unfurled in the events of 1968, and after, spoke not of neo-liberal reforms or the marketization of higher education, but of political and socialist change powered by a radical left. The onset of the global recession in the 1970s saw the involvement of the IMF and World Bank in structural adjustment on the continent. Universities were one of the principal targets of these reforms. Students were now thrown into the eye of the crisis and though they often spoke in the old politics of privilege – as the slogan of the Zimbabwean student movement in the 1990s expressed, 'the voice of the voiceless' – they were now, more and more, part of the convergence of popular forces emerging to contest structural adjustment and economic crisis.

But this new convergence emerged with the collapse of the Stalinist regimes in 1989, so generations of student activists were unlike their 1968 counterparts. Their voices – though loud and strident in the transitions – lacked the political confidence of the early period of activism and were unable to construct political alternatives to challenge neo-liberal reforms on the continent. The governments that emerged from the turmoil and uprisings of the transition resumed the politics of adjustment – the privatization and underfunding of higher education – rejected by the movements that had brought the new regimes to power. '1968' still stands as the radical turning point for a generation of militants on the continent. Re-examining the movements and politics of 1968 in Africa insists that we shift our focus to other voices that began to speak of liberation and political renewal that year.

Notes

1. I am aware of the dangers of Africa-wide generalization, but believe a broad picture of its political and economic transformation is both possible and necessary.
2. It is important to stress the fluidity of this category so that members of the colonial civil services and trade union leaders were also frequently recent graduates.

3. While these communities might not have been very numerous, their national unions certainly were. Diané (1990: 55–64) notes 14 African student organizations in France formed between 1947 and 1956, many with their headquarters (and leading activists) in France.
4. 'on apprenait à vivre, à penser, à agir en commun, une école [FEANF] surtout où nous fîmes nos premières classes politiques. C'est au sein de la FEANF que les étudiants africains ont pris conscience du fait national africain...Par l'analyse et la pratiques des luttes syndicales, ils se sont forgés cet idéal de liberté'.
5. Nwafor Orizu later became the first president of the Nigerian Senate.
6. Public Record Office, Colonial Office 968/121/4. I have referenced Colonial Office papers held in the Public Records Office as PRO CO followed by their relevant catalogue number as well as title or date and so on where available.
7. It is interesting that the solution was regarded as 'better funding' to prevent students falling in with anti-imperialist groups. How it could conceivably have been financially beneficial to fall in with the anti-colonial left is not made clear in the files. Maybe, however, they were paid to address meetings, write and so on. Public Record Office, Colonial Office 968/121/4.
8. This idea is still an important one to student activists today. As one student described to me, 'our parents speak from an African culture...whereas ours comes from Europe' ['les parents parlent de culture...africaine, [et] une culture qui nous vienne de l'Europe qu'on nous a apprise'] (Mor Faye interview, 5 February 2004). These ideas are also discussed in Ngugi's classic *Decolonizing the Mind* (1987).
9. 'Le pouvoir au peuple: liberté syndicale', 'Nous voulons du travail et du riz'.
10. 'on avait l'impression que le pouvoir était devenu vacant...les ministres avaient été consignés aux buildings administratifs...et de hauts responsables du parti et de l'Etat s'étaient cachés dans leurs maisons!'
11. Term used in Senegal to describe students who have exhausted almost all of their chances (literally their 'cartridges'), giving them just one more chance in the annual exams (Bianchini 2002: 368).

10
Riding the Waves: Feminism, Lesbian and Gay Politics, and the Transgender Debates

Sally Hines

I. Introduction

The social movements of the 1960s have been well documented in relation to the impact upon the political cultures and the lived experiences of women (Mitchell 1973; Allen *et al.* 1974; Rowbotham *et al.* 1981; Wilson 1982; Rowbotham 2000) and sexual minorities (D'Emillo 1983, 2004; D'Emilio and Freedman 1988; Weeks 2000, 2007; Carter 2004). Yet the role of transgender people in these social transformations has received scant attention. Alongside other chapters in this volume that articulate the 'other voices' excluded from dominant discourses of 1968, this chapter will address the role of transgender people in the social and political changes of this time.

The chapter begins by examining two events that 'sandwich' 1968, where transgender people fought alongside feminist and lesbian and gay activists: *Compton's Cafeteria Riots* of 1966 and the *Stonewall Riots* of 1969. These events will be explored to illustrate the role of trans activism in 1960s gender and sexual movements. The chapter will move on to map subsequent relationships between transgender communities and gender and sexual politics. At times, the chapter draws on data from my own research on practices of transgender identity, intimacy and care.[1] This research suggests a tense and contentious relationship between feminist, lesbian and gay, and transgender communities on both a personal and a political level. Yet, despite continued strands of transphobia within some sections of feminist, and lesbian and gay communities, my research suggests that, in the main, relationships between these communities have improved in recent years. In conclusion, the chapter will argue for the need to recognize past links, and the necessity to forge present and future connections, between transgender, feminist, and lesbian and gay theory and politics.

II. Compton's Cafeteria Riots

In the 1960s, Compton's Cafeteria in the Tenderloin district of San Francisco was an all-night meeting point for street prostitutes and homeless people. It was also one of the few places in San Francisco where transgender people felt able to be publicly visible. Throughout the 1950s and 1960s, cross-dressing was illegal in California and transgender people were unwelcome in most gay bars (Stryker 2008). In her 2005 documentary, 'Screaming Queens', Susan Stryker locates the Compton's Cafeteria Riots as the starting point for a new type of radical politics led by gender and sexual minorities:

> It's a hot August night in San Francisco in 1966 – three years before the famed Stonewall. Compton's Cafeteria, in the seedy Tenderloin district, is hopping with its usual assortment of transgender people, young street hustlers, and down-and-out regulars. The management, annoyed by the noisy crowd at one table, calls the police. When a surly cop, accustomed to manhandling Compton's clientele, attempts to arrest one of the queens, she throws her coffee in his face. Mayhem erupts – windows break, furniture flies through the air. Police reinforcements arrive, and the fighting spills into the street. For the first time, the drag queens band together to fight back, getting the better of the cops, whom they kick and stomp with their high-heeled shoes and beat with their heavy purses. For everyone at Compton's that night, one thing was certain – things would never be the same again.
>
> (Stryker 2008)

Though many gay and lesbian organizations and venues were unwelcoming to transgender people, the year leading up to the events at Compton's saw links being forged between some lesbian, gay and transgender communities. Many of those involved in the riots were members of *Vanguard*, the first known gay youth organization in the US, which had been organized earlier that year with the help of radical ministers working with Glide Memorial Church, a centre for progressive social activism in the Tenderloin. Others were members of *Street Orphans*, a group of homeless people and street prostitutes. Thus, prior to the Compton riots, alliances had existed between these marginalized groups. Following the riots, transgender people were barred from entering Compton's, leading to frequent and often violet pickets of the cafeteria organized by lesbian, gay, transgender and street people. According to Stryker, the riots marked a turning point in the LGBT (Lesbian, Gay, Bisexual and Transgender) movement:

> It was the first time that people who were discriminated against because of their gender identity banded together to resist their oppression. And it had results. In the years after the riot, trans activists and allies began to make real progress in meeting the unique social and medical needs of trans people.

(Stryker 2008)

In the months following the riots at Compton's, then, a network of transgender social and support services were developed, which led to the creation in 1968 of the 'National Transsexual Counselling Unit', the first transgender-run support and rights advocacy organization in the world.

III. The Stonewall Riots

While the Compton's Cafeteria Riots have largely been ignored in LGBT history, in stark contrast, the New York Stonewall Riots have become synonymous with the birth of the modern lesbian and gay movement in the West. A mythological positioning of Stonewall though is contentious (Murray 1996) and certainly, lesbian and gay political organizations had existed in preceding decades – most notably in the 1950s with the 'Mattachine Society' and the 'Daughters of Bilitis'. Yet it is widely agreed by sexual historians (Weeks 2000; D'Emilio 2004) that these early lesbian and gay organizations were generally conservative about the route to social change. The goal was to work within the system to organize for social acceptance. The civil rights, Black power, anti-war, and women's movements of the mid- to late 1960s, however, seemed to have inspired a more militant politics in younger lesbian and gay activists. It is not my intention here to explore these wider debates around Stonewall. Rather, my point of reference is to discuss the relationship between transgender and lesbian and gay activists at the time.

As John D'Emilio (1983) discusses, raids on the 'Stonewall Inn' were nothing new. Yet in 1969, New York was in the middle of a mayoral campaign and the clean-up of the bar took on a new impetus. It operated without a liquor license, it had ties to organized crime, it was popular with Black and Hispanic gay men, trans women and drag queens, and as D'Emilio remarks, 'offering scantily clad go-go boys as entertainment, it brought an "unruly" element to Sheridan Square' (D'Emilio 1983: 231). In Emilio's account of Stonewall, the events of 28 June can be distinguished from previous raids by both the size and the anger of the reacting clientele. The riots lasted for five days and a crowd of, according to David Carter's (2004) research on Stonewall, around 2000 protesters continued to fight back at attempts to arrest them.

In most retellings of Stonewall, it is trans woman Sylvia Rivera who is identified as initiating the Stonewall uprising by throwing a bottle at the police. Trans activist and writer Riki Anne Wilchins describes the Stonewall Inn as 'a sanctuary for genderqueers, who were unwelcome at the city's tonier gay bars' (Wilchins 2002). Rivera was a member of the 'Gay Activists Alliance', and a founding member of the 'Gay Liberation Front', yet many lesbian and gay rights groups distanced themselves from Rivera – seeing her gender queerness as a political liability. As she said in an interview in 1995, 'when things started getting more mainstream [...] it was like, "we don't need you no more"' (quoted by Wilchins 2002). With Marsha Johnson, Rivera went on to form the first transgender political organization and safe house 'Street Transvestite Action Revolutionaries' (STAR). Yet funding was often withheld from STAR by other lesbian and gay organizations, and both Rivera and Johnson returned to sex work to financially support themselves and STAR (Wilchins 2004). The disowning of transgender people by lesbian and gay organizations is further illustrated by Matt Foreman, the executive director of the National Gay and Lesbian Task Force in the US. Foreman remembers,

> There was a time when nobody wanted to even mention transgender issues or have transgender people accompany you on lobbying visits to members of your state assembly because that was pushing the envelope too far [...] There was a myth in our community, and frankly I was part of that myth, that including transgender people would set our cause back.
>
> (quoted in Leff 2008)

Foreman's narrative explicitly illustrates the ways in which transgender people were excluded from many lesbian and gay organizations in the 1960s. As the next section of the chapter will address, transgender people were also unaccounted for within the gender politics of feminism at this time.

IV. 1968: The left, women's liberation and gender politics

Recent memoirs (DuPlessis and Snitow 1998; Rowbotham 2000; Segal 2007) written by women who were activists in left political organizations in the late 1960s, and who went on to be key players in feminist organizations and politics, highlight the sexism at play within the left-based liberation movements of this time. Issues central to women's lives – inequality and low pay in the workforce, domestic labour and childcare, sexual autonomy and safety – were sidelined within the political left. The argument from male activists was that a focus upon women's issues was divisive; that it would dissipate attention from the 'real' cause – class revolution. Moreover, it was not only women's 'issues' that were marginalized. Women themselves were frequently on the outside. For some women activists, childcare responsibilities meant that they played a diminished political role. In this way, Sue O'Sullivan recalled,

> 1968, a political marker in the history books and in many other people's lives, was for me a lead-up year – of demonstrations in Grosvenor Square where I stuck to the side because of my pregnancy, of Martin Luther King's assignation, of student uprisings which I was moved by, but outside of. I was sometimes on my own with a baby in a part of London where I knew no one, while my husband was off working and taking part in meetings and demonstrations.
> (1988: 51)

Other women activists were relegated to the periphery by male activists who saw their role in the movement as predominately a supportive one. Thus Sheila Rowbotham remembers a meeting with the collective of the Left magazine *Black Dwarf*: '[...] he (the male activist) simply assumed it was the men's job to talk politics. [...] he sent me off to the bedroom to stuff envelopes with the other women' (Rowbotham 2000: 177). This state of affairs became increasingly frustrating for women activists. As Lynne Segal states,

> [...] *after* working with our 'brothers' to oppose the evils of the Vietnam War, *after* supporting workers in the struggle in an era of trade union militancy, *after*, above all, seeing ourselves the hip chick

of the 60s sexual liberation, facing ever cruder sexist pin-ups and porn in the underground press, confronting the sexism of our comrades – after this, many women glimpsed that we needed a bit of liberation of our own. And this was the birth of women's liberation.

(quoted in Weeks 2007: 18)

From the late 1960s, women activists began to meet separately in women's workshops and consciousness raising groups in order to talk about the issues that affected them as women; as distinct from men. Speaking about the US, Jo Freeman recalled,

> For months they met quietly to analyze their perpetual secondary roles in the radical movement, assimilate lessons learned in study groups, or reflect on their treatment in the civil rights movement. They were constantly ridiculed by the men they worked with and continually told that what they were doing was 'counter-revolutionary' because it would further splinter an already badly fragmented movement. In many ways this very ridicule served to feed their growing rage. One immediate result was that all the groups, independently banned men from their meetings.
>
> (1971: 150)

Following the rebuffing of women's issues within male-dominated left politics, then, women activists began to meet in women-only spaces. These groups provided an arena for women to share their experiences. As Sue O'Sullivan remembers,

> I found myself sitting somewhat self-consciously in a living room, talking with other women about isolation, feelings of inadequacy, ambivalences towards motherhood, and hearing sympathetic voices confirming, identifying and expanding.
>
> (1988: 52)

Moreover, women's groups were to be spaces where women organized politically around issues such as childcare, abortion, cultural representations of women and low pay – issues that became central to feminist demands over the next decades.

Retrospectively, these spaces can be seen to be based on traditional understandings of difference that link sex and gender. While at this point feminist activists were not explicitly excluding transgender people, implicitly, a politics of identity that tied gender identity and experience to biological sex was to pave the way for the marginalization of transgender people within feminism. Moreover, as the next section of the chapter will address, the preceding decades gave rise to an explicitly anti-transgender feminism.

V. Who are you?: Identity politics and the disowning of trans

Second-wave feminism was one of the first academic fields to respond to the growing public awareness of modern Western transgender practices (Hird 2002). As I have suggested elsewhere (Hines 2006; 2007b), transgender raises key questions concerning the epistemological status and the ontology of 'sex' and 'gender'. Additionally, transgender problematizes the relationship between these categories, evoking complex questions about the construction, deconstruction and ongoing reconstruction of both gender and sexual taxonomies. These issues have long been central to feminist thought. Yet, on a theoretical, political and cultural level, feminism developed a high level of antagonism towards transgender people. Raymond's (1980) critique of trans sexuality as a construction of servile women by a patriarchal medical system instigated a feminist politics of hostility towards transgender people. More recently, other feminist writers (Jeffreys 1997; Greer 1999; Bindel 2003) have echoed Raymond in positioning transgender practices as unfeminist acts. Trans women have been seen to reinforce a stereotypical model of femininity, while trans men have been located as renegades seeking to acquire male power and privilege. In problematizing a unified concept of gender, transgender practices pose central questions to feminist theories and politics of identity. As Feinberg states,

> The development of the trans movement has raised a vital question that's being discussed in women's communities all over the country. How is woman defined? The answer we give may determine the course of women's liberation for decades to come.
> (1996: 109)

A radical feminist response to these complexities, however, has been to reinforce a gender and sexual binary model in order to regulate gendered belonging. Further, a radical feminist critique of transgender can be seen to have moved beyond those who directly identify as radical feminists and into a mainstream feminist agenda, as illustrated by feminist author and scholar Germaine Greer's public outing of a trans female colleague at Cambridge University, UK, in 1996. Another example of transphobia within feminist and lesbian and gay communities occurred in 2008 at 'London Pride' when a trans woman was denied access to a female toilet. When she, and other trans people, challenged this, they were told by an LGBT liaison officer that they had to show their gender recognition certificates[2] before using the toilets, or to use the disabled toilets.

A range of key, and highly problematic, issues around gender identity and recognition are raised here. A radical feminist biologically based politics of gender underscores the incident discussed above. 'The Gender Recognition Act' (GRA 2004) aimed to end the discrimination of transgender people by implementing the rights and recognition of self-identified gender. Though there are limitations in the Act in relation to these aims (see Hines 2007a), the Act importantly marks a departure from a biologically based legal understanding of gender, which arises directly from 'sex' as defined at birth. Yet, if one follows Raymond's premise that 'It is biologically impossible to change *chromosomal* sex. If chromosomal sex is taken to be the fundamental basis for maleness and femaleness, the man who undergoes sex conversion is *not* female' (1980: 10), the conceptual framework of the GRA is based on a false premise. Thus, from this perspective, the legislation is, at the most, grudgingly conceded. A gender recognition certificate can be seen here to be a further tool in the policing of gender by sections of feminist and lesbian and gay communities who desire to regulate the gender and sexual make-up of their communities.

Furthermore, although gender recognition, as framed through the GRA, recognizes that gender may be distinct from 'sex' as defined at birth, it remains tied to a binary model of gender that recognizes only two genders and, moreover, separates gender discreetly into these two categories. As I have argued elsewhere (Hines 2007b), there is a danger that 'gender recognition' will work to further marginalize those who inhabit non-binary genders. More detailed debate around the GRA is beyond the scope of this chapter, yet the issues discussed here are important in relation to the impact of a biologically based identity politics on participants in my research.

Exclusion based on a social ordering of sexual and gendered practices appears as a frequent theme in transgender people's narratives. Many trans men faced critiques of trans masculinity as an unethical way of women accessing male power and privilege. Illustrating this, research participant Svar said, 'There was actually from the dyke feminist scene, there was quite a lot of opposition to female to male transsexuality.

I mean one friend did actually say to me "Oh I see...so you're abandoning the female race then?" [...] There was some accusations, you know, "you're trying to have power, get power"' (Svar, age 41).

The impact of a radical feminist critique on transgender practices was, then, both personally and politically problematic for trans men, and many found themselves excluded from feminist and lesbian communities. At the core of feminist discussions around trans femininity is the concept 'woman'. In explaining the marginalized histories, experiences and social and political demands of women, the women's movement applied 'woman' as a fixed category, which was distinct from 'man'. For the most part, feminist theory has assumed that there is some existing identity, understood through the category of 'woman', who not only initiates feminist interests and goals within discourse, but constitutes the subject for whom political representation is pursued.

Because the definition of 'woman' became inextricably tied to biological 'sex', trans women also experienced difficulty as they attempted to define their gender and sexual identity and fit into lesbian and/or feminist spaces. Many trans women I interviewed thus spoke of rejection from second-wave feminist and lesbian communities. Talking about her attendance at an early Lesbian and Gay Pride event, research participant Gabrielle, for example, said, 'I do remember feeling like it wasn't my day, it was for gay and lesbian people and we were not viewed necessarily with inclusiveness by the community, and weren't made to feel as though they wanted us to be part of the community' (Gabrielle, age 45).

Questions around the position of trans women within feminism cut to the heart of discussions around the constitution of 'woman'. As with feminist communities, transgender people were often marginalized within many strands of lesbian and gay activism. Boyd (2007) has shown how transgendered bodies have troubled lesbian politics. This was also borne out in my research. Research participant Rebecca, who identities as 'bigendered', for example, said,

> For some trans people their sexuality will follow their sex so they might start out as a male with female partners and end up as a female with male partners. And then there are people like me who just muddy the water (laugh). The objects of my desire are women and that hasn't changed. I don't know whether that makes me a female homosexual or a male lesbian, I'm not quite sure. I don't think it's either of those and there's a lack of language to describe my sexuality.
> (Rebecca, age 55)

The locking of gender into sexuality, or vice versa, is problematic for theorizing trans sexualities, which demand a more complex reading of the relationship between gender and sexuality as both interconnected *and* distinct (Hines 2007b). The complexities of sexual sensibilities, identities and expressions might also be apparent after the process of self-identification as transgender and before surgery or hormone therapy. In this way, many participants spoke of the problems when potential partners misunderstand gender and sexual identity categories. For example, Dave said, 'I had a relationship with a woman and I told her straight away that I was transsexual but she thought of me as being a lesbian so the relationship didn't work because that's not what I was' (Dave, age 26).

Narratives of trans sexuality illustrate the limitations of existing classificatory systems of gender, sex and sexuality (Hines 2007a). A number of issues are raised here about how transgender people are situated within identity politics. While identity-based feminist politics developed around the uniform concept of 'woman', lesbian and gay identity politics spoke of the shared experiences of lesbians and gay men. Thus transgender identities are often perceived as a challenge to notions of shared experience based upon sexual identity. As Devor and Matte (2006) argue,

> Homosexual collective identity, especially in the days before queer politics, was largely framed as inborn, like ethnicity, and based primarily on sexual desires for persons of the same sex and gender. However, such definitions make sense only when founded on clearly delineated distinctions between sexes and genders. It becomes considerably harder to delineate who is gay and who is lesbian when it's not clear who is male or a man, and who is female or a woman. Like bisexual people, transgendered and transsexual people destabilize the otherwise easy divisions of men and women into categories of straight and gay because they are both and/or neither. Thus there is a long standing tension over the political terrain of queer politics between gays and lesbians, on the one hand, and transgendered and transsexual people, on the other.

Yet, as the final section of the chapter will suggest, some contemporary movements around gender and sexuality can be seen to be more welcoming to transgender people.

VI. Who are we?: Queering identities

The all-embracing notion of 'woman' began to fracture through a series of challenges from feminists who argued that their experiences remained unarticulated in a predominately white, middle-class and educated movement. Thus it became more appropriate to talk of a range of feminisms than to discuss a uniform body of feminist thought. Recognition of diversity also became apparent in sexual rights politics. Rubin (1992) appealed for a greater tolerance of transgender people within lesbian and gay communities, and suggested a common history, though not identity, between lesbians, gay men and transgender people. Feinberg (1996) also argued for a coalition politics in support of transgender civil rights. Rubin and Feinberg stress the specificities of transgender experience, while arguing for alliances between lesbians, gay men and gender diverse people.

A move towards diversity parallels the focus on difference within queer theory. In taking the discursive formations of gender and sexuality as its starting point, queer theory has engaged directly with transgender. Queer theorists have argued that traditional lesbian and gay theory and politics have been exclusive in their attitudes towards those whose identities fall outside of that which is deemed to be 'correct' or 'fitting'. Thus queer theory has positively embraced difference and has argued against the representation of identity categories as authentic. In viewing all gendered or sexual identities as socially constructed, queer theory aims to dissolve the naturalization and pathologization of minority identities.

Both trans male and female participants in my research located contemporary feminism and lesbian and gay movements as more welcoming spaces than those of the 1970s and 1980s. The shift away from restrictive gender identity politics within feminism was mirrored by less restrained understandings of sexual identity politics. Illustrating this, research participant Gabrielle reflected, 'Having being to Pride for may be ten years in a row and always feeling out of it 'cuz we weren't included and then we were included and it was magical... And yeah, I do feel included... And I remember going to Pride and going in the women's tent and it was fantastic, scary but fantastic, really exciting' (Gabrielle, age 45). Despite experiencing alienation from feminist and lesbian spaces in the past, then, many participants speak positively about their relationships with current feminist and queer communities, often linking contemporary relationships between trans men and feminist and lesbian communities to broader changes in attitudes towards transgender.

While I celebrate the increased engagement with transgender from strands of feminism and queer cultures, as I (Hines 2006; 2007b) and others (Felski 1996; Rubin 1996; MacDonald 1998; Prosser 1998; Namaste 2000) have argued, there are limitations with queer approaches to transgender – namely that queer theory has a tendency to neglect the material and embodied contours of transgender lives. Queer theory's focus upon transgender as a symbolic site of gender deconstruction means that transgender subjectivities remain under-explored; leaving many transgendered people's experiences unaccounted for. Crucially, though, queer theory's deconstruction of an inside/outside binary detracts from essentializing hierarchies, which marginalize those who, through factors of structure and/or agency, inhabit gender borderlands.

VII. Conclusions

As the chapter began by addressing, transgender people were central to two of the key events in the late 1960s, which paved the way for a more radical and visible gender and sexual politics. Yet, in the main, transgender people's role in feminist and lesbian and gay liberation movements has been marginalized. I have, somewhat tentatively, suggested that queer theory and political activism have effected a departure from sexual identity politics that are informed by rigid notions of entitlement to community membership – marking a move beyond what Devor and Matte (2006) have described as 'a dark corner in the struggle for gay and lesbian rights'.

Yet, in arguing for the forging of present and future connections between transgender, feminist, and lesbian and gay theory and politics, I do not wish to portray a linear account of a theoretical or cultural trajectory from conservative feminist and sexual politics to queer. As this chapter has indicated, a feminist critique of transgender remains vocal in certain feminist politics and theory and within some sections of lesbian and gay communities; moreover, the recognition and celebration of sexual and gender diversity was more than apparent 40 years ago in the riots of Compton's and Stonewall. Thus, queer imaginaries, radical gender and sexual politics, or, what Plummer refers to as 'deviant imaginations' (Chapter 3, this volume), preceded queer theory by four decades. In recognizing past links, then, this chapter argues that it is important to reflect back in order to move forward.

Notes

1. The empirical material on which this chapter draws was gathered during two research projects. The first was completed in the School of Sociology and Social Policy at the University of Leeds between 2000 and 2004 as part of the Economic and Social Research Council (ESRC) research project 'Care, Values and the Future of Welfare' (CAVA). The aims of the research were to examine individual and collective transgender practices of identity and intimacy. Data was generated through two-stage in-depth interviews with 30 transgender women and men in the UK over a 9-month period in 2002. Participants were recruited through research calls posted on electronic transgender forums, social contacting and campaigning websites, and through snowballing techniques. Seventeen participants were transgender women and 13 were transgender men. Participants were at different stages of transition, and the sample included people who use hormone therapy and/or a range of surgical modifications and those who reject such interventions. All participants lived in the UK. The second research project was completed in the School of Sociology and Social Policy at the University of Leeds between 2005 and 2006, and was funded by an ESRC postdoctoral fellowship. The aims of this project were to revisit the original data in relation to the theme of transgender politics and visibility.
2. The 2004 'Gender Recognition Act' (GRA) enabled transgender people to change their birth certificates from the gender as defined at birth to their self-identified gender.

11
Subjectivization, State and Other: On the Limits of Our Political Imagination

Mihnea Panu

This chapter explores, tentatively, the connections between, on the one hand, a form of political imagination that in Western nation-states looks for inspiration to the '1968' moment and, on the other, an understanding of the political as 'critical ontology of ourselves'. The main *problematique* is the contemporary conceptualization of 'difference', analysed as an imperative of all our political involvements. And the analytical concern is with the persisting desire of academics to posit '1968' as the organizing principle of a symbolic, theoretical and political order or reality. I argue that by using '1968' as the ordering principle of history and of the present we create a narrative in which global history is subsumed to and made sense of only in relation to the history of Europe. And we anchor our political practices to technologies of power that function by positing the difference between 'Us' and 'Them' as one of substance, thus acting in synergy with the dominations and exclusions we should rather struggle against. More precisely, that all contemporary political forms that borrow their political ontology from the 1968 moment – various forms of feminism, post-structuralism, multiculturalism, grass-roots movements, identity politics and the list can go on – cannot but support the similar technologies of subjectivization that (neo-)liberal apparatuses use to dominate and exclude. And cannot but make unlikely forms of political and theoretical action that would challenge the fixation as inferior and ultimately expandable of certain sexes, genders, sexualities, phenotypes, genotypes, cultures, geographical locations, histories, religions or socio-economic situations. The imagination of '1968' works today to maintain in place all the relations of power and domination the 1968 events thought they were directed against.

Before proceeding with the argument I must add that I found it interesting to see a chapter problematizing the use of 'difference' as substance and the construction of identity in relation to an irreducible Other included in the 'Alterity' part. To my mind, this part signals the editors' intention to emphasize the split between dominant and marginal discourses in general as well as when '1968' is concerned. Those 'Other Voices' then problematize, rather than reiterate through exegesis or commentary, the European theoretical and political canon usually mobilized to represent '1968'. From this perspective, the inclusion might signal those voices as being themselves Othered: placed in a separate, peripheral ontological category that has yet to acquire the authority or resonance of the main representations of 1968.[1] Then, by signalling this power relation, such placing constitutes a most welcome political practice and can/may help the ensuing argument become more convincing.

I. Politics, identity and the liberal bio-Political apparatuses

Politics is framed here as a 'critical ontology of ourselves', that is, as a 'historic-practical test of the limits we may go beyond' (Foucault 1997: 316), thus implying that politics represents a permanent exercise in the deconstruction/reconstruction of identity. And that the outcome of such a critical exercise is never final, is not the moment of full self-awareness from which unambiguous political activity flows, but is a moment of becoming uncertain of who we are from which a politics founded on 'identity-as-uncertainty' might be attempted. This approach to politics ensues, of course, from an understanding of subjectivity, agency and autonomy as the result of kaleidoscopic power relations rather than as the immanent force that always resists power. Further, it considers that the very power/knowledge relations we denounce as being oppressive or unjust are operating, partly, through the trope of the self-referential, known and closed identity. In other words, if we consider any identity – and, indeed, any reality – to result from one's positioning into a system of differences (same/different, I/Other, true/false, good/bad) as a result of various strategies of power. And if, moreover, we accept that in order to imagine the political, the subjects of the Western nation-state need to mobilize a non-ambivalent self-identity that is constructed within those systems of differences and in relation with Others they rigidly position, then subjectivization, understood as the practices of power through which one is made into a known object and self-knowing subject, represents a central political moment.

While a political strategy constructed in terms of a non-ambivalent, self-same, coherent and unitary identity that is fully immanent, what I shall call here an 'identity-as-substance',[2] cannot but reiterate the exclusions and dominations that found any identity posited as 'full presence'. The conducts[3] that seem politically self-evident to a subjectivity formed within a particular configuration of power and knowledge relations are, indeed, the same conducts that tend to reiterate those constitutive relations and to reduce political action to a momentary tactic of 'fight-or-flight'. In other words, as long as we do not engage in a permanent critique of our political identities, we cannot but continuously act as 'relays' or vessels for the very forms of power we try to overcome, that is, we cannot but contribute to the reiteration and propagation of those power relations without even being aware of it. This is because, if we consider that our deepest impulses result from the internalization of the power relations that form our subjectivity, then a subject's first impulse in a political situation is to engage in conducts that reiterate those formative power relations. For example, it is not at all surprising that certain feminists think of politics as 'politics of the female body' and of sexuality, reproduction and maternity as a political resource in fighting patriarchy. It is precisely as embodied, sexed and reproductive subjects that women are formed and ruled by a patriarchal liberal order and it is precisely the body, sexuality and reproductive characteristics of women that are politically relevant to such an order. It is an obvious tactic to mobilize those most easily accessible resources for political struggles.

At the same time, those 'body politics' are political manoeuvres that do not interrogate critically the relation between, on the one hand, the systems of power and knowledge that form an inferior, Other or particular subject – in this case the liberal patriarchal systems that form one as woman – and, on the other hand, that subject's desires, goals, conducts or politics. Rather, since those 'body politics' are founded exclusively on the resources and ontological traits of the subject 'woman' as defined by liberal patriarchy, in the long run they end up reinforcing the system's ability to fix such subjects as Other. This is not to say that those struggles that use the female body as tactical resource are not a necessary and often productive political tactic in resisting liberal patriarchy and misogyny. But it is to wonder if they can go beyond the 'fight-or-flight' reaction I was previously mentioning, in the sense that their exclusive confinement to the field of liberal patriarchal power might not succeed in ever dismantling the relations that lock women as inferior. And maybe this tactical cul-de-sac has something to do with the surprisingly efficient smothering of the radical and compelling critiques feminism put forward by the flaccid patriarchal truisms some call 'post-feminism'. What this chapter argues then is, first, whenever a political struggle is organized around an identity that is closed, it acts to strengthen the processes of Othering that make political struggle necessary in the first place. Second, Othering represents a central political technology of most contemporary systems of domination and especially of (neo-)liberal systems. Third, the political imagination spawned by the 1968 moment stimulates precisely those political projects operating through Othering. Thus, continuing to use 1968 to fuel our political imagination helps to strengthen any dominant identity that is defined in relation to its Other and all power relations that are structured by such binaries, including colonialism, racism, patriarchy, homophobia, pauperism[4] or eugenics. To argue these points I shall start with a brief analysis of the liberal governmental apparatuses, since it is hard to contest that those apparatuses determine, in one form or another, all contemporary subjectivities.

I shall think of 'government' as the attempt to structure the possible actions of others, that is, to elaborate governmental apparatuses that aim to shape the conduct of subjects by acting on their environment, circumstances or will according to specific ideas of 'truth' and 'good'. Then, to govern involves bringing into being a version of the reality of the governed objects – that is to say, of the population in its various guises from bio-medical to sociological, consumerist, working or electoral – amenable to specific intervention tactics and technologies (see Foucault 1991; Rose and Miller 1992; Rose 1999). Those realities remain structured by the Enlightenment idea of governing as an enterprise for linking the progress of truth and the history of liberty (Foucault 1997: 312). And I would argue that liberalism, as the dominant governing regime of our time and space, has two crucial characteristics. First, liberal apparatuses, in their reliance on a version of truth that did not set itself free from the Enlightenment ideals of knowledge and science, recodify in law and norm the violences that found Enlightenment universalism (see Foucault 1998: 378): positivism, patriarchy, Eurocentrism, colonialism, racism, heterosexism, homophobia, eugenics, slavery and genocide. To mention but a well-known example, both liberal biopolitical apparatuses and the liberal subject are crucially concerned with sexuality and reproduction, nodal points whose systematically racialized and gendered nature has in liberalism genealogies going back to empire and slavery. And we can systematically trace those genealogies of liberal brutality, ontological and physical, in all liberal apparatuses that aim to constitute or preserve 'bourgeois subjectivity' (see Stoler 1995), that is, in the governmental apparatuses regulating the family, child-rearing, domesticity, ownership, self-restraint, work ethic, criminality, deviance and so on.

Second, liberal apparatuses depend on a construction of identity-as-substance and implicitly of difference-as-difference-of-substance. Evidently, liberal apparatuses depend on a type of scientific expertise that cannot read reality, thus cannot make identities intelligible and possible to affect, unless in terms of an unambiguous 'substance'. The scientific segmentations and taxonomies of the social on which governing reality depends operate exclusively with objects whose natural, unambivalent and true identities are revealed to the observer using the correct methodology. I would therefore argue that liberal subjectivization operates through Othering, where Othering is understood precisely as the ontological fixation of difference as a difference-of-substance. While at the same time, which among the observed differences are considered to have ontological weight, that is, to express the nature of the objects, is determined by the above-mentioned genealogy of liberal governing. Then, within a grid of intelligibility shaped by liberal apparatuses, I can perceive the different substance of the Other, her full presence or absolute absence, because who I am is 'worked entirely from within' (see Nancy 1991) and non-ambivalent; because the truth of objects is revealed to me in an unmediated and undistorted manner; and because identities, especially the 'I', can be known in a complete and final manner. Othering makes difference completely external to both the 'I' and the 'I/Other' relation and thus dissociates difference from the strategies of truth and power that form reality and place it outside the reach of our critical analyses of reality (see Butler 1990: 184).

Othering fulfils several functions in liberalism: (1) it helps to accommodate the contradiction between its understanding of freedom as negative and its 'will to govern'. Liberalism cannot define non-compliant subjects as autonomous individuals that chose to 'do Otherwise', nor as a result of the systematic failure of the liberal bio-politics to secure the well-being and prosperity of the polity. However, if the non-compliant citizens are different-in-substance from the ideal-type liberal citizen, they cease being autonomous individuals towards which liberal governing has responsibilities, either of non-intervention or of support. On the contrary, those Others fail to attain autonomy as a result of their own incompatibility with the universalism of liberalism.

(2) Othering aligns with political goals the irresolvable liberal tension between the universal and the particular by making it possible,

whenever necessary, to translate those governmentally defined as 'particular' into those governmentally defined as 'Other', and vice-versa. As Marxist, feminist and post-colonial studies have exhaustively argued, when the 'normal' liberal individual is made universal all specificity is removed from him. He is outside any sexuality, culture, gender, race or ethnicity. On the contrary, in liberal polities the 'particular' is the citizen that does not fit the 'universal' ontological category and is therefore identified as racialized, ethnic, gendered, sexualized or 'cultural'. An identification that utilizes precisely the same nodal points to fix 'difference-as-substance' as liberal Othering. Thus, 'particular' or 'special' and Other are made the same in the liberal discourses. Paradoxically, that means that the liberal governmental gaze is always-already 'particularized'; that is, it sees and aims to regulate preferentially those defined as ontologically different or particular. Moreover, since contemporary bio-politics operate through the double bind of 'individualizing' and 'totalizing' power, they can retreat into one of those guises ('same' or 'different') when the other arm is under attack and thus create the social *qua* polity as an entity with fluctuating boundaries, retracted or extended according to the governmental logics of the moment, to include or exclude certain social identities from society. This double bind keeps the identities constituted as 'particular/Other' in an 'in/out' wavering position: the presence of the 'abject Other' (see Butler 1993: 57–93) that polices the boundaries of normality remains well hidden when liberal political structures adopt their universalizing mode, while being spectacularly displayed in their particular mode (e.g., in multiculturalism or the 'War on Terror').

(3) Othering prevents the dislocation of the liberal systems of power/knowledge. Since Othering makes the critical interrogation of wider systems of subjectivization (patriarchy, neo-colonialism, racism, positivism, Eurocentrism) increasingly difficult, the same rules of truth-formation are repeated with each governmental investigation of socio-pathology, 'finding' each time the same subjects as pathological (the unemployed; the poor; the homeless; the single and/or incompetent mothers; the dissolute women; the 'abnormal family'; the immigrants; the racialized and ethnicized and especially the Black race, family, cultures or genders; the addicts; the perverts; the lazy; the 'dependent'; the 'illiberal'). Through such systematic reiteration of the nodal points and organizing dichotomies that shape 'bourgeois subjectivity', Othering stabilizes the differential systems of the liberal discourse that equate this subjectivity with 'good' and 'freedom'.

II. 1968 and the contemporary political imagination

To what extent is a political imagination inspired by 1968 acting in synergy with liberal Othering? And what are the understandings of power and subjectivity that we reiterate when tracing our political roots to 1968? Of course, the May 1968 moment went through a chain of interpretive moments, from being described as the crucial revolution in politics to being described as opening the road for the neo-liberal individualist hedonism of the 1980s. A definitive interpretation is probably out of our reach. Nevertheless, I think we can confidently identify a set of recurrent themes that our political imagination – including that of theorists like Bourdieu, Lefebvre, Lefort or Castoriadis (see Seidman 2004) – attributes to those events, themes that include the moment of a momentous change in conducts and ideas that inaugurated a new political order; a revolutionary cultural, social and political crisis; the refusal of a decomposing society and a major challenge to the bureaucratic-consumer society; a challenge to university, hierarchy, a repressive state and traditional politics; a cultural rebellion that led to a more emancipated society; the reconquest of urban spaces; the reinvention of participatory democracy, collective action, including *autogestion* (the self-management of worker's control); the birth point of contemporary feminism; or a radical resocialization through the connection of individual liberation and collectivity.

The question this chapter asks therefore can now be rephrased: 'Is it that, as long as we persist in analysing 1968 as that revolutionary moment described by these themes, and as long as we strive to recycle these themes as foundations of our political investments, we are supporting and reproducing the above-mentioned strategies, tactics and technologies of Othering?' The remainder of this chapter will argue that, indeed, harnessing our political imagination to the 1968 moment works in synergy with liberal apparatuses and that such an alignment of liberal subjectivization and 'civil' political imagination creates 'dense transfer points' of power that thwart politics as 'critical ontology of ourselves' (see Brown 1995; Foucault 1997).

I have already argued that, whenever they assume their identity as a 'substance', the subject is not that which resists power but the medium through which power circulates. This is since, simply by 'being ourselves', we reproduce those obligatory 'passage points' of subjectivity without which we cannot make sense of who we are in the contemporary social configuration: our sex, gender, race, ethnicity, desires, thoughts and so on. How does this mechanism work in the case of the liberal subject? The political imagination of this subject is structured by the nodal points of liberal subjectivization and therefore thinks politics in the register of freedom, autonomy from repression and more generally from power, equality in difference, representative democracy or sovereignty. This subject hopes to achieve fulfilment and/or emancipation through legal or human rights, sex, (ethical) consumption, liberal achievement (education, financial status, social status, employment status, habitus), improved individualism (securing and defending personal space, making one's voice heard in the liberal socio-political arena, being recognized as special or particular), self-affirmation (discovering and asserting one's real self, removing obstacles towards self-fulfilment, letting one's specialness shine) and so on. All those political tactics remain firmly grounded in liberal understandings of the self and the political and therefore are impotent in contesting liberal rule and least of all its subtle technologies of Othering. On the contrary, they affirm a compulsive – and probably masochistic (see Brown 2001: 45–62) – desire for liberal order and Othering even while they antagonize it. In what follows I will discuss some of those tactics to exemplify how our desire for the 1968 moment is instrumental in maintaining us within this enfeebling and narrow political field. More specifically, I will argue that our desire for 1968 insidiously makes our politics dependent on forms of Othering like Eurocentrism, understandings of power as repressive and of political ontologies as a-relational, and identity-politics.

Eurocentrism

If we think identity as a historically contingent construction, then, especially after the European colonial endeavour, it is difficult to imagine any identity relevant to the 'analysis of ourselves' that is formed outside a relation between an identity posited as 'Western' and one posited as 'non-Western'. Any contemporary identity, in as much as it participates in a discursive economy structured by 'truth', 'capitalism', 'science', 'progress', 'freedom', 'democracy', 'prosperity' or 'civilization', needs to critically problematize its relation with 'Europe'. Positing 1968 as the origin point of all that is significant in contemporary politics does not engage in this problematization in any politically interesting manner. Rather, seeing a global political landscape through the lens of an event happening in Europe, as the endless commentary on 1968 does, consolidates Europe and Europeanism as 'entirely worked from within' in a global perspective and reiterates the racialized core of the European Enlightenment that liberal apparatuses so subtly incorporate. This desire for 1968 seems to mark our compulsive longing to reposition authentic politico-ontological reflexivity and authentic transformative political action in its traditional European centre. In other words, to reaffirm Europe as the 'theatre of history' and the engine of global progress. Of course, the choice of '1968' as the ordering principle of contemporary history and as origin and end-point of transformative politics is made self-evident by the attention this hyped event instantly commands for any politico-theoretical project and by the present status of '1968' as a signifier of radical political struggle. However, selecting this 'ready-made' signifier of radicalism can transform a project that aspires to be politically radical into an innocent vessel of Eurocentric power and implicitly of liberal-capitalist narratives of modernity. Often those reiterations of Eurocentrism are done with the good intention of praising global political struggle. Nevertheless, the imperative of using '1968' as the historical grid of intelligibility means that those global historical events often become political satellites orbiting the sun of 'Paris 1968' – and more generally student revolts or workers' struggles – in the overdeveloped world. Decade long anti-colonial struggles are put on a *par* with the three weeks of upheaval in Paris. Genealogies are constructed that, following a pattern extensively used in classical nationalist narratives of the birth of the Nation or liberal narratives of modernity, arrange heterogeneous global events, from the Tet Offensive to the Civil Rights Movement and to the birth of the Palestine Liberation Organisation (PLO), into historical continuities of which '1968' is both the final purpose and the moment of rupture from which a new world history irradiates. However, whenever we discuss '1968' as being a global phenomenon we elide the fact that what we fundamentally mean by '1968' are the socio-political and theoretical events of France. Thus, all those projects end up engulfing under the '1968' signifier, all generically 'anti-bourgeois' moments of revolt or social unrest happening around the world in the late 1960s and subsequently universalizing the European, and specifically French,[5] 1968 moment into an original model that, yet again, galvanizes and educates the rest of the world. They contribute to the erasure of the particularities of those other events and subsume the differences between their genealogies to a master European narrative. I would suggest that we reanalyse our 'bringing home' of progress, history and reflexivity to Europe using the mythical progressive moment of 1968. And, moreover, that obsessively repositing students as the revolutionary class might be suggestive of our own desire as academics to be represented as the original revolutionary (super?) class.

At the same time, the more reflexive contemporary avatars of 'Eurocentrism' include a form of 'respect of the Other' that collapses identity making into European solipsism, thus further calcifying the Europe/Rest difference. When this European 'respect of the Other' posits the experience of the Other as irreducible to my own – European – experience, it cannot but isolate the Other on one side of an Us/Other dichotomy that maintains 'truth' and 'the good' as defining traits of 'Us'. I will illustrate this idea with two examples of Othering in the fathers of some of our political thinking. Thinking about the difference between the Whites and the primitive Negro, Kant asserts, 'So fundamental is the difference between these two races of man, and it appears to be as great in regard to mental capacities as in colour' (in Eze 1997: 55). While Hegel (in Eze 1997: 127) affirms that in general 'in the interior of Africa, the consciousness of the inhabitants has not yet reached an awareness of any substantial and objective existence'. The African, therefore, remains as foundationally different and incomprehensible to the self-aware European as a dog, or as an ancient Greek (Hegel in Eze 1997: 128). It is in the name of this difference that Hegel legitimizes slavery of the African and European colonialism. In our political times, the peril in the moves that posit ethics to be the acceptance of the Other as irreducibly different is to construct the political around a moment of solipsism that can be used to erase both the political significance of responsibility for the Other and the presence of the Other in the Self. To insist: if intelligible reality results from strategies of truth-formation and, therefore, both I and the Other are known and affected through practices of power tributary to those strategies of truth, then positing the acknowledgement that we cannot reduce the Other to our own categories (emotional, cognitive and so on) as the defining political-ethical moment – while resulting from an understandable fear of repeating the genocidal violence of recent European history – cannot account for the collective construction of onto-epistemological frameworks. It suggests the possibility of boundaries that separate me completely from any Other (Nancy 1991). And, more importantly, refuses to submit to critical analysis precisely that which I consider to be the political object par excellence: the strategies of truth-formation. In this guise, the Western-liberal political actor risks being defined as the monadic subject that cannot know and that, therefore, remains the passive object of the power/knowledge relations that form it. In a nutshell, when positing the Other as irreducible difference, our fear of 'totalitarianism' runs the risk of mutating into an upholding of 'difference as substance', as opposed to prompting an analysis of 'difference' as a political moment of truth-formation. An image of the social that remains too close for comfort to the liberal understandings.

Power as repressive and the subject as (individual) agent

Othering, and especially liberal Othering, depends on the positing of identities as 'worked entirely from within' and, therefore, as developed independently of and in opposition to power. The political imagination spawned by the 1968 moment puts forward the same neo-liberal understandings of freedom as absence of power, of liberty as the antagonism of regulation and thus of radical individualism, counter-cultural libertarianism and focus on pleasure. Think only of some of the slogans engendered by the 1968 moment and given cult status today: *'Il est interdit d'interdire*; No God and no master; God is me; Live without dead time; Enjoy without obstacles; Take your desires for reality; Boredom is counter-revolutionary; I came on the cobblestones; The more I make revolution the more I want to make love'. To go back to the previous comment on the 'body politics' of feminism, it is striking that in a politico-theoretical landscape that circulates – but seems to give no weight to – Lacanian psycho-analysis, post-structuralist feminism and queer studies, we still need to hark back to those discourses that relentlessly converge in their emphasis on personal liberation *through* desire and sexuality. Such constructions of sexuality as liberation set 'sex' as the core of subjectivity, as the pre-social and either hidden or repressed truth of the subject that awaits liberation, as the explanatory and emancipating nodal point of contemporary subjectivity. A nostalgia that cannot but confine our truth and freedom within the circuits of various expert technologies of sex, while stubbornly refusing to engage critically with sex as a 'fictitious unity' that is strategically essential to the construction and ruling of the contemporary liberal-capitalist subject (see Butler 1990; Foucault 1990; Rose 1989). In fact, all those imaginings of the political as emancipation of desire and/or the true self from technocratic, State and expert control act in synergy with a liberal bio-politics equally sceptical of the State's possibility to know and equally convinced of the need to respect, nurture and elicit the natural order of the social, population, individual or market. They further fail to see how our longing for emancipation from repression makes us especially prone to being seduced by the liberal apparatuses that operate through enticement, channelling, arousal – in a word, through the *construction* of subjectivity. Thus, giving in to such seduction replaces the analysis of the power-knowledge strategies that shape our subjectivities with a compulsive desire for a conservative form of 'self-affirmation'. The critiques of the State and of professions and expertise that bloomed in the late 1960s and exploded in 1968 are based on a renewed emphasis on personal needs and expression, on difference, on the culture of the self and its actualization. They equate political activity with various techniques of consciousness raising, empowerment, self-esteem, alternative pedagogy; with the rhetoric of voice and representation; with a focus on 'active citizenship', 'active society' (Dean 1999: 161); and with a 'post-modern libertarianism' that, in its insistence on 'responsibility' and 'self-determination' as the crucial political moment, plays the game of neo-liberal definitions of the social space as divided into 'private' and 'public' and as structured by 'pluralism'. The contemporary liberal subject is a product of those critiques and techniques and in its compulsive search for self-affirmation as freedom actively reinvests its desire for self-discovery into the neo-liberal apparatuses that work to reiterate the making of the bourgeois selfhood around the compulsory moments of gender, sex or race and in opposition to its gendered, sexualized and racialized Others.

Moreover, those understandings of politics as the fight of the repressed and oppressed against power make us think of an emancipatory politics as exclusively 'bottom-up', that is, in opposition to a centre of power most frequently associated with the State. This thinking, itself reiterated each time we think of 1968 as an event to be emulated, marks the dominant contemporary political trends like 'strategic essentialism' that will be discussed below. For the moment, I would suggest that any understanding of politics in terms of a top and a bottom must be approached with caution. Its problematic nature is double: it not only reifies the State as the centre of power but also falls back on the sentimentalism of the 'authentic subject', untouched by power and, therefore, in a privileged relation to truth – what Wendy Brown (1995) terms a 'politics of resentment'. First, it is dubious that the State is a coherent machine of social control. One look at how liberal apparatuses function will reveal heterogeneous – and frequently ill-coordinated or contradictory – discourses and technologies at work. Moreover, the foundational assumptions of liberalism do not originate in the State nor do they express the will of a ruling class.[6] Rather, the State is one of the factors that contributes to the organization, hierarchizing and co-ordination – thus to the propagation and intensification – of disparate clusters of power relations that originate in the social nexus and that render the functioning of governing apparatuses possible (Foucault 1980: 122). The great molar centres are always 'immersed in the molecular soup that nourishes them and makes their outlines waver' (Deleuze and Guattari 1988: 225). Thus, the formation of the contemporary subject – including as able to imagine herself as free and self-actualizing – is not prior to its relation with the governing apparatuses that regulate 'bourgeois selfhood', but takes place in relation to (expert) knowledges and technologies that are at some point engendered by, encouraged by, organized by or intersecting such apparatuses. If this is the case, then positing power as always forbidding or the State as the unambiguous centre of power can only enhance our uncritical want for those liberal apparatuses that function 'at a distance' and through enticement of desire, apparatuses that equate freedom with 'unconstrained choice'.

Political uses of identity: 'strategic essentialism'

To conclude this chapter, I will discuss a model of the political use of identity: strategic essentialism. The relevance of this discussion for the present topic is that this strategy, like all identity-politics, is founded on the I/Other dichotomy. In other words, it addresses and contests liberal universalism from the position of particular or Other it is ascribed or, if you prefer, pursues political gains through self-Othering. Moreover, in their claims for difference, self-discovery, self-affirmation and freedom from the power regime of liberal universalism, identity-politics are types of political practices that anyone positing 1968 as the opening of a new and radical political horizon would logically have to condone. Once again, my discussion should not be taken as dismissing such politics 'en bloc'. The necessity for such resistances is not doubted and their political outcomes impossible to predict. At the time of writing, the struggle for a separate Afrocentric educational system in Ontario, Canada, seems a most refreshing and hope-inducing one. There is an undisputable need to rupture the insidiously racist technologies of liberal governing and opting out of the universal liberal polity might be one interesting modality of doing it. What this discussion rather doubts is the ability of present strategic essentialism or multiculturalism strategies to achieve such a rupture, or in fact their ability to achieve anything more than commanding more resources – rights, recognition, money, institutional networks – within a political landscape defined in liberal terms.

To counterbalance the by now impossible to ignore critiques of a 'worked-from-within' identity on which politics are to be founded, while continuing to keep political struggle on the terrain of identity as self-affirmation, contemporary critics envisage 'essentialism' as a momentary strategy to be surpassed once political gains are obtained. As a conservative moment that makes possible a more radical future political struggle. However, can this strategic reconfiguration of identity-politics transcend a reduction of identity to a 'centre' more easily than its older, 'un-strategic' versions? Or is it forced to reduce the collective selves to a defining trait of what we 'are', be that race, gender, sexuality, ethnicity, religion or genotype? If this is the case, then there ensues a cascading list of political consequences. Strategic uses of identity-politics do not and cannot militate for an ontological dislocation of the liberal framing of difference since they depend on this frame to self-define as special and thus to justify their demands. The political critique of liberal Othering is then reduced to an apolitical competition for resources within a liberal-pluralist framework. Moreover, since essentializing erases the formative 'I/Other' relationship from its make-up, each such political affirmation of self-identity unsuspectingly internalizes and reiterates the original ontological hierarchy. Thus, strategic uses of identity-politics reiterate the universalism of the dominant identity – White, European, bourgeois, man, heterosexual – and its own Othering with every reiteration of self-identity. And, once an identity is strategically made into a substance, both the political demands placed on the State in its name and the processes of identity-formation subsequent to those demands being met work towards the further naturalization of the identity in question. That is, the deconstructive moment that we expect to follow from the moment of strategic essentialism is made increasingly improbable and difficult precisely by this political strategy's consolidation of identity in the liberal language of law or science; or in the subsequent mechanics of identity-formation of those liberal subjects defined by this identity. The more resources are demanded or mobilized in the name of one's difference, the more rigid the boundaries of that social group have to be and the more self-evident the liberal game of universal/particular seems.

III. In(stead of) conclusion: (an)Other rethinking of the political?

As long as they continue to define themselves in relation to presumed founding events like 1968, contemporary political imaginings remain inextricably linked to, and depend for their self-conceptualizations on, the liberal nation-state project and thus on the Enlightenment project of discovering true and final identities. Therefore, they make impossible understandings of politics as the permanent contestation of 'who we are now' – and it is maybe this denial of fluidity that creates the contemporary political resignation, fatalism, anger and frustration. However, the present critique is not a resolution and there is no talking about the political as if its nature and implications are sorted once and for all. In fact, even looking at the 'problem' of politics in terms of a 'solution' might prove to be an unfruitful approach. Moreover, cowardly, the chapter proposed this critique without offering substantive solutions. However, isn't it that such cowardice, at least in our present political configuration, constitutes a valid political strategy in itself, maybe the only strategy I can justify within an understanding of reality as 'relational' and as consisting of 'events'? If there is no political identity and no political position that is free of power or 'worked entirely from within'. If the political represents the never-concluded clearing of political spaces from power/knowledge relations that aim to fix them as immutable. And if, finally, we need to rethink history as strings of 'events' that are both contingent and – possibly infinitely – multifaceted, then, both placing any of those events as compulsory origins and aiming to construct political projects in terms of utopias are irrelevant political strategies. However, if our political goals are to enable the possibility of no longer being, doing, or thinking what we are, do or think (Foucault 1997), then engaging critically in deconstruction, even while shying away from putting forward incontrovertible solutions, represents a valid political stance.

Notes

1. I am thinking here of Latour's (1987: 92–3) definition of reality as the ability to elaborate definitions that resist the trials of strength a contestant could subject them to – the Latin *res* means 'to resist'.
2. I borrow this term from Gilles Deleuze. See May (2005) for an introduction to the concept.
3. Extrapolating from Foucault's (1991) formulation of governing as the 'conduct of conduct', I use conduct to mean not only acts or behaviours but also desires, drives, goals, thoughts, emotions, or indeed whatever capabilities we consider to found our (political) identities.
4. By 'pauperism', I mean the construction of poverty as abnormal and of the poor as the Other of the normal citizen.
5. We should not forget that the 1968 events in Paris made copious use of the rhetoric and symbols of past *French* revolutionary events.
6. The issue of the relation between truth and the 'ruling class' is too complex to be discussed in this context. However, rather than adopting an idea of a bourgeoisie that builds an ideology to serve its purpose, I would argue that the bourgeoisie was itself born into and through the workings of a set of discourses and power relations. Like all subjects, the bourgeoisie is as much an effect of those relations as it is a relay for them.

Conclusion: When Did 1968 End?

William Outhwaite

My 1968 began promptly on New Year's Day when I caught the slow cross-country train from Manchester to Harwich and thence to Hoek van Holland and by train to Basle. After that, the year was substantially one of missed opportunities. I spent the next four months learning German in the Black Forest and a further four months consolidating it in a temporary job in Basle. By then, the German movement was substantially over. (*Die Zeit* recently published a photo of Ralf Dahrendorf and Daniel Cohn-Bendit debating at an open-air meeting in nearby Freiburg, but that was the previous year.) In Basle, I was only a tram ride from the French border, and crossed it occasionally, but there was nothing to see in the small border town and with the general strike no obvious way of getting to Paris. I again missed seeing Cohn-Bendit when he was replaced on a visit to a student meeting in Basle by another member of the *Mouvement du 22 mars*, which seemed to have been worried about a personality cult developing round him. There were some more demonstrations and meetings, including one addressed by Elmar Altvater, but that was about it as far as I was concerned. Back in England in the autumn, and beginning to study PPE (Politics, Philosophy, Economics) at Oxford, I went on the big anti-Vietnam demonstration in London at the end of October, which so scared the BBC that they sent programme tapes to Birmingham in case their buildings were occupied, but I opted out of the more adventurous side-trip to attack the US Embassy. For as long as it lasted, I was a member (not that there was anything as formal as membership) of the Oxford Revolutionary Socialist Students (ORSS).

Nostalgia isn't what it used to be, and having already accepted an invitation to write a kind of memoir, in the volume edited by Alan Sica and Stephen P. Turner (Outhwaite 2005), I am one of the last people who should be indulging in any more Mayalgia. There is however a sense in which the Western 1968 (the Eastern European one was very different, though to some extent overlapping)[1] is a year defined by process rather than outcome, inviting a focus on its phenomenology rather than an analysis of its material causes and consequences. In other words, the memory, true or false, is to a substantial extent the reality.

An excellent edited volume by Gerd-Rainer Horn and Padraic Kenney (2004) on *Transnational Moments of Change: Europe 1945, 1968, 1989* puts 1968 into an appropriate context. '1968' differs, however from the other two years, I think, in that they both brought a specific outcome: the end of dictatorship and, for much of Europe, occupation, war and genocide. We may be nostalgic for the demonstrations or for the breaching of the Berlin Wall in the wonderful autumn of 1989 and, if we are old enough, for the celebrations of victory or liberation in 1945, but these are in a sense ancillary to the main events: in 1968, the main event *was* the *événements*.

'1968' is often likened to two revolutionary years in the nineteenth century: 1848 and 1871 (the year of the Paris Commune). Here, also, the outcomes were disappointing, especially if compared (a little harshly) to the great revolution of 1789. Their after-lives were largely on the terrain of memory: as the 'springtime of peoples' or as the rehearsal for the expected socialist revolution which finally came, in a rather unexpected form and venue, in 1917.[2]

'1848', like 1989, is a relevant comparison year for another reason: the international character of the movements and the way in which events in one location served as a model for others. But whereas 1989 displays a relatively simple domino pattern, ironically imitating in reverse motion the Western strategists' earlier image of the spread of communism, the temporalities of 1968 were significantly different in different parts of the West. In France, of course, most things happened in May, but in Germany the movement was by then already in decline, with a last failed attempt to prevent the government's emergency legislation finally passed at the end of the month. In Italy the student movements had peaked earlier in the spring, though the workers were beginning a series of movements lasting into the mid-1970s which gave the 'hot autumn' of 1969 and the '68 years' their names and led Colin Crouch and Alessandro Pizzorno, perhaps over-influenced by the Italian case, to write of the 'Resurgence of Class Conflict in Western Europe Since 1968' (Crouch and Pizzorno 1978).

Before we ask, then, when 1968 ended, we should ask when it began. In France, as Maud Anne Bracke notes in her chapter, it has become common to speak of 'the '68 years' (*les années 68*) as running from the end of the Algerian War in 1962 to the presidential election of 1981 which brought the socialist François Mitterand to power. Yet as late as 15 March 1968, a journalist could write in *Le Monde* that 'France is bored'; a week later the *Mouvement du 22 mars* had occupied the university at Nanterre and the rest, as they say, is history.

As Patricia Hill Collins reminds us in her chapter, which neatly links the mobilization for Obama's election victory in 2008 with the 1968 struggles,[3] we should go back a little earlier and to the largely Marxism-free zone of the US, where students had been involved in the Civil Rights Movement from the beginning of the 1960s. The Berkeley Free Speech Movement of 1964 had a typically banal origin in the university's attempt to ban activity of a Hyde Park Corner type from a site on the edge of the campus. A few months later, the Vietnam War had become the *cause célèbre* which it remained until the US was driven out in 1973. In Europe, student movements in Belgium, Italy, Germany and finally France became a significant force in 1966 and 1967. But the protests against the Vietnam War and against the militarization of West Germany had earlier roots in the Campaign for Nuclear Disarmament in the UK and the German 'Easter marches' modelled on it.

The intellectual bases of the student and related movements had also been laid in the early 1960s by the European and North American New Left (The British *New Left Review* was launched in 1960) and boosted by such books as Marcuse's *One Dimensional Man* of 1964. Neo-Marxist theory was one important element, finding institutional expression in new political parties like the French PSU (Parti Socialiste Unifié), the British and French Trotskyist *groupuscules* and student organizations like the US and German SDS (Students for a Democratic Society and Sozialistische Deutsche Studentenschaft, respectively).[4] The new left, as Horn (2007: 212) points out, came together with sections of the old left (communists in Italy though not in France; in West Germany and the UK there were hardly any) in what can be called a new far left, often theoretically dogmatic and practically utopian but anti-authoritarian. (The anti-authoritarian dimension, drawing on the critical theory of what had come to be called the Frankfurt School, was particularly strong in Germany, for obvious historical reasons.)

Also important was Situationism, a movement with affinities to surrealism and a substantial physical presence in the Amsterdam Provos and Kabouters. An early student movement event was the publication of a Situationist pamphlet on 'the misery of the student condition' in Strasbourg in November 1966, and Raoul Vaneigem's *Traité de savoir-vivre à l'usage des jeunes générations* was published in 1968.

178 Conclusion: When Did 1968 End?

The choreography of the demonstrations, occupations and other events and their textual counterpart in leaflets and posters owed as much to Situationism as to the more stolid traditions of revolutionary Marxism.

The components of the 1968 movements, then, were diverse, as were their temporalities in different countries and cities. And yet there were all sorts of geographical and sectoral cross-overs and linkages, including, in France and Italy, the much-desired opening to the workers. A causal analysis of the movements is confronted with something that Montesquieu recognized in the mid-eighteenth century: the need to relate long-term trends with specific events. If a Berlin policeman had not shot dead a student demonstrating against a visit by the Iranian Shah and dictator in 1967, the Berlin movements might well not have spread to the rest of the country. Conversely, if De Gaulle's helicopter ride on 29 May 1968 to visit the commander of French forces in Germany had not strengthened his resolve, his regime might have fallen. There were political specificities which contributed to the success of the movements. De Gaulle was ageing and had been in power for ten years ('dix ans, ça suffit' was one slogan); the contradictions between his confrontational strategy ('reform yes, fuck-up no') and that of his more conciliatory prime minister, Pompidou, were an important source of weakness. In Germany, a 'grand coalition' of Christian Democrats and Socialists had made the need for an opposition outside parliament (APO) seem particularly obvious, and the country's Nazi past made emergency laws and police brutality more than usually sensitive issues. Or if, on the other hand, Harold Wilson had given in to US pressure, as of course British prime ministers habitually do, and sent some troops to Vietnam, the demonstrations which formed the main theme of the British movement might have been even better supported.

When, then, did 1968 end? The 1968 movements in the 'West' had few immediate and concrete results. There were pay increases in France, rapidly eroded by inflation, and some organizational reforms in higher education there and in West Germany. Only in Italy was there a lasting demonstration effect on working-class militancy. In Britain, as Mick Jagger complained, there was 'no place for a street-fighting man in sleepy London town'. The effects of 1968 have rather to be seen in longer-term cultural and generational terms. As Ken Plummer writes in his chapter, 'A range of movements existed before 1968 in relative isolation and quietness, but the furore of 1968 helped them to develop in the years between 1969 and 1975...' At the same time, however, as Stephen Frosh writes, 'The capacity of an administered society to absorb dissent... is nowhere more visible than in the consequences of the 1968 revolts.'

In one sense, '1968' was over well before the end of the calendar year. In France, it was pretty much over by the end of May. The factories and universities were back at work; the Gaullist regime was secure again, though the General made his long-threatened and overdue departure in the following year, and the hopes and fears of insurrection rapidly dissipated. The 1973 'oil shock' and the restriction of pay increases and state spending, later consecrated by the ideological and electoral successes of neo-liberalism, could be seen as a further milestone or tombstone for the end of 1968. We should probably pay more attention to 1973–74 as a crucial turning-point for Western capitalism and the welfare state. This was the end of the 'thirty glorious' post-war years of prosperity and the beginning of an age of welfare cutbacks (often coinciding with growing expenditure) and of what we can now recognize as the increasing marginalization of Europe and North America in global capitalism.

Another, more local and political milestone might be the *Berufsverbot* in West Germany in 1972, introduced by Willy Brandt's socialist-dominated government which followed the grand coalition and banning those linked with 'anti-constitutional' movements from public employment (both of these terms being broadly defined). Here again we must note the very different political climates across otherwise similar Western European democracies. In Italy or France, to be a communist was perfectly normal. In Britain, it was statistically abnormal, but something of little interest, except perhaps to the security services. In Germany, it could lose you your job. In Germany, too, 1977 marked the effective end of leftist terrorism (which itself was, of course, one desperate response to the perceived failure of 1968), with only a few sporadic repeat attempts in the following few years. In France, there was no continuity between 1968 and the later terrorism of *Action Directe* (Wieviorka 1998: 281); here, there also remained a serious Trotskyist political presence. In Northern Ireland, 1968 meant a different kind of protest, demanding fair access to jobs and other resources for the Catholic population; the Unionist backlash against what it saw as just another wave of republicanism led to a serious political and military confrontation which has only recently ended.

'1989' is of course another crucial landmark in relation to 1968 (Armbruster *et al* 2009; see also Jarausch 1998). In Czechoslovakia and across the Soviet bloc as a whole, it marked a clear end to the period initiated by the 'Eastern' 1968 of reform in the spring followed by repression in August and 'normalization' thereafter. The failure of 1968 in that part of the world was, along with those of 1953 in East Germany and 1956 in Hungary, a further unmasking of state socialism as a viable alternative to capitalism. Later on, for leftists in the West, 1989 was the demise of a real, if unattractive, alternative, which could be seen either positively, as the removal of a distraction to the pursuit of socialism in the West, or, more pessimistically, as a sign of its unviability. But to the extent that 1968 was a *communist* movement (Touraine 1968), the events of 1989 might be seen as another end-point.

This raises a broader issue. Not surprisingly, since they were substantially student movements, the 1968 movements attracted a lot of attention from academic contemporaries, some of whom were themselves active in the movements. Opinions divide roughly between those sympathetic to the movements (though often critical as well) and more dismissive ones, such as Raymond Aron's book on the 'Elusive Revolution', in which Marxism is presented as (in the title of another of his books) 'The Opium of the Intellectuals', or Erwin Scheuch's collection called 'The Anabaptists of the Welfare Society' – the term refers to an extremist early protestant revolutionary sect. Alain Touraine's book provides a sympathetic, but critical, discussion of the 'utopian communism' of the movement as a rather confused reaction to the emergence of a post-industrial society in which conflicts around the use of *knowledge* would become as important as those over the (other) forces of production.

In Germany, the student movement divided the critical theorists of what had come to be called the Frankfurt School, following the return of the Institute for Social Research to Frankfurt in 1950. Adorno (1903–69), the director of the Institute after 1958, like Horkheimer (1895–1973), deplored what he saw as the dangerous 'adventurism' of the movements, whereas Herbert Marcuse (1898–1979), based in California but making occasional visits to Germany, strongly supported them. He wrote to Adorno in April 1969: 'We cannot avoid the fact that these students are influenced by us (and certainly not least by you)' (Gilcher-Holtey 1998: 168).

Marcuse, unlike Adorno and Horkheimer, had been politically active at the end of the First World War. Habermas, born in 1929, was a generation apart from them. A teenager in the final years of the Second World War, he describes himself as 'a product of re-education', coming to terms with the horror of the regime under which he had grown up. He had been closely involved with university issues from the end of the 1950s, when he worked on a research project on students' political attitudes, documenting their rather unpolitical state. His book of 1962, *Structural*

Transformation of the Public Sphere, documented a parallel decline in the quality of public debate, as politics became dominated by what we would now call 'spin'. He had formed, with Wolfgang Abendroth, a socialist support group for the SDS, wrote a preface to a book they published on university reform, and joined in campaigns against the Vietnam War and the emergency laws. He was therefore very sympathetic to the aims of the movement but parted company with its strategy of provoking the state into revealing its oppressive character. Its importance, for him, lies in its modernizing effect on West German political culture.

I suggested earlier that the real effects of 1968 should be seen in broader cultural and generational terms. Here is a rather cool reaction by someone from the generation immediately following that of 1968, writing of West Berlin in the late 1970s (Garton-Ash 1997: 37–8; 41):

> I had mixed feelings about the sixty-eighters...I could sympathize with some of their political projects...However, they seemed to me often hysterical, self-obsessed and self-indulgent. I tired of their moaning about problems that struck me either as self-created or as minor compared with those in the East.

Garton-Ash (1997: 150) was of course working a good deal in Poland in 1980, and interacting with *Solidarity* activists who were also substantially of the 1968 generation.

> There were things, important things, that they had in common with the sixty-eighters in Germany: the casual way of dressing, the programmatic informality (straight to *ty*, rather than the formal *pan*), the attitude to sex and to personal relations more generally. But other, more important things were utterly different. The German sixty-eighters had never themselves lived under Nazism. The Polish sixty-eighters had lived and still lived under communism.

'1968' in Poland was of course notable for the regime's anti-intellectual and anti-Semitic pogrom, an ill wind which blew, eventually to the UK, some leading thinkers such as Zygmunt Bauman, Włodzimierz Brus and Leszek Kołakowski. But the differences in the *political* 1968 in East and West go along with a trans-Iron-Curtain *cultural* shift, tracked for the West by R. F. Inglehart in *The Silent Revolution*. Inglehart's book, published in 1977, was of course extremely influential in the English-speaking world; the German translation of 1982 had even more impact there.

If this shift, to a post-materialism which should perhaps really be seen as another version of consumerism, with a focus on self-realization and 'experiences' (the *Erlebnisgesellschaft* described by Gerhard Schulze [1992]), a corporate world where a laid-back atmosphere of sofas and first names co-exists uneasily with a reality of increasing stress and insecurity, is a paradoxical legacy of 1968, there is also a more genuinely post-materialist alternative culture finding political expression in local and global social movements. The 1968 movements display a paradoxical combination: on the one hand, a deeply serious concentration on issues like class inequality and war which mainstream opinion tended to marginalize, and on the other hand an imaginative and playful political choreography. They leave us with the question of what we should understand by *serious* politics in the twenty-first century: protest movements which seem utopian or the increasingly formalistic rituals of post-democracy (Crouch 2004). Rudi Dutschke announced the need for a 'long march through the institutions', which he was tragically unable to make himself.[5] In their different ways, Daniel Cohn-Bendit and Joschka Fischer can be seen as doing this, as can their British and North American counterparts in politics and intellectual life[6] now reaching the end of their careers and marking a further milestone in the road on from 1968. This political generation, for all its sometimes narcissistic combination of pseudo-intransigence with willingness to compromise, has surely played a positive part in the political modernization of our societies.[7] It is less easy to judge what the future of our politics is likely to be, but if the 'outcomes' of 1968 were substantially 'learning outcomes' (to borrow for a moment the vile jargon of UK academic bureaucracy), the learning still goes on.

Notes

1. See, for example, Michael Lühmann (2008).
2. Caroline Humphreys' classic ethnographic study of the *Karl Marx Collective: Economy, Society and Religion in a Siberian Collective Farm* (Humphreys 1983) recounts how the fishers of Lake Baikal prayed for a good catch to the spirits of two Communard heroes.
3. We should also recall the less happy parallel with the 1968 assassinations of Martin Luther King and Robert Kennedy: the concern for Obama's physical safety during the campaign. Collins suggests another temporary end-point to 1968 with her claim that Reagan's election in 1980 'can be seen as a direct response to the radicalism of 1968'. In France nearly 30 years later, the future President Sarkozy lashed out in public, for no obvious reason, at the ideas of 1968.

4. The German SDS, which had fizzled out at the end of the 1960s, was recently reincarnated in association with the new socialist party, *Die Linke*.
5. At the other end of the political spectrum, Niklas Luhmann (1992: 152–3) wrote that society 'does not have an address. If one wants something from it, one has to address oneself to organizations.'
6. On intellectuals, see, for example, Fleck *et al.* (2009).
7. See, for example, the ironical cover of *Spiegel* No. 44, 29.10.07. 'Es war nicht alles schlecht. Gnade für die 68er.' ('It wasn't all bad. Give the sixty-eighters a break.')

Bibliography

Abdallah, M. H. and Réseau No Pasaran 2000. *J'y suis, J'y reste! Les Luttes de l'Immigration en France Depuis les Années Soixante.* Paris: Editions Reflex.
Abramson, M. and Young Lords Party 1971. *Palante: Young Lords Party.* New York: McGraw-Hill.
Adi, H. 1998. *West Africans in Britain: 1900–1960.* London: Lawrence and Wishart.
Adorno, T. 1974. *Minima Moralia.* London: New Left Books.
Adorno, T. and M. Horkheimer 1972. *Dialectic of Enlightenment.* New York: Herder and Herder.
Alexander, J. C. 1984. *Theoretical Logic in Sociology, Vol. IV: The Modern Reconstruction of Classical Thought: Talcott Parsons.* London: Routledge and Kegan Paul.
—— 1985. 'Introduction' in J. C. Alexander (ed.) *Neofunctionalism.* Beverley Hills, California: Sage.
Allen, S., L. Sanders and J. Wallis 1974. *Contradictions of Illusion: Papers from the Women's Movement.* Leeds: Feminist Books.
Amin, S. 1971. *L'Afrique de l'ouest bloquée, l'économie politique de la colonisation, 1880–1970.* Paris: Ed. Minuit.
Anderson-Bricker, K. 1999. ' "Triple Jeopardy": Black Women and the Growth of Feminist Consciousness in SNCC, 1964–1975' in K. Springer (ed.) *Still Lifting, Still Climbing: African American Women's Contemporary Activism.* New York: New York University Press.
Appiah, K. A. 2006. *Cosmopolitanism: Ethics in a World of Strangers.* London: Allen Lane.
Appignanesi, L. 1988. *Simone de Beauvoir.* London: Penguin.
Archer, M. 1988. *Culture and Agency.* Cambridge: Cambridge University Press.
Armbruster, C., M. Cox and G. Lawson (eds) 2009. *The Global 1989.* Cambridge: Cambridge University Press.
Aron, R. 1968. *La Révolution Introuvable. Réflexions sur les Evénements de Mai.* Paris: Fayard.
Aronowitz, S. and R. Ausch 2000. 'A Critique of Methodological Reason', *The Sociological Quarterly*, 41 (4), 699–719.
Artières, P. 2008. 'Portrait: Amor le Marocain et la Grève de Pennaroya-Gerland, Lyon, 1972' in P. Artières and M. Zancarini-Fournel (eds) *1968, Une Histoire Collective (1962–1981).* Paris: La Découverte.
Atkinson, D. 1971. *Orthodox Consensus and Radical Alternative: A Study in Sociological Theory.* London: Heinemann Educational Books.
Badiou, A. 2008. 'Spectres of 68', *New Left Review*, 49 January/February, 29–46.
Baez, J. 2008. 'To Bobby' http://www.lyricsdownload.com/joan-baez-to-bobby-lyrics.html, date accessed 25 March 2008.
Baltzell, E. D. 1972. 'Epilogue: To Be a Phoenix – Reflections on Two Noisy Ages of Prose', *American Journal of Sociology*, 78, 202–20.
Barkan, J. D. 1975. *An African Dilemma: University Students, Development And Politics in Ghana, Tanzania and Uganda.* Nairobi: Oxford University Press.

Bathily, A. 1992. *Mai 68 à Dakar ou la Révolte Universitaire et la Démocratie*. Paris: Chaka.
Bathily, A., M. Diouf and M. Mbodj 1995. 'The Senegalese Student Movement from its Inception to 1989' in M. Mamdani and E. Wamba-Dia-Wamba (eds) *African Studies in Social Movements and Democracy*. Dakar: Codesria.
Baxandall, R. F. 1998. 'Catching the Fire' in R. B. DuPlessis and A. Snitow (eds) *The Feminist Memoir Project: Voices from Women's Liberation*. New York: Three Rivers Press.
de Beauvoir, S. 1988. *The Second Sex*, translated by H. M. Parshley. London: Picador.
Beck, U. 2005. *Power in the Global Age: A New Global Political Economy*. Cambridge: Polity.
Beemyn, B. 2003. 'The Silence is Broken: A History of the First Lesbian, Gay, and Bisexual College Student Groups', *Journal of the History of Sexuality*, 12 (2), 205–23.
Bell, D. 1960. *The End of Ideology: The Exhaustion of Political Ideas in the Fifties*. New York: Free Press.
Benhabib, S. 1984. *Critique, Norm, and Utopia: A Study of the Foundations of Critical Theory*. New York: Columbia University Press.
Benoit, J. 1980. *Dossier E Come Esclaves. Le Dossier Noir de l'Immigration en France*. Paris: Editions A. Moreau.
Berry, M. F. 1994. *Black Resistance, White Law: A History of Constitutional Racism in America*. New York: Penguin Press.
Bianchini, P. 2002. 'Le mouvement étudiant Sénégalais. Un essai d'interprétation' in Diop, MC *La Société Sénéglaise entre le local et le global*. Paris: Karthala.
Bianchini, P. 2004. *Ecole et Politique en Afrique Noire. Sociologie des Crises et des Réformes du Système d'Enseignement au Sénégal et au Burkina Faso (1960–2000)*. Paris: Karthala.
Bindel, J. 2003. *The Telegraph*. 15 October.
Boltanski, L. and E. Chiapello 2005. 'The Role of Criticism in the Dynamics of Capitalism: Social Criticism versus Artistic Criticism' in M. Miller (ed.) *Worlds of Capitalism: Institutions, Governance and Economic Change in the Era of Globalization*. London: Routledge.
Boltanski, L. and L. Thevenot 1991. *De la Justification. Les Economies de la Grandeur*. Paris: Gallimard.
Boren, M. E. 2001 *Student Resistance: A History of the Unruly Subject*. New York: Routledge.
Boubeker, A. 2003. *Les Mondes de l'Ethnicité: la Communauté d'Expérience des Héritiers de l'Immigration Maghrebienne*. Paris: Editions Balland.
Boyd, H. 2007. *She's Not the Man I Married: My Life with a Transgender Husband*. Berkeley, California: Sela Press.
Boyer, D. 2002. 'The African Crisis in Context: Comparative Encounters with Educational Rationalization', *African Studies Review* 45 (2), 205–18.
Brown, W. 1995. *States of Injury: Power and Freedom in Late Modernity*. Princeton: Princeton University Press.
—— 2001. *Politics Out of History*. Princeton: Princeton University Press.
Brunkhorst, H. 1997. 'Culture and Bourgeois Society: The Unity of Reason in a Divided Society' in A. Honneth, T. McCarthy, C. Offe and A. Wellmer

(eds) *Cultural-Political Interventions in the Unfinished Project of Enlightenment*. Cambridge. Massachusetts: MIT Press.
—— 2005. *Solidarity: From Civic Friendship to a Global Legal Community*. Cambridge, Massachusetts: MIT Press.
Burger, T. 1977. 'Talcott Parsons, the Problem of Order in Society and the Program of an Analytical Sociology', *American Journal of Sociology* 83, 320–34.
Butler, J. 1990. *Gender Trouble: Feminism and the Subversion of Identity*. London: Routledge.
—— 1993. *Bodies That Matter: On the Discursive Limits of 'Sex'*. New York: Routledge.
Bynoe, Y. 2004. *Stand and Deliver: Political Activism, Leadership, and Hip Hop Culture*. Brooklyn, New York: Soft Skull Press.
Cabral, A. 1969. *Revolution in Guinea: an African People's Struggle*. London: Stage 1.
Caffentzis, G. 2000. 'The World Bank and Education in Africa' in Alidou, O, Caffentzis, G. and Federici, S. (eds) *A Thousand Flowers. Social Struggles Against Structural Adjustment in African Universities*. Eritrea: Africa World Press Inc.
Calvert, G. 1991. *Democracy from the Heart: Spiritual Values, Decentralism, and Democratic Idealism in the Movement of the 1960s*. Eugene: Communitas Press.
Carson, C. and K. Shepard 2002. *A Call to Conscience: The Landmark Speeches of Dr. Martin Luther King, Jr.* New York: Warner Books.
Carter, A. 1998. 'Truly, It Felt Like Year One' in S. Maitland (ed.) *Very Heaven: Looking back at the Sixties*. London: Virago.
Carter, D. 2004. *Stonewall: The Riots That Sparked The Gay Revolution*. New York: St. Martin's Press.
Chambrier Rahandi, M. E. 1990. 'Introduction' in C. Diané (ed.) *La FEANF: Et les Grandes Heures du Mouvement Syndical Etudiant Noir*. Paris: Chaka.
Chhachhi, A. and H. Nicholas 2006. 'Cosmopolitanisms: An Examination of Frontiers of Justice', *Development and Change* 37 (6), 1227–334.
Cissé, S. 2001. De la Provenance des 'Espèces', *Comprendre le Sénégal*. Dakar: Le Soleil.
Clay, A. 2006. ' "All I need is one mic": Mobilizing Youth for Social Change in the Post-Civil Rights Era', *Social Justice* 33 (2), 105–21.
Clemens, J. and R. Grigg 2006. 'Introduction' in J. Clemens and R. Grigg (eds) *Jacques Lacan and the Other Side of Psychoanalysis*. London: Duke.
Cliff, T. 1963. 'Deflected Permanent Revolution', *International Socialism* 1 (12), 15–22.
Collins, P. H. 1998. *Fighting Words: Black Women and the Search for Justice*. Minneapolis: University of Minnesota Press.
—— 2002. 'Introduction to On Lynchings' in Ida B. Wells-Barnett (ed.) *On Lynchings*. Amherst: Humanity Books.
—— 2004. *Black Sexual Politics: African Americans, Gender, and the New Racism*. New York: Routledge.
—— 2006. *From Black Power to Hip Hop: Essays on Racism, Nationalism and Feminism*. Philadelphia: Temple University Press.
—— 2009. *Another Kind of Public Education: Race, Schools, the Media and Democratic Possibilities*. Boston: Beacon Press.
Combahee River Collective 1995. 'A Black Feminist Statement' in B. Guy-Sheftall (ed.) *Words of Fire: An Anthology of African-American Feminist Thought*. New York: The New Press.

Connery, M. 2008. *Youth to Power: How Today's Young Voters are Building Tomorrow's Progressive Majority*. Brooklyn: Ig Publishing.

Crouch, C. 2004. *Post-Democracy*. Cambridge: Polity.

Crouch, C. and A. Pizzzorno 1978. *The Resurgence of Class Conflict in Western Europe Since 1968* (2 vols). Basingstoke: Macmillan.

Curthoys, A. 2000. 'Adventures of Feminism: Simone de Beauvoir's Autobiographies, Women's Liberation and Self-Fashioning', *Feminist Review* 64, 3–18.

Dahl, M. 2008. 'Young voter turnout likely sets new record', MSNBC, http://www.msnbc.msn.com/id/27562023/?GT1=43001, date accessed 11 May 2008.

Dahrendorf, R. 1958. 'Out of Utopia: Toward a Re-orientation of Sociological Theory', *American Journal of Sociology* LXIV, 115–27.

Davidson, B. 1992. *The Black Man's Burden: Africa and the Curse of the Nation-State*. London: James Currey.

Dean, M. 1999. *Governmentality: Power and Rule in Modern Society*. London: Sage.

Debray, R. 1978. *Modeste Contribution aux Cérémonies Officielles du Dixième Anniversaire*. Paris: Cahiers libres, Ed. Maspéro.

Deleuze, G. and Guattari, F. 1988. *A Thousand Plateaus: Capitalism and Schizophrenia*. London: Continuum.

D'Emilio, J. 1983. *Sexual Politics, Sexual Communities*. Chicago: University of Chicago Press.

—— 2004. *The World Turned: Histories on Gay History, Politics and Culture*. Durham, North Carolina: Duke University Press.

D'Emilio, J. and E. Freedman 1988. *Intimate Matters: A History of Sexuality in America*. New York: Harper and Row.

Devor, A. H. and N. Matte 2006. 'One Inc. And Reed Erickson: The Uneasy Collaboration of Gay and Trans Activism, 1964–2003' in S. Stryker and S. Whittle (eds) *The Transgender Studies Reader*. New York and Abingdon: Routledge.

Dewey, J. 1954. *The Public and Its Problems*. Athens, Ohio: Ohio University Press.

Diané, C. 1990. *La FEANF: Et les Grandes Heures du Mouvement Syndical Etudiant Noir*. Paris: Chaka.

Diaw, A. 1993. 'The Democracy of the Literati' in M. C. Diop (ed.) *Senegal Essays in Statecraft*. Dakar: CODESRIA.

Diop, M. C. 1993. 'Student Unionism: Pluralism and Pressure Politics' in M. C. Diop (ed.) *Senegal Essays in Statecraft*. Dakar: CODESRIA.

Douglass, F. 1962. *The Life and Times of Frederick Douglass*. New York: Collier.

Driver, S. (ed.) 2008. *Queer Youth Cultures*. Albany: State University of New York Press.

DuPlessis, R. B. and A. Snitow 1998. *The Feminist Memoir Project: Voices from Women's Liberation*. California: Three Rivers Press.

Dynes, W. R. 2002. 'Stephen Donaldson (Robert A. Martin): (1946–1996)' in V. L. Bullough (ed.) *Before Stonewall: Activists for Gay and Lesbian Rights in Historical Context*. New York: Harrington Park Press.

Dyson, M. E. 2000. *I May Not Get There With You: The True Martin Luther King, Jr.* New York: Touchstone.

—— 2003. *Open Mike: Reflections on Philosophy, Race, Sex, Culture, and Religion*. New York: Basic Books.

Epstein, B. 1998. 'On the Origins of the Women's Liberation Movement from a Strictly Personal Perspective' in A. Snitow and R. DuPlessis (eds) *The*

Feminist Memoir Project: Voices from Women's Liberation. New York: Three Rivers Press.
Eze, E. C. 1997. *Race and the Enlightenment: A Reader.* Oxford: Blackwell.
Fanon, F. 1963. *The Wretched of the Earth.* New York: Grove Press.
Feinberg, L. 1996. *Transgender Warriors: Making History from Joan of Arc to Dennis Rodman.* Boston: Beacon Press.
Felski, R. 1996. 'Fin de Siècle, Fin de Sexe: Transsexuality, Postmodernism and the Death of History', *New Literary History* 27 (2), 137–53.
First, R. 1970. *The Barrel of a Gun: Political Power in Africa and the Coup d'État.* London: Allen Lane.
Fleck, C., A. Hess, A. and E. S. Lyon 2009. *Intellectuals and their Publics. Perspectives from the Social Sciences.* Aldershot: Ashgate.
Foster, P. and I. Sutton 1989. *Daughters of De Beauviour.* London: Women's Press Ltd.
Foucault, M. 1980. *Power/Knowledge.* C. Gordon (ed.). Brighton: Harvester Press.
—— 1990. *The History of Sexuality,* Vol. 1. London: Penguin.
—— 1991. 'Governmentality' in G. Burchell, C. Gordon and P. Miller (eds) *The Foucault Effect: Studies in Governmentality.* Brighton: Harvester Wheatsheaf.
—— 1997. 'What Is Enlightenment?' in P. Rabinow (ed.) *Ethics: Subjectivity and Truth.* New York: The New Press.
—— 1998. 'Nietzsche, Genealogy, History' in J. D. Faubion (ed.) *Aesthetics, Method and Epistemology.* New York: The New Press.
Foucher, V. 2002. 'Les "Évolués", la Migration, l'Ecole: Pour une Nouvelle Interprétation du Nationalisme Casamançais' in M. C. Diop (ed.) *Le Sénégal Contemporain.* Paris: Karthala.
Franklin, V. P. 1992. *Black Self-Determination: A Cultural History of African-American Resistance,* 2nd edn. Brooklyn: Lawrence Hill.
—— 2003. 'Patterns of Student Activism at Historically Black Universities in the United States and South Africa, 1960–1977', *Journal of African American History* 88 (2), 204–17.
Frederici, S. 2000. 'The New Student Movement' in O. Alidou, G. Caffentzis and S. Federici (eds) *A Thousand Flowers. Social Struggles Against Structural Adjustment in African Universities.* New York: Africa World Press.
Freeman, J. 1971. 'The Revolution is Happening in Our Minds' in J. Sochen (ed.) *The New Feminism in Twentieth Century America.* Lexington: D. C. Heath and Co.
Freud, S. 1919. 'On the Teaching of Psychoanalysis in Universities' *Standard Edition of the Collected Works of Sigmund Freud,* Vol. 17, London: Hogarth Press.
—— 2001 [1916–1917]. 'Introductory Lectures on Psycho–Analysis, Part III' in J. Strachey (trans. and ed.) *The Standard Edition of the Complete Psychological Works of Freud,* Vol. XVI. London: Vintage.
Friedan, B. 1963. *The Feminine Mystique.* New York: Norton.
Garton-Ash, T. 1997. *The File.* New York: Random House.
Gastaut, Y. 1994. Le Rôle des Immigrés Pendant les Journées de Mai-Juin 1968. *Migrations Société,* Centre d'Information et d'Etudes sur les Migrations Internationales, no. 32.
—— 2000. *L'Immigration et l'Opinion Publique en France Sous la Ve République.* Paris: Editions du Seuil.
Georgakas, D. and M. Surkin 1998. *Detroit, I Do Mind Dying: A Study in Urban Revolution.* New York: South End Press.

Bibliography 189

Giddens, A. 1984. *The Constitution of Society*. Cambridge: Polity.
Gilcher-Holtey, I. 1998. 'Kritische Theorie und Neue Linke', in Gilcher-Holtey (ed.) *1968. Vom Ereignis zum Gegenstand der Geschichtswissenschaf*. Göttingen: Vandenhoeck & Ruprecht.
Ginwright, S., P. Noguera and J. Cammarota (eds) 2006. *Beyond Resistance! Youth Activism and Community Change: New Democratic Possibilities for Practice and Policy for America's Youth*. New York: Routledge.
Giovanni, N. 1968. *The Collected Poetry of Nikki Giovanni: 1968–1998*. New York: Harper Collins.
Gitlin, T. 1980. *The Whole World is Watching*. Berkeley: University of California Press.
Giudice, F., 1992. *Arabicides: Une Chronique Française, 1970–1991*. Paris: La Découverte, Enquetes.
Global Exchange 2008. http://www.globalexchange.org (home page), date accessed 15 October 2008.
Goff, K. 2008. *Party Crashing: How the Hip-Hop Generation Declared Political Independence*. New York: Basic Books.
Gordon, D. 2003. Il est Recommandé aux Etrangers de ne pas Participer. *Migrations Société*, Centre d'Information et d'Etudes sur les Migrations Internationales, nos. 87–8.
Gouldner, A. 1970. *The Coming Crisis of Western Sociology*. London: Heinemann.
—— 1973. 'Romanticism and Classicism: Deep Structures in Social Science', *For Sociology: Renewal and Critique in Sociology Today*. London: Allen Lane.
Granotier, B. 1979. *Les Travailleurs Immigrés en France*. Paris: Ed. Maspéro.
Grayling, A. C. 2007. *Towards the Light*. London: Bloomsbury.
Greer, G. 1971. *The Female Eunuch*. Harmonsworth: Penguin.
—— 1999. *The Whole Woman*. London: Random House.
Groot de, G. 2008. *The 60s Unplugged: A Kaleidoscopic History of a Disorderly Decade*. Basingstoke: Palgrave Macmillan.
Habermas, J. 1971 [1968]. 'Technology and Science as "Ideology"' in *Toward A Rational Society: Student Protest, Science and Politics*, translated by J. J. Shapiro. London: Heinemann.
—— 1972. *Knowledge and Human Interests*, translated by J. J. Shapiro. London: Heinemann.
—— 1976. *Legitimation Crisis*, translated by T. McCarthy. London: Heinemann.
—— 1981. 'Talcott Parsons: Problems of Theory Construction', *Sociological Inquiry* 51, 173–96.
—— 1984 [1981]. *The Theory of Communicative Action, Vol. I: Reason and the Rationalisation of Society*, translated by T. McCarthy. London: Heinemann.
—— 1987 [1981]. *The Theory of Communicative Action, Vol. II: Lifeworld and System*, translated by T. McCarthy. Cambridge: Polity.
—— 2001. *The Post-National Constellation*, translated by M. Pensky. Cambridge: Polity Press.
—— 2003. *Truth and Justification*, translated by B. Fultner. Cambridge: Polity Press.
—— 2008. *Between Naturalism and Religion*. Cambridge: Polity Press.
Hajjat, A. 2006a. 'L'Expérience Politique du Mouvement des Travailleurs Arabes', *Contre Temps*, No. 16, May.

—— 2006b. 'Les Comités Palestine (1970–1972). Aux Origines du Soutien à la Cause Palestinienne en France', *Revue d'Etudes Palestiniennes*. No. 98, Winter, 74–92.

Hall, S. 1989. 'The First New Left' in The Oxford University Socialist Discussion Group (ed.) *Out of Apathy: Voices of the New Left 30 Years On*. London: Verso.

Halperin, M. 2008. 'How the Powell Endorsement Boosts Obama' *Time Magazine*, http://www.time.com/time/nation/article/0,8599,1851832,00.html?imw=Y, date accessed 19 October 20008.

Halsey, H. 2004. *A History of Sociology in Britain*. Oxford: Oxford University Press

Hanna, W. J. 1975. 'Students, Universities and Political Outcomes' in W. J. Hanna and J. Hanna (eds) *University Students and African Politics*. London: Africana Publishing Company.

Hanna, W. J. and J. L. Hanna 1975. 'Students as Elites' in W. J. Hanna and J. L. Hanna (eds) *University Students and African Politics*. London: Africana Publishing Company.

Harrigan, R. 1982. 'The German Women's Movement and Ours', *Jump Cut: A Review of Contemporary Media* 27, 42–44.

Harris, C. I. 1993. 'Whiteness As Property', *Harvard Law Review* 106 (8), 1707–91.

Harrison, G. 2002. *Issues in the Contemporary Politics of Sub-Saharan Africa: The Dynamics of Struggle and Resistance*. New York: Palgrave.

Hegel, G. W. F. 1929. *Science of Logic*, translated by W. H. Johnston and L.G. Struthers. New York: Macmillan.

Hill, J. 2006. 'Excerpts from a Life Standing at the Well', *Black Scholar* 36 (1), 31–5.

Hines, S. 2006. 'What's the Difference?: Bringing Particularity to Queer Studies of Transgender', *Journal of Gender Studies*, 15 (1), 49–66.

—— 2007a. 'Social/Cultural Change and Transgender Citizenship', *Sociological Research Online* 12 (1), available at http://www.socresonline.org.uk/12/1hines.htm.

—— 2007b. *TransForming Gender: Transgender Practices of Identity, Intimacy and Care*. Bristol: Policy Press.

Hird, M. J. 2002. 'For a Sociology of Transsexualism', *Sociology*, 36 (3), 557–95.

Holmwood, J. 1996. *Founding Sociology? Talcott Parsons and the Idea of General Theory*. London: Longman.

—— 1999. 'Radical Sociology: What's Left?' in P. Bagguley and J. Hearn (eds) *Transforming Politics: Power and Resistance*. Houndmills: Macmillan.

Honneth, A. 1999. 'The Social Dynamics of Disrespect: Situating Critical Theory Today' in P. Dews (ed.) *Habermas: A Critical Reader*. Oxford: Blackwell.

Horkheimer, M. 1982. 'The End of Reason' in A. Arato and E. Gebhardt (eds) *The Essential Frankfurt School Reader*. New York: The Continuum Publishing Company.

Horn, G-R. 2007. *The Spirit of '68. Rebellion in Western Europe and North America 1956–1976*.Oxford University Press.

Horn, G-R. and P. Kenney 2004. *Transnational Moments of Change: Europe 1945, 1968, 1989*. Lanham: Rowman and Littlefield.

Howe, N. and W. Strauss 2000. *Millennials Rising: The Next Great Generation*. New York: Vintage.

Humphreys, C. 1983. *Karl Marx Collective: Economy, Society and Religion in a Siberian Collective Farm*. Cambridge: Cambridge University Press.

Huyssen, A. 2003. *Present Pasts: Urban Palimpsests and the Politics of Memory*. Stanford: Stanford University Press.
Inglehart, R. 1990. *Culture Shift in Advanced Industrial Society*. Princeton: Princeton University Press.
Jalali, R. and S. M. Lipset 1998. 'Racial and Ethnic Conflicts: A Global Perspective' in M. W. Hughey (ed.) *New Tribalisms: The Resurgence of Race and Ethnicity*. New York: New York University Press.
James, S. M. and Abena P. A. Busia 1993. *Theorizing Black Feminisms: The Visionary Pragmatism of Black Women*. New York: Routledge.
Jarausch, K. 1998. '1968 and 1989. Caesuras, Comparisons, and Connections' in C. Fink, P. Gassert and D. Junker (eds) *1968: The World Transformed*. New York: Cambridge University Press.
Jay, M. 1973. *The Dialectical Imagination: A History of the Frankfurt School and the Institute of Social Research, 1923–1950*. Boston: Little, Brown and Company.
Jeffreys, S. 1997. 'Transgender Activism: A Feminist Perspective', *The Journal of Lesbian Studies*, 1 (3/4), 55–74.
Jones, W. D. 1999. *The Lost Debate: German Socialist Intellectuals and Totalitarianism*. Chicago: University of Illinois Press.
Kelley, R. D. G. 2002. *Freedom Dreams: The Black Radical Imagination*. Boston: Beacon.
Kellner, D. 1989. *Critical Theory, Marxism and Modernity*. Cambridge: Polity Press.
—— 2003. *Media Spectacle*. New York: Routledge.
—— 2005. *Media Spectacle and the Crisis of Democracy: Terrorism, War, and Election Battles*. Boulder: Paradigm Publishers.
King, R. H. 1996. *Civil Rights and the Idea of Freedom*. Athens: University of Georgia Press.
Kitwana, B. 2002. *The Hip Hop Generation: Young Blacks and the Crisis in African-American Culture*. New York: Basic Books.
Kunzel, R. 2008. *Criminal Intimacy: Prison and the Uneven History of American Sexuality*. Chicago and London: University of Chicago Press.
Lacan, J. 1967. 'The Proposition of October 9, 1967 on the Psychoanalyst of the School', quoted on www.wapol.org/en/elpase/Template.asp, date accessed 3 November 2008.
—— 1991. *The Other Side of Psychoanalysis: The Seminar of Jacques Lacan Book XVII*. New York: Norton.
Latour, B. 1987. *Science in Action: How to Follow Scientists and Engineers Through Society*. Cambridge, Massachusetts: Harvard University Press.
Lawson, B. E. and D. F. Koch 2004. *Pragmatism and the Problem of Race*. Bloomington: Indiana University Press.
Lawson, S. 2002. *How Simone De Beauvoir Died in Australia : Stories and Essays*. Seattle, Washington: University of Washington Press.
Leff, L. 2008. 'As Gay Pride hits Stride, Transgendered find More Acceptance' Associated Press, USATODAY.com (home page), date accessed 10 July 2008.
Lemire, V. 2008. 'Nanterre, les Bidonvilles et les Etudiants' in P. Artières and M. Zancarini-Fournel (eds) *1968, Une Histoire Collective (1962–1981)*. Paris: La Découverte.
Lo, M. 1987. *Sénégal: Syndicalisme et Participation*. Paris: L'Harmattan.
Lockwood, D. 1956. 'Some Remarks on *The Social System*', *British Journal of Sociology* 7, 134–46.

—— 1964. 'Social Integration and System Integration' in G. Zollschan and W. Hirsch (eds) *Explorations in Social Change*. London: Routledge and Kegan Paul.

—— 1992. *Solidarity and Schism: The Problem of Disorder in Durkheimian and Marxist Sociology*. Oxford: Clarendon Press.

Lucas, C. J. 1994. *American Higher Education: A History*. New York: St. Martin's Press.

Luhmann, N. 1992. 'Universität als Milieu' in A. Kieserling (ed.) *Kleine Schriften*. Bielefeld: Haux.

—— 1995 [1984]. *Social Systems*, translated by J. Bednarz Jr and Dirk Baecker. Stanford, California: Stanford University Press.

Lühmann, M. 2008. 'Geteilt, ungeliebt, deutungsschwach? Die 68-er Generation der DDR', *Deutschland-Archiv* 41. 1: 102–7.

MacDonald, E. 1998. 'Critical Identities: Rethinking Feminism through Transgender Politics', *Atlantis* 23 (1), 3–12.

Mailer, N. 1971. *The Prisoner of Sex*. Boston: Little, Brown.

Malcolm, X. 1965. *The Autobiography of Malcolm X*. New York: Grove Press.

Mamarbachi, A. 2008. 'Palestine' in A. Artous, D. Epsztajn and P. Silberstein (eds) *La France des Années 1968*. Paris: Editions Syllepse.

Mamdani, M. 1994. 'The Intelligentsia, the State and Social Movements in Africa' in M. Diouf and M. Mamdani (eds) *Academic Freedom in Africa*. Dakar: Codesria.

Mannheim, K. 1954. *Ideology and Utopia: An Introduction to the Sociology of Knowledge*. New York: Harcourt, Brace and World.

Marcuse, H. 1941. *Reason and Revolution*. Oxford: Oxford University Press.

—— 1955. *Eros and Civilization: A Philosophical Inquiry into Freud*. Boston: Beacon Press.

—— 1964. *One-Dimensional Man*. Boston: Beacon Press.

—— 1968. *Negations: Essays in Critical Theory*. Boston: Beacon Press.

—— 1998 [1941]. 'Some Social Implications of Modern Technology' in D. Kellner (ed.) *Technology, War and Fascism: Collected Papers of Herbert Marcuse*, Vol. I. New York: Routledge.

—— 1998a. 'State and Individual Under National Socialism' in D. Kellner (ed.) *Technology, War and Fascism: Collected Papers of Herbert Marcuse*, Vol. I. New York: Routledge.

—— 1998b. 'The New German Mentality, Supplement Three: On Psychological Neutrality' in D. Kellner (ed.) *Technology, War and Fascism: Collected Papers of Herbert Marcuse*, Vol. I. New York: Routledge.

—— 2001 [1961]. 'The Problem of Social Change in the Technological Society' in D. Kellner (ed.) *Towards a Critical Theory of Society: Collected Papers of Herbert Marcuse*, Vol. II. New York: Routledge.

—— 2001 [1965]. 'The Containment of Social Change in Industrial Society' in D. Kellner (ed.) *Towards a Critical Theory of Society: Collected Papers of Herbert Marcuse*, Vol. II. New York: Routledge.

Martindale, D. C. 1971. 'Talcott Parsons' Theoretical Metamorphosis from Social Behaviourism to Macro-functionalism' in H. Turk and R. L. Simpson (eds) *Institutions and Exchange: The Sociologies of Talcott Parsons and George Caspar Homans*. New York: Bobbs-Merrill.

Martins, L. 2002. *Kabila et la révolution congolaise, panafricanisme ou neocolonialisme? Tome 1*. Anvers: Editions EPO.

Marwick, A. 1998. *The Sixties: Cultural Revolution in Britain, France, Italy, and the United States, 1958–1974*. Oxford: Oxford University Press.
Marx, K. 1984. *The Eighteenth Brumaire of Louis Bonaparte*. London: Lawrence and Wishart.
Matza, D. 1961. 'Subterranean Traditions of Youth', *Annals of the American Academy of Political and Social Science* 338 (1), 102–18.
May, T. 2005. *Gilles Deleuze: An Introduction*. New York: Cambridge University Press.
McCarthy, T. 1991. *Ideals and Illusions*. Cambridge, Massachusetts : MIT Press.
McDermid, A. 1988. 'Paris in the Springtime' in S. Maitland (ed.) *Very Heaven: Looking back at the Sixties*. London: Virago.
McKee, J. B. 1993. *Sociology and the Race Problem: The Failure of a Perspective*. Urbana: University of Illinois Press.
Miller, M. 2005. 'Introduction' in M. Miller (ed.) *Worlds of Capitalism: Institutions, Goverance and Economic Change in the Era of Globalization*. London: Routledge.
Miles, M. W. 1973. *The Radical Probe: The Logic of Student Rebellion*. New York: Atheneum Books.
Millett, K. 1989. 'Untitled' in P. Forster and I. Sutton (eds) *Daughters of de Beauvoir*. London: Women's Press.
Mills, C. W. 1951. *White Collar: The American Middle Class*. New York: Oxford University Press.
—— 1959. *The Sociological Imagination*. Oxford: Oxford University Press.
—— 2000. *The Sociological Imagination*. New York: Oxford University Press.
Mitchell, J. 1973. *Women's Estate*. Harmondsworh: Penguin.
Mouzelis, N. 1995. *Sociological Theory: What Went Wrong?: Diagnosis and Remedies*. London: Routledge.
Muñoz, C. 1989. *Youth, Identity, Power: The Chicano Movement*. New York: Verso.
Murray, S. O. 1996. *American Gay*. Chicago: University of Chicago Press.
Namaste, K. 2000. *Invisible Lives: The Erasure of Transsexual and Transgendered People*. Chicago: The University of Chicago Press.
Nancy, J-L. 1991. *The Inoperative Community*. Minneapolis: University of Minnesota Press.
Nkongolo, M. N. 2000. *Le Campus Martyr*. Paris: L'Harmattan.
Nzongola-Ntalaja, G. 2002. *A People's History of the Congo*. London: Zed Books.
O'Brien, D. C. 1996. 'A Lost Generation? Youth Identity and State Decay in West Africa' in R. P. Werbner and T. O. Ranger (eds) *Post-colonial Identities in Africa*. London: Zed Books.
O'Sullivan, S. 1988. 'From 1969' in S. Sebestyen (ed.) *'68, '78, '88: From Women's Liberation to Feminism*. Dorset: Prism Press.
Offe, C. 1968. 'Technik und Eindimensionalitat: Eine Version der Technokratiethese?' in J. Habermas (ed.) *Antworten auf Herbert Marcuse*. Frankfurt am Main: Suhrkamp.
—— 1997. 'Bindings, Shackles, Brakes: On Self-Limitation Strategies' in A. Honneth, T. McCarthy, C. Offe and A. Wellmer (eds) *Cultural-Political Interventions in the Unfinished Project of Enlightenment*. Cambridge, Massachusetts: MIT Press.
—— 2005. 'The European Model of Social Capitalism: Can it Survive European Integration?' in M. Miller (ed.) *Worlds of Capitalism: Institutions, Governance and Economic Change in the Era of Globalization*. London: Routledge.

Outhwaite, W. 2005. 'From Switzerland to Sussex' in A. Sica and S. P. Turner (eds) *The Disobedient Generation: Social Theorists in the Sixties*. Chicago and London: Chicago University Press.
Parker, I. 2008. 'Temptations of Pedagogery: Seventeen Lures (review of Lacan's Seminar XVII)' *Subjectivities* 24, 376–9.
Parsons, T. 1937. *The Structure of Social Action*. New York: Free Press.
—— 1951. *The Social System*. London: Routledge and Kegan Paul.
—— 1954 [1950]. 'The Prospects of Sociological Theory', *Essays in Sociological Theory*. New York: Free Press.
—— 1954 [1953]. 'A Revised Analytical Approach to the Social Stratification', *Essays in Sociological Theory*, revised edn. New York: Free Press.
—— 1966. *Societies: Evolutionary and Comparative Perspectives*. Englewood Cliffs: Prentice-Hall.
—— 1967. 'Some Comments on the Sociology of Karl Marx', *Sociological Theory and Modern Society*. New York: Free Press.
—— 2007. *American Society: A Theory of the Societal Community*. Boulder, Colorado: Paradigm Publisher.
Pitti, L. 1994. *Les Ouvriers Algériens à Renault-Billancourt, de 1954 à 1973*. Unpublished DEA thesis, Université de Paris 8.
—— 2006. Une Matrice Algérienne? Trajectoires et Recompositions Militantes en Terrain Ouvrier, de la Cause de l'indépendance aux Grèves d'OS des années 1968–1975. *Politix* 19 (76), 143–66.
Pope, W., J. Cohen and L. Hazelrigg. 1975. 'On the Divergence of Weber and Durkheim: A Critique of Parsons' Convergence Thesis', *American Sociological Review* 40, 417–27.
Popkin, A. 1979. 'The Personal is Political' in D. Cluster (ed.) *They Should Have Served that Cup of Coffee*. Boston: South End Press.
Postman, N. 1993. *Technopoly: The Surrender of Culture to Technology*. New York: Vintage.
Prévost, G. and A. Kadri 2008. 'Immigrés' in A. Artous, D. Epsztajn and P. Silberstein (eds) *La France des Années 1968*. Paris: Editions Syllepse.
Prosser, J. 1998. *Second Skins: The Body Narratives of Transsexuality*. New York: Columbia University Press.
Raymond, J. 1980. *The Transsexual Empire*. London: The Women's Press.
Reitan, R. 2007. *Global Activism*. London: Routledge.
Renton, D. Seddon, D. and Zeilig, L. 2006. *The Congo: Plunder and resistance*. London: Zed Books.
Rex, J. 1961. *Key Problems of Sociological Theory*. London: Routledge and Kegan Paul.
Rich, A. 2008. 'Planetarium', http://www.americanpoems.com/poets/adrienne_rich/7091, date accessed 25 March 2008.
Rioux, J. P. 1990. *La Guerre d'Algérie et les Français*. Paris: Fayard.
Robinson, E. 1968. *The New Polytechnics: The People's Universities*. London: Penguin.
Robinson, P. 2009. *The Changing Worlds of Gay Men 1950–2000*. Basingstoke: Palgrave Macmillan.
Rodney, W. 1981. *How Europe Underdeveloped Africa*. Washington, DC: Howard University Press.

Rooks, N. 2006. *White Money/Black Power: The Surprising History of African American Studies and the Crisis of Race in Higher Education*. Boston: Beacon Press.

Rose, N. 1989. *Governing the Soul: The Shaping of the Private Self*. London: Routledge.

—— 1999. *Powers of Freedom: Reframing Political Thought*. Cambridge: Cambridge University Press.

Rose, N. and P. Miller 1992. 'Political Power beyond the State: Problematics of Government'. *British Journal of Sociology* 43 (2), 173–205.

Rosenthal, J. 1975. 'Black Student Activism: Assimilation vs. Nationalism', *The Journal of Negro Education* 44 (2), 113–29.

Ross, K. 1996. *Fast Cars, Clean Bodies. Decolonization and the Re-ordering of French Culture*. Cambridge, Massachusetts: MIT Press.

Roudinesco, E. 1986. *Jacques Lacan and Co.: A History of Psychoanalysis in France, 1925–1985*. London: Free Association Books.

—— 1994. *Jacques Lacan*. Cambridge: Polity.

Rowbotham, S. 1972. *Women, Resistance, and Revolution: A History of Women and Revolution*. London: Pantheon Books.

—— 1973. *Women's Consciousness, Man's World*. London: Pluto Press.

—— 1988. 'A Muggins Twice Over', *New Statesman & Society*, June 10, 26.

—— 2000. *Promise of a Dream: Remembering the Sixties*. London: Penguin.

Rowbotham, S., L. Segal and H. Wainwright 1981. *Beyond the Fragments: Feminism and the Making of Socialism*. Boston: Alyson Press.

Rubin, G. 1992. 'Of Catamites and Kings: Reflections on Butch, Gender and Boundaries' in J. Nestle (ed.) *The Persistent Desire. A Femme-Butch-Reader*. Boston: Alyson Press.

Rubin, H. 1996. 'Do You Believe in Gender?' *Sojourner* 21 (6), 7–8.

Sayad, A. 1999. *The Suffering of the Immigrant*. Paris: Editions du Seuil.

Sandoval, C. 2000. *Methodology of the Oppressed*. Minneapolis: University of Minnesota Press.

Schor, J. 1999. *The Overspent American: Why We Want What We Don't Need*. New York: Harper Perennial.

—— 2004. *Born to Buy: The Commercialized Child and the New Consumer Culture*. New York: Scribner.

Schulze, G. 1992. *Die Erlebnisgesellschaft. Kultursoziologie der Gegenwart*. Frankfurt: Campus.

Scott, J. F. 1963. 'The Changing Foundations of the Parsonian Action Scheme', *American Sociological Review* 28, 716–35.

Seddon, D. 2002. 'Popular Protest and Class Struggle in Africa: An Historical Overview' in L. Zeilig (ed.) *Class Struggle and Resistance in Africa*. Cheltenham: New Clarion.

Seddon, D. and Zeilig, L. 2005. 'Class and Protest in Africa: New Waves', *Review of African Political Economy* 31(103), 9–27.

Segal, L. 2007. *Making Trouble: Life and Politics*. London: Serpents Tail.

Seidman, M. 2004. *The Imaginary Revolution: Parisian Students and Workers in 1968*. New York: Berghahn Books.

Shelby, T. 2005. *We Who Are Dark: The Philosophical Foundations of Black Solidarity*. Cambridge: Harvard University Press.

Shulman, A. K. 1978. *Burning Questions*. New York: Knopf.

—— 1998. 'A Marriage Disagreement, or Marriage by Other Means' in R. B. DuPlessis and A. Snitow (eds) *The Feminist Memoir Project: Voices from Women's Liberation*. New York: Three Rivers Press.

Le Soleil 2001. 'Le Raz de Marée de Mai 68: Quand Etudiants et Ouvriers font Cause Commune'; 'Le Regard Rétrospectif des Acteurs de l'Histoire', 28 February.

Stansill, P. and D. Z. Mairowitz 1971. *BAMN: Outlaw Manifestos and Ephemera 1965–70*. Harmondsworth: Penguin.

Stoler, A. 1995. *Race and the Education of Desire: Foucaults History of Sexuality and the Colonial Order of Things*. Durham NC: Duke University Press.

Stryker, S. 2008. comptonscafeteriariot.org (home page), date accessed 1 June 2008.

Sznaider, N. 2001. *The Compassionate Temperament: Care and Cruelty in Modern Society*. Boulder: Rowman and Littlefield.

Taylor, V. 1989. 'Social Movement Continuity: The Women's Movements in Abeyance', *American Sociological Review* 54, 761–75.

Thioub, I. 1992. 'Le mouvement étudiant de Dakar et la vie politique sénégalaise: la marche vers la crise de mai-juin 1968' in D'Almeida-Topor, H. Coquery-Vidrovitch, C. Goerg, O. and Guitart, F. (eds) *Les Jeunes en Afrique: la politique et la ville*. Tome 2 Paris: L'Harmattan.

Thompson, E. P. (ed.) 1970. *Warwick University Ltd*. Penguin: Harmondsworth.

Thompson, J. B. 2005. 'The New Visibility', *Theory, Culture & Society* 22 (6), 31–51.

Tilly, C. 2004. *Social Movements 1768–2004*. Boulder: Paradigm.

Touraine, A. 1968. *Le mouvement de mai ou le communisme utopique*. Paris: Seuil.

—— 1971. *The May Movement: Revolt and Reform*. New York: Random House.

Touraine, A. 1988. *Return of the Actor: Social Theory in Postindustrial Society*, translated by M. Godzich. Minnesota: University of Minnesota Press.

—— 1997. *What is Democracy?*, translated by D. Macey. Boulder, CO: Westview Press.

—— 2000. *Can We Live Together? Equality and Difference*, translated by D. Macey. Cambridge: Polity Press.

Trappo, H. 1990. De la Clandestinité à la Reconnaissance. *Plein Droit*, no. 11.

Tripier, M. 1990. *L'Immigration dans la Classe Ouvrière en France*. Paris: L'Harmattan.

Turner, B. 2006. *Vulnerability and Human Rights*. Pennsylvania: Pennsylvania State University Press.

Turner, S. and J. H. Turner 1990. *The Impossible Science: An Institutional Analysis of American Sociology*. Newbury Park, CA: Sage Publications.

Urry, J. 2003. *Global Complexity*. London: Sage.

Valk, A. M. 2008. *Radical Sisters: Second-Wave Feminism and Black Liberation in Washington, D.C.* Urbana: University of Illinois Press.

Vigna, X. 2007. *L'Insubordination Ouvrière dans les Années 68. Essai d'Histoire Politique des Usines*. Rennes: Presses Universitaires de Rennes.

Walsh, P. 2008. 'Beyond the Consumer Society: Herbert Marcuse and Contemporary Social Theory' in H. Dahms (ed.) *No Social Science without Critical Theory, Current Perspectives in Social Theory*, Vol. 25, 235–60.

Warner, R. S. 1978. 'Towards a Re-definition of Action Theory: Paying the Cognitive Element its Due', *American Journal of Sociology* 83, 1317–49.

Weeks, J. 2000. *Making Sexual History*. Cambridge: Polity.

—— 2007. *The World We Have Won*. London: Routledge.
Wieviorka, M. 1998. '1968 und der Terrorismus' in I. Gilcher-Holtey (ed.) *1968. Vom Ereignis zum Gegenstand der Geschichtswissenschaft*. Göttingen: Vandenhoeck & Ruprecht.
Wilchins, R. A. 2002. 'A Woman for Her Time: In Memory of Stonewall Warrior Sylvia Rivera', *Village Voice*, Tuesday, 26 February 2002, available at http://www.villagevoice.com/2002-02-26/news/a-woman-for-her-time/.
—— 2004. *Queer Theory, Gender Theory: An Instant Primer*. Boston: Alyson Press.
Willer, D. and J. Willer 1973. *Systematic Empiricism: Critique of a Pseudo- Science*. Englewood-Cliffs: Prentice-Hall.
Willie, C. V. and D. Cunnigen 1981. 'Black Students in Higher Education: A Review of Studies, 1965–1980', *Annual Review of Sociology* 7, 177–98.
Wilson, E. 1982. *Mirror Writing: An Autobiography*. London: Pandora.
World Bank 2000. *Higher Education in Developing Countries: Peril and Promise*. Washington, DC.
Zancarini-Fournel, M. 2002. La Question Immigré Après '68. *Plein Droit*, nos. 52–3.
—— 2008. *Le Moment '68. Une Histoire Contestée*. Paris: Editions du Seuil.
Zaretsky, E. 2008. 'Narcissism, Personal Life and Identity: The Place of the 1960s in the History of Psychoanalysis', *Psychoanalysis, Culture & Society* 13 (1), 94–104.
Žižek, S. 2006. '*Objet a* in Social Links' in J. Clemens and R. Grigg (eds) *Jacques Lacan and the Other Side of Psychoanalysis*. London: Duke.

Index

1848 revolutions, 176
1989 revolutions, 176, 179

African Americans
  education, 9–11, 24, 25
  freedom, 8, 24, 25
  student protests at Harvard University, 15
anti-capitalist movements
  Global Exchange, 77, 83
  Jubilee 2000, 29, 85
  similarities with 1968, 84–6,
  Third World Network, 83
  use of media, 82, 85
anti-colonial struggles, xiii, 169
Aron, Raymond, 180

Black Feminism, 16
Black Studies, 15
Bracke, Maud Anne, xvii, 176

Collins, Patricia Hill, xiv, xv, 177
Compton's Cafeteria Riots, 147–9
critical theory, xvi, 73–4, 177, 180
  see also Habermas, Herbert Marcuse, Frankfurt School

Eastern Europe, 179–80
end of 1968, xix, 177–8, 182
Eurocentricism, xii, xiv, xviii, 120, 128, 131, 133, 160–1, 167–70

Fanon, Frantz, 20, 25
Foucault, Michel, 100, 102, 127, 161, 163, 166, 170, 171, 174
Frankfurt School, xvi, 74, 95, 98, 177
  see also Habermas, Jurgen; Marcuse, Herbert
French left and immigrants, 120–3
French unions, 121–3, 126
Frosh, Stephen, xvi, 178

gay and lesbian organizations, 148, 150

gay rights, 55–6
Greer, Germaine, 35, 41

Habermas, Jurgen, xvi, 60, 66–71, 77, 85, 180
  see also critical theory; Frankfurt School
Hegel, Georg Wilhelm Friedrich, 74, 169
hegemonic cultures, 52
Hines, Sally, xvii
Holmwood, John, xii, xv
Hornstein, Sarah, xvi

immigrants (France), xvii, 117–20

King Jr, Martin Luther, 7, 12, 14, 151

Lacan, Jacques
  master, 106
  on rebelling students, 104–5, 107
Lockwood, David, 64–5

Marcuse, Herbert, xvi, 180
  critical judgement, 88–9
  freedom, 94
  rationality, 86, 94
  technological rationality, 90–1
  terroristic and non-terroristic technocracies, 92–4
  totalitarianism, 88, 97–9
  see also critical theory
Mitchell, Juliet, 30, 36, 41

National Transsexual Counselling Unit, 149
New Left, 30–1, 40–1, 177
New Right, xii
1989 revolutions, 176, 179
Northern Ireland, 179

Obama, Barack, xiv, xviii–xix, 3, 19–21, 177, 182

othering, xviii, 85, 161, 163–5, 167, 172–4
Outhwaite, William, xii, xviii

Panu, Mihnea, xviii
Parson, Talcott, xvi, 59–62
Plummer, Ken, xv, 178
psychoanalysis
   institutionalization of, 101
   revolution, 100, 111
   training and qualification, 108–10

queer theory, 157–8

Rowbotham, Shelia, 30, 33, 34, 36, 37, 151

Sarkozy, Nicolas, 182
Segal, Lynne, xv, 151
situationism, 177
Skillington, Tracey, xvi
social movements, 51–4, 81–4
standpoint, 47, 49–51

Stonewall Riots, 33, 147, 149–51
strategic essentialism, 172
student activism
   Africa, xvii, 27, 127–41, 135, 145
   Black American, xiv, *see also* African Americans
   Europe, xii, 82, 177
subjectivization, 161, 165, 167

Thatcher, Margaret, xii, 31
Touraine, Alain, 75, 180
transgender people, xvii
   and feminism, 15, 153, 157–8
   gender and sexual taxonomies, 153, 158
   and lesbian and gay organizations, 148, 150, 156–8

women's liberation, 36–9, 151–3

X, Malcolm, 12–13, 26

Zeilig, Leo, xvii